Possessing the City

OXFORD HISTORICAL MONOGRAPHS

The *Oxford Historical Monographs* series publishes some of the best Oxford University doctoral theses on historical topics, especially those likely to engage the interest of a broad academic readership.

Possessing the City

Property and Politics in Delhi, 1911–1947

ANISH VANAIK

OXFORD
UNIVERSITY PRESS

OXFORD
UNIVERSITY PRESS

Great Clarendon Street, Oxford, OX2 6DP,
United Kingdom

Oxford University Press is a department of the University of Oxford.
It furthers the University's objective of excellence in research, scholarship,
and education by publishing worldwide. Oxford is a registered trade mark of
Oxford University Press in the UK and in certain other countries

First Edition published in 2020

Impression: 1

Published in the United States of America by Oxford University Press
198 Madison Avenue, New York, NY 10016, United States of America

British Library Cataloguing in Publication Data
Data available

Library of Congress Control Number: 2019941473

ISBN 978–0–19–884875–2

DOI: 10.1093/oso/9780198848752.001.0001

Printed and bound by
CPI Group (UK) Ltd, Croydon, CR0 4YY

Acknowledgements

I was warned early in the process that research inevitably involves loneliness, lack of confidence, and boredom. Friendships across three continents have ensured that this was only rarely true. That this text exists is testament to prods (gentle and brutal), guidance, and comradeship that have sustained me through the process.

The thesis and its subsequent avatars were, in large part, guided by Dr Nandini Gooptu's close and acute reading. Prof Neeladri Bhattacharya has been, since my formative academic years at JNU, a constant source of ideas and good advice. Prof Tanika Sarkar and Dr Radhika Singha taught courses that shaped my academic work.

This research would not have been possible without the support of the Clarendon Fund, the Balliol College C. R. Parekh Scholarship, the Institute for Historical Research and Royal Historical Society's Marshall Fellowship, and the Beit Fund. I am particularly grateful to Prof Bhikhu Parekh and Prof Peter Marshall for their generous endowments.

The librarians and archivists at the Department of Delhi Archives and Teen Murti changed numerous times during this research but were unfailingly helpful. The same holds true for the staff at the British Library in London. Mr Maan and Om Prakash at Town Hall cheerfully accommodated me at the payroll office even when my tugging at piles of municipal registers left their workspace saturated with dust. Kevin Greenbank, Barbara Roe, and Rachel Rowe at CSAS responded with characteristic good cheer to my monopolistic designs on the microfilm machine over a period that seemed unfairly interminable, even to this eager researcher.

Presentations organized by Ravi Ahuja (at Goettingen), Stephen Legg and Prashant Kidambi (at Nottingham), Eleanor Newbigin and Upal Chakrabarti (at SOAS), and Carlos Galvis and Prof Richard Dennis (at IHR) were occasions to air rudimentary versions of many ideas that have improved greatly as a result of feedback and criticisms. Contributing to Janaki Nair's textbook on urban history helped clarify much of the urban theory that I eventually used. A special debt must be recorded to Ammi (Khadija Azeem), who sat patiently with me for weeks trying to decipher documents drafted by careless clerks at the turn of century. Much that is interesting in this book would have been impossible without her help. During the final stages of my PhD dissertation, and again after, I had the immense good fortune to attend the summer school on Marxism organized at Dehradun by the Centre for Marxist Studies. It was a galvanizing moment for me, and continues to shape my intellectual and political trajectories. To its organizers, and especially to Willy, Anil, and Vivek, I owe my compass.

Without Layli and Sumeet, whose cynicism, humour, and affection kept me grounded, Oxford would have been a much stranger bubble, and it was not the same without them around. Andrea and Amr shared a passion for travel, movies, and many a long and winding conversation. Dinners and discussions with Anup and Agrima were eagerly anticipated and never disappointed. The SSL gang (of four?)—Anisha, Dhvani, and Simin—helped make an otherwise tense and constricting writing-up period memorable, full of expansive and varied disquisitions, jokes, and movie and music recommendations. Gabor's love–hate relationship with Cheddarland and Cheddarman were productively diverting. Juta, Tom, and Karin were companions to many a Katweazle and football match, and, along with Nicole, Nike, and Marcin, made the Randolph the warm house that it was. I was fortunate in having Kasturi living in Oxford, as her generosity over the years meant that I always had a second home as well. The memorable Dylan, chess, and cricket evenings with Maan and Manav were discovered regrettably late. Moid, Indrajit, George Karekwaivanane, Chris Oldiges, Rakesh, Samina, Youness, and Ibrahim all made Oxford a stimulating place.

Akhila and Parth have been hosts, comrades, and confidants for a long time. Bhochka will find that parts of this book emerge from conversations scattered across almost two decades. As a rule I take Antara's advice on everything, and it is always correct; her being in England was a wonderful happenstance. Post-BL evenings with Deepak were a delightful summative conclusion to the workday, as were Umar's provocations. Raghav could be relied on to share an interest in Delhi's *kuchas* where others would be bored stiff. Reconnecting with Manu and Samiksha was one of the many glorious fringe benefits of being in England, and both their warmth and meticulous scholarship are worthy of emulation. Upal and Sukanya in Cambridge were generous hosts during research trips. Thanks also to Emile, and Gautam Appa.

My time with the NREGA surveys in Jhusi and work in Seelampur was full of ideas and experiences of which I am still trying to make sense. Jean and Reetika made most of it possible. With Siddhartha, Sunil, Pushpam, and Anirban, arguments and ideas from every shade of political commitment worth holding were aired and tested. In the US, Matt, Casey, Teht, Padmini, Andrew, Carlos, Juan, and Allison all made Lafayette and New York full of warm memories.

Working at Purdue was a period of growth as first jobs often are. I am grateful to have had mentors and bosses as caring as Rhonda and Emily at the Honors College. From my many colleagues and students there I learned my first lessons in life as a teacher and am grateful for the many models and friendships I was able to draw on. Dwaine and Natasha, Bill, Tithi, and Shayari are inspirational in ways separate and collective. Thanks for all the happy times in West Lafayette.

The variously styled Frunch Forum, Reading Group, Pretend-reading Group, and 4S drunkards brought all the passion, camaraderie, intellect, and humour that makes academic work a satisfying endeavour. From them and Sunalini, Kriti, and Vrinda—as a collective and as individuals—I have learned about making meaning in life and work. With Mijie I have often had the eerie sense of looking into a mirror; thanks for sharing anxieties and for having different strengths from me—the best kind of friendship. Neha is co-founder of the only humour club that counts , and here in Delhi I miss her.

Jindal University has, somewhat unexpectedly, been a stimulating environment in which to teach and learn in troubled times. Credit for this is due entirely to the presence of Vanessa and Avishek. I would not change any part of our journey together over the last three years or so. Indeed, I look forward to reading Capital (again!) together soon. Rakesh, though he is not here any more, has been inspirational in many ways. His departure has in some ways been compensated by having Laurence around to collaborate with and to confabulate various schemes for promoting history around campus. Sumeet's presence at Jindal is also a welcome return to old conversations and collaborations and many new ones. Many thanks also to Albeena, Serohi, Sannoy, and Krithika for their good cheer and conversation.

Suresh, Bali, Mike, and Liz have not only opened up their homes but have supplied me with examples of how politics, ideas, writing, and professional skills can be combined. My gratitude for their struggles, courage, convictions, and commitment are impossibly entangled with viewing them as inspiration, motivation, and model.

Dadaji did not live to see how this turned out, but his enthusiasm for the past is a tangible source of my own. Dadima tolerated a too-often truant grandson with many an indulgent 'naughty boy', and barfi and Chinese food besides. They are both missed. Pasha's formidable intellect, commitment to pedagogy, and ideas have often made me see things in striking new light, and are a model for the best that academia can be. Pam's inexhaustible energy and infectious enthusiasm are enviable, and keeping up with her fiction reading is the next challenge that I intend to take up. Both Pam and Pasha have welcomed me into their home and lives to the point where a time before it is unimaginable. Achin and Pamela created a home in which politics, ideas, music, writing, laughter, books, sports, and TV were necessities. They ensured that my earliest lessons in respect, integrity, and principled activity were not just theoretical. I have borrowed freely from each of their very different interests and personalities, and would not have it any other way. Samar's accomplishments meant that I was the second doctor in the family. As he would no doubt remind me, only one of these is 'real'. His humour, grit, companionship, and compassion have sustained and inspired me at many places and times.

Megha's role in this book is probably more than even she knows. I have learnt from her and continue to do so every day, about academics, politics, music, movies, food, people, art . . . in short, about life. I rely on her immense strength, and would be lost were we not able to share our vulnerabilities, disappointments, and joys. In every sense of the phrase, we have grown up together. It is reassuring to think that, important as this book is to me, it is merely a drop in the shared pool of memories and experiences we have created.

Contents

List of Figures

List of Tables

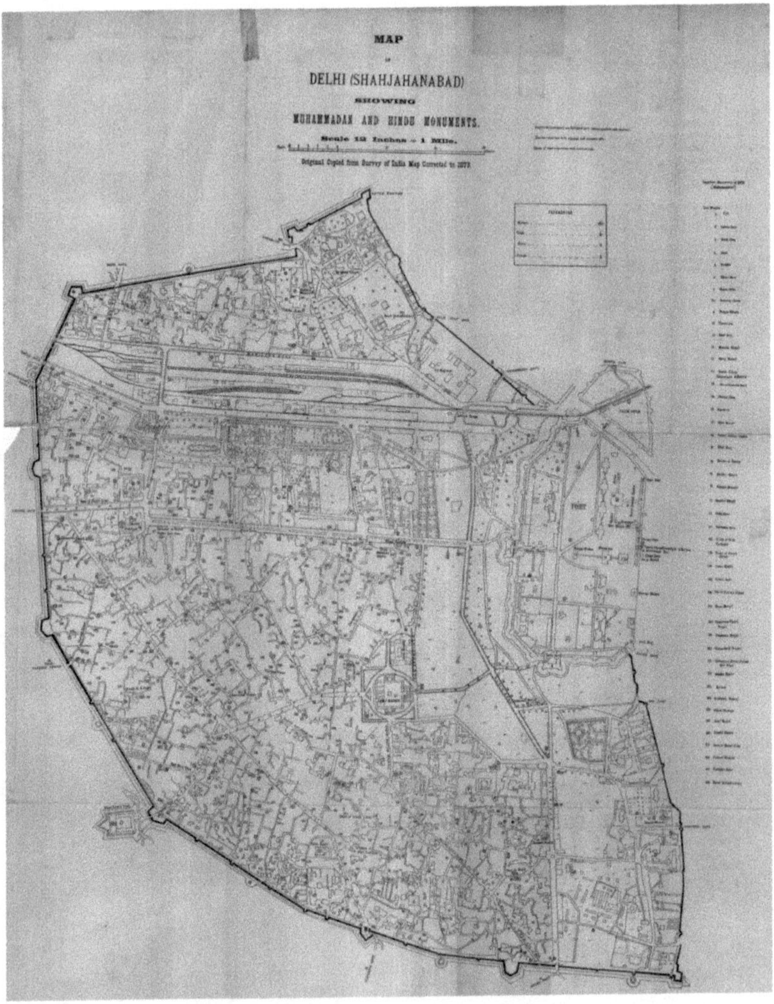

Map 1. Map of Shahjahanabad, Delhi[1]

[1] DDA, Map Collection, S no. 178.

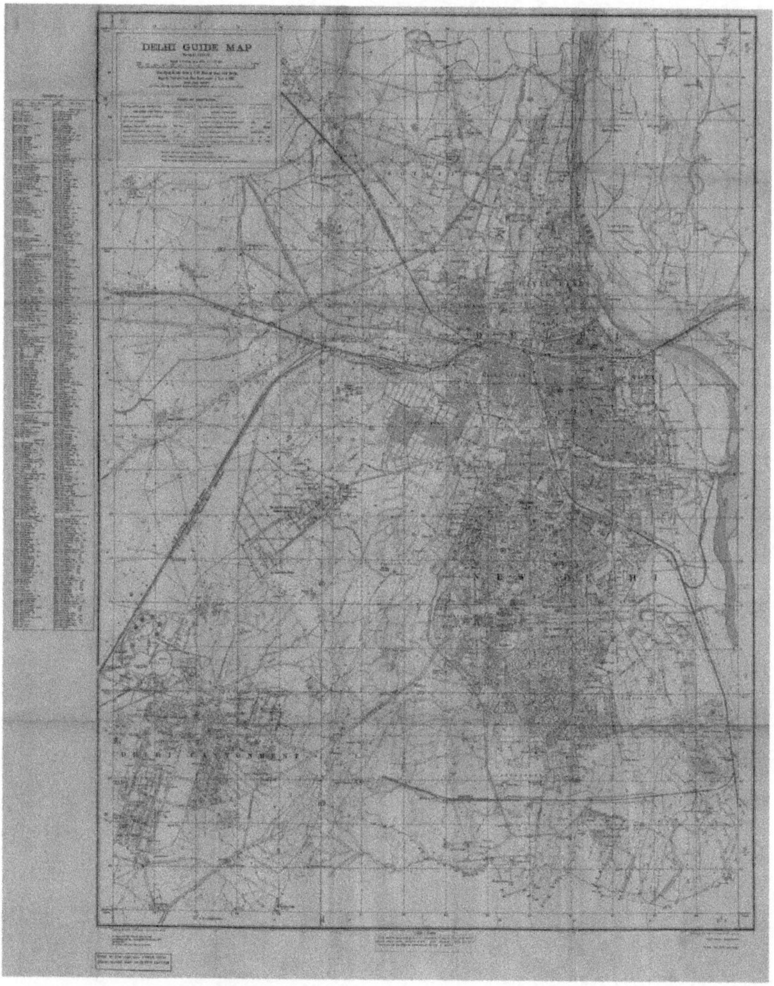

Map 2. Delhi Guide Map ca. 194[2]

[2] DDA, Map Collection, S no. 56.

Introduction

> The agricultural owners [in the suburbs] have not reached that stage of development that marks the desertion of traditional means of livelihood for a general economic outlook. They look askancc if asked to pool their properties and... [create] a plot of land with a front on a developed road; they don't see in it a building plot and enhanced value but rather a market garden partly ruined.
>
> Personal Secretary to the Chief Commissioner Delhi, 1912[1]

> The completion of the protective 'ring' is clearly a matter of urgent importance; private development has already begun, especially in the northern areas, and unless strict control is established the outskirts of Delhi will be irretrievably ruined.
>
> Chief Commissioner Delhi, 1939[2]

These two statements, just twenty-seven years apart and coming from the same office, tell a story about the treatment of land as a commodity in Delhi. The contrast between the two is striking. The first expresses dismay about the lack of an instinct for turning a profit from urban space in the agrarian outskirts of Delhi, for how could a city 'develop' without such entrepreneurialism? The second laments the existence of that very instinct for nearly 'ruining' the city. Between these two assessments can be discerned the outline of both the ramifying consequences of private enterprise in the property market and the knots into which the state tied itself when confronted with these consequences.

In the three-and-a-half decades preceding Partition that are examined in this book, Delhi's cityscape was shaped by a clutch of crucial transformations

[1] DDA, CC Records, Home, Pt. B., F no. 379, 1915: note by G. F de Montmorency, 14 November 1912.

[2] DDA, CC Records, LSG-LB, F no. 1(44), 1939, CC to Secy. to GoI, Dept. of EHL, 30 March 1939.

Possessing the City: Property and Politics in Delhi, 1911–1947. Anish Vanaik, Oxford University Press (2020).

DOI: 10.1093/oso/9780198848752.001.0001

spanning the market, the state, and mass politics. I concentrate on the parts of Delhi that came to be called 'Old Delhi' after 1911 when the declaration of Delhi as the capital dictated that a new city be built. Old Delhi included parts of the city that had a history stretching back to the seventeenth century, and these remained the main population centre of the city throughout the period of the study. More severely modernist New Delhi was developed and maintained largely for purposes of state and administration. Between 1920 and the 1940s, Delhi underwent an economic depression and recovery. In going through and emerging from these ructions, urban administration and the property market were transformed in lasting ways. At around the same time, Delhi also became the site for mass politics—of nationalist and communal stripes. Mobilizational politics (pickets, processions, and riots) and institutional representation (committees, voting, and so on) each emerged as theatres that re-created urban life.

Against this turbulent background, this book tracks the changes in the property market at three levels. First, the place of private property development in Delhi's economy. Even as this period was marked by large-scale state initiatives such as the Delhi Improvement Trust, profit-oriented, decentralized, and market-based initiatives of urban construction created the Delhi cityscape to a far greater degree than did the halting initiatives of the state. In order to more clearly delineate the role of the property market, it has been necessary to take up a second issue: the relationship between the state and market in the development of urban property. In particular, I bring into focus a number of mechanisms other than urban planning—driven by aesthetic, sanitary, or security concerns—that shaped the relationship of the state to urban space. What, for instance, might it mean for the state to intervene in urban space during an economic depression? Resolutions of these kind of dilemmas were sought and embedded into the quotidian practices of local government throughout these decades. The third overarching level of analysis is the relationship between the commodification of land and opposition to it. This emerged as a crucial axis of political struggles in Delhi. Rents and prices of urban property were directly at issue in tussles over housing. The question of commodification can, however, also be discerned in clashes that were not ostensibly about economic issues. The instance taken up for extended examination is violence over religious sites in the city.

Concentration on urban property affords a useful frame to connect these levels of Delhi's history: the property market, the state, and popular protests. Both the early historiography of cities in European cities and more recent urban theory have highlighted the far-reaching implications of the modern commodification of urban space,[3] and the rarity of full-length treatments of urban property in Indian history writing is therefore something of a curiosity. History in South Asia, including urban history, has taken up each of the three levels that this book explores: property relations, the state, and social protests. How, then, can we understand the marginalization of urban property from this body of work?

Property, Economic History, and the City

The theme of property relations and their transformations during the colonial period has been one of the canonical preoccupations of South Asian history. This preoccupation, however, has been overwhelmingly focused on agrarian and forest settings, and a conspicuous absence within this literature has been the fate of urban property in the colonial city. The literature on the history of agrarian property in India is formidable in its scope and complexity. Ranajit Guha's *A Rule of Property for Bengal* and Eric Stokes' *English Utilitarians and India* examined colonial land policy in terms of its intellectual formation.[4] Contending against their approach were accounts that foregrounded administrative officials' experience of existing institutional arrangements in the countryside.[5] The net result has been the excavation of a wealth of empirical evidence about the concrete effects of property arrangements on different social groups across ecological regions. These questions, posed largely in the 1960s and 1970s, were put on the back-burner as agrarian history moved onto different terrain. In the 1990s, environmental histories brought back the issue of property relations, with much of the focus being on the displacement of older ways of relating to space and the erosion of rights in the commons. Cities, however, were absent from this historiographical trajectory.

[3] The work of H. J. Dyos is a good example of the centrality of property to early urban histories. Dyos (1968), 'The Speculative Builders and Developers of Victorian London', *Victorian Studies*, 11 (Supplement: Symposium on the Victorian City), 641–90. For urban theory, David Harvey's work explored here is a key reference point.

[4] Ranajit Guha (1963), *A Rule of Property for Bengal; an Essay on the Idea of Permanent Settlement* (Paris: Mouton). Eric Stokes (1959), *The English Utilitarians and India* (Oxford: Clarendon Press).

[5] For an overview of the debates, see Neeladri Bhattacharya (1986), 'Colonial State and Agrarian Policy', in Sabyasachi Bhattacharya and Romila Thapar (eds.), *Situating Indian History: For Sarvepalli Gopal* (Delhi: Oxford University Press).

The most likely cause for the absence of urban property amid this interest in land relations is that it does not display the manifest links with imperial revenues characteristic of agrarian property. Particularly for north and central India, direct taxes relating to urban land, such as house tax, were always a far less significant source of revenue than were indirect taxes on commercial activity in the city, such as the octroi.[6] Urban property tended to confront colonial officials in the form of a practical everyday problem, rather than, as was the case in the countryside, as a foundational issue generating polarized opinion and counter-opinion. There is certainly nothing like the debates within the colonial bureaucracy over the Permanent Settlement or other kinds of revenue settlement in the archival deliberations on urban property.[7] History writing seems to have followed administrative deliberations in downgrading the significance of urban property.

There is another reason for the marginalization of urban property in mainstream economic history. Scholarly treatment of property relations had derived from wider formulations of the relationship between colonialism and capitalism. This meant that research into property forms was closely tied into larger debates within the economic history of the colonial period. The central thematic progression within Indian economic history—the 'Drain of Wealth', deindustrialization of traditional crafts, commercialization of agriculture, and the rise of modern industry—was a narrative of India's integration into the wider colonial economy. Agriculture, the revenue settlements, and consequently the property forms evolved in the countryside were central to the economic history of the eighteenth and nineteenth centuries. The economic history of the twentieth century has been traditionally dominated by discussion of international financial arrangements, international trade, and its impact upon Indian industrialization.[8] The classic narrative, in fact, sketches out connections between these three processes. It takes up the issue of tariff barriers, the need to maintain exchange rates between Britain and India, and, post-World War I,

[6] Hugh Tinker (1954), *The Foundations of Local Self-Government in India, Pakistan, and Burma* (London: Athlone Press).

[7] William Glover makes a similar point. William J. Glover (2008), *Making Lahore Modern: Constructing and Imagining a Colonial City* (Minneapolis: University of Minnesota Press), p. 32.

[8] Prasannan Parthasarathi suggests that the dominant influence of the themes of agriculture and industry in the economic history which emerged in the 1960s and 1970s was largely an outcome of the canonical status of the earlier pre-1930s nationalist economic history. Parthasarathi Prasannan (2015), 'The History of Indian Economic History', in Daniele Boldizzoni and Pat Hudson (eds.), *Routledge Handbook of Global Economic History* (London: Routledge).

the hesitant, contradictory, and sometimes confrontational rise of indigenous Indian-owned industry from out of the ranks of those engaged in domestic trade and finance. Since it did not contribute to industrialization or agrarian revenues, urban property and real estate have received scant attention in the overarching plot lines of economic history.[9]

An exemplary instance of the effect of these emphases can be found in the colonial history of Bombay. Urban histories of the latter have been able to draw on economic history far more than is the case for Delhi. However, this has been an economic history shaped by the overarching question of industrialization.[10] The results have been paradoxical. On the one hand, certain kinds of connections between the economy and urban space have been central to accounts of Bombay: the role of business and commercial elites in city development are well etched, and an interest in industrial labour has led historians into working-class localities. On the other hand, what might be seen as the most direct projection of the economy onto urban space—the property market—has until fairly recently been marginal.[11] A. D. D. Gordon's work, for instance, dwells for the most part on the fortunes—economic and political—of the traders and industrialists of Bombay.[12] Somewhat incongruously, a central chapter on the progress of municipal politics introduces 'landlords' as a crucial set of actors with distinct political motivations, only for them to disappear again in the rest of his book. Without an account of their economic activities comparable to the one about traders and industrialists, landlords remain an undertheorized

[9] Tirthankar Roy's survey of the post-1983 historiography underlines the important role played by regional studies (usually village and agrarian) in illuminating broader themes in economic history, but does not even identify history of urban land as a significant direction for future research, let alone noticing its absence. Tirthankar Roy (2004), 'Flourishing Branches, Wilting Core: Research in Modern Indian Economic History', *Australian Economic History Review*, 44 (3), 221–40.

[10] More generally, it is striking that industrial towns—Ahmedabad, Kanpur, and Calcutta for instance—are able to draw upon much more well developed histories of the (local) economy than those cities where industry was relatively marginal. Anindita Ghosh's complaint that 'urban histories of colonial India have traditionally been considered within the rigid framework of political economy or dominant colonial ideologies' is therefore more applicable to Calcutta or Mumbai than to places such as Delhi or Lucknow. Anindita Ghosh (2016), *Claiming the City: Protest, Crime and Scandals in Colonial Calcutta, c.1860–1920* (New Delhi: Oxford University Press).

[11] Nikhil Rao (2013), *House, but No Garden: Apartment Living in Bombay's Suburbs, 1898–1964* (Minneapolis: University of Minnesota Press). Mariam Dossal (2010), *Theatre of Conflict, City of Hope: Mumbai: 1660 to Present Times* (New Delhi; Oxford: Oxford University Press).

[12] A. D. D. Gordon (1978), *Businessmen and Politics: Rising Nationalism and a Modernising Economy in Bombay, 1918–1933* (New Delhi: Manohar).

group, and consequently their interests are read straightforwardly from the supply and demand of housing stock.

Broadly speaking, interest in the history of Indian trade and finance has usually derived from the contribution (or lack thereof) of commerce and finance to the emergence of industry. Such a paradigm, relegates urban property to the footnotes. In pointing this out, I do not mean to argue that the links between commerce, finance, and industry are unimportant. There are, however, economic processes that the economic frame just outlined has neglected. Prominent among these must be counted the links between finance, real estate, and the development of urban infrastructure. David Harvey's theoretical work points to the centrality of these connections, for the circulation of capital in general quite as much as for the production of urban space. With respect to economic history, then, urban property acquires significance only with a more careful integration of the spatial dimension into accounts of the economy. In short, the dominant perspective that makes the countryside and industrialization the key economic questions about colonial India has conditioned a silence on urban property. A better understanding of colonial urban development must incorporate new theoretical perspectives on the political economy of urban space.

Power, the State, and Urban Space

Where the conventional interpretation of economic history has been marked by a silence on urban real estate, a quite different marginalization of urban property can be seen in the literature on state power in the South Asian city. In this body of work, urban property has, in fact, been ubiquitous. Ironically enough, however, urban property's inclusion has been eclectic, rarely extending to an analytical understanding of the linkages between the state, the market, and urban space. The result has been a resolutely static relationship between the state and the urban property market.

Urban histories of South Asia have brought the state into their discussions in three broad ways. First, as the site of competition among Indians for institutional control of urban politics—municipalities in particular.[13] Second,

[13] The urban in these texts is important as a setting for schools, administration, and trade. For all their intricate tracing of the politics of groups and factions in urban areas, these are analyses that separate politics from spatial practice. Christine E. Dobbin (1972), *Urban Leadership in Western India: Politics and Communities in Bombay City, 1840–1885* (Oxford: Oxford University Press). C. A. Bayly (1975), *The Local Roots of Indian Politics: Allahabad,*

as developing, articulating, and executing plans for urban development. Third, in the form of the coercive presence of the police to put down strikes and nationalist protests or quell communal riots. In the first body of work, urban landlords appear as important political actors with little analysis of either their property holdings or their impact on urban space independent of municipal agencies. In the third body of work, symbolic contestations over space, or strategic deployments of the coercive apparatus of the state, have been foregrounded.[14] Most directly concerned to link the state to space, however, are approaches that take up urban planning.

Two classic histories from the 1980s by Narayani Gupta on Delhi and Veena Oldenburg on Lucknow investigated the post-Mutiny reorganization of these north Indian cities in terms of an almost Hausmannesque state-directed transformation of urban space.[15] Oldenburg encapsulates the authoritarian exercise of power at this moment through a series of imperatives that formed the titles of her chapters: 'The City must be Clean', 'The City must Pay', 'The City must be Safe', and so on. The underlying assumption here was the plasticity of space to the aims of the ruling elite.[16] The decisive transformations of the cityscape were ultimately shaped by the decisive actions of the colonial state.[17] These explanations, on one hand, leave little room for other forces to mould urban space. On the other hand, they rely on a unitary understanding of the state, its planning apparatus, and its ability to translate ambition into reality.

More recent accounts of planning, such as that of Janaki Nair, have rejected such a unitary understanding, tending to present plans as heterogeneously conceived and often ineffective. They instead choose to highlight

1880–1920 (Oxford: Clarendon Press). Rajat Kanta Ray (1979), *Urban Roots of Indian Nationalism: Pressure Groups and Conflict of Interests in Calcutta City Politics, 1875–1939* (New Delhi: Vikas). Howard Spodek's work—rooted in the actions of leading Ahmedabadi personalities—might be considered a recent reanimation of this approach. Howard Spodek (2012), *Ahmedabad: Shock City of Twentieth-Century India* (Hyderabad: Orient BlackSwan).

[14] Rajnarayan Chandavarkar (1998), *Imperial Power and Popular Politics: Class, Resistance and the State in India, c.1850–1950* (Cambridge: Cambridge University Press).

[15] Narayani Gupta (1981), *Delhi between Two Empires, 1803–1931: Society, Government and Urban Growth* (Delhi: Oxford University Press). Veena Talwar Oldenburg (1984), *The Making of Colonial Lucknow, 1856–1877* (Princeton: Princeton University Press).

[16] Narayani Gupta's work, less closely focused on statecraft and empirically richer, is nevertheless framed by the plans of the colonial state.

[17] Partho Datta's account of colonial Calcutta is a throwback to a relatively unproblematic account of official plans shaping urban reality. Partho Datta (2012), *Planning the City: Urbanization and Reform in Calcutta, c.1800–c.1940* (New Delhi: Tulika Books).

sites of contestation and often failure.[18] Urban planning itself, especially in the twentieth century, saw the emergence of a variety of intellectual currents whose relationship to the colonial project and state power was not univocal.[19] More generally in this literature, competing visions of space—both within state institutions and between state and non-state actors—are presented as transforming the meanings of planning. With all this complexity, however, histories of planning in Indian cities have tended not to open onto the workings of property markets. Even where plans and planning are seen as constituted by complex and cross-cutting factors, the mechanisms of planning have not been linked to the dynamics of the economy. In doing so, the crucial connections between the state, economy, and urban space are made into black boxes rather than objects of enquiry.

Awadhendra Sharan's statecentric account of housing in his pioneering environmental history of Delhi presents an illustrative contrast to the approach of this book.[20] Sharan points to the discourse of 'congestion' that became a key reference point for planners in the Delhi Improvement Trust (DIT) from the 1930s onwards. Public housing was envisioned by the state as a response to congestion, and congestion remained a useful stick with which to beat the poor after the failures of public housing. In Sharan's account, a key role in planning failure is played by the fiscal conservatism of the colonial state.[21] Unwilling to subsidize housing for the poor who needed it but could not pay, only a quarter of the housing planned by the Delhi Improvement Trust was ultimately built. A secondary cause of the failures of DIT was the gross underestimation of the population that streamed into the city. In Sharan's account, these two factors—fiscal conservatism and inadequate demographic projections—remained the root cause of the inability to address urban congestion well into the post-colonial period. The lack of any dynamic relationship between the market and the

[18] Janaki Nair (2005), *The Promise of the Metropolis: Bangalore's Twentieth Century* (Delhi: Oxford University Press). Preeti Chopra (2011), *A Joint Enterprise: Indian Elites and the Making of British Bombay* (Minneapolis, MN: University of Minnesota Press). Swati Chattopadhyay (2005), *Representing Calcutta: Modernity, Nationalism and the Colonial Uncanny* (London: Routledge).

[19] Peter Hall (2002), *Cities of Tomorrow: An Intellectual History of Urban Planning and Design in the Twentieth Century*, 3rd ed. (Oxford: Blackwell).

[20] Awadhendra B. Sharan (2014), *In the City, Out of Place: Nuisance, Pollution, and Dwelling in Delhi, c.1850–2000*, 1st edn. (New Delhi: Oxford University Press).

[21] Stephen Legg's account of the failures of DIT plans also cite fiscal conservatism as the chief cause. In his account, colonial aesthetic considerations are also given significant if subsidiary weight. Stephen Legg (2007), *Spaces of Colonialism: Delhi's Urban Governmentalities* (Malden, MA; Oxford: Blackwell).

economic considerations of the state is characteristic. In fact, as will be demonstrated later, spikes and troughs in the property market elicited different kinds of responses from the colonial state. Again, as illustrated in the epigraph at the beginning of this Introduction, the very action of planning layouts was sparking speculation in the areas in which the Trust operated. We hear little about this from Sharan's account, and, consequently, even the comparatively late institution of an Improvement Trust in Delhi is unsatisfyingly attributed to the rise of a discourse of congestion.[22] The political economy of property, as this book will demonstrate, played an enormous role in the establishment and ongoing operations of the DIT. The market in urban land threw up specific dilemmas with which urban administration had to grapple.

It is not only the political economy of property that is ignored in Sharan's account, however. The provision of housing and the ability of the state to deny provision, defer it, or supply it promptly, was also determined by the political strength of the mobilizations that occurred (or did not occur) around the issue. Sharan's sole referencing of an exchange between the Chief Commissioner and the Congress Municipal Councillor Asaf Ali is not part of a wider effort to track how popular politics grappled with commoditized urban land.[23] The scant mention of housing, or the commoditization of urban land in the extensive literature on urban protests, is a lacuna complementary to the stilted approach to urban property in the work on planning and state power in the city.

Protest, Mobilizations, and Social Conflict in the City

The literature on social protests in the city shares, with the work on the urban economy, a tendency to invisibilize the property market. That literature can be thought to have a number of components. Histories of labour and the urban poor have added a dynamic sense of urban space to their exploration of mass politics.[24] Rajnarayan Chandavarkar's history of working-class Bombay

[22] Most colonial cities—Bombay, Calcutta, Madras, Kanpur, and so on—had already begun to establish Improvement Trusts in the first two decades of the twentieth century. Delhi's Improvement Trust in 1937 emerged well after this cycle.

[23] Stephen Legg's account of resistance to the Delhi Ajmere Gate Scheme of DIT is only slightly more elaborate.

[24] The term 'urban poor' is designed in part to avoid the imputation of a class as the organizing basis for the mobilizations, politics, and culture of groups below the middle classes. Gooptu's work is a pioneering instance of the employment of this category. Nandini Gooptu

unearths dynamic connections between labour militancy and neighbourhood configurations, as do Nandini Gooptu and Chitra Joshi for the north Indian cities that they study.[25] These were cities in which the labouring poor struggled against the burden of being seen as immoral and insanitary. Urban elites ensured that municipal 'improvements' were applied to selected portions of the city, even as coercive regimes of inspection and policing 'nuisance' operated in slums. Equally, however, working-class neighbourhoods evolved spatial layouts and a cultural ethos of their own. Chandavarkar points to the ways in which the cramped tenements of Girangaon forced a dissolution of the divide between public and private lives. Joshi discusses the sense of territoriality in the 'Garh' (fort) that was Gwaltoli, the working class suburb of Kanpur. The working classes and labouring poor contributed to the making of the city quite as much as did elite planners. These histories from below have done much to shift the historian's gaze beyond the urban elites who dominated early accounts of the city. This is a valuable perspective that links mass politics to the creation of the colonial city. But what are the ways in which the economy of urban space has appeared in these histories?

Unsurprisingly, where the economy is discussed, it has been in terms of the trajectory of industrial capital highlighted previously. The neighbourhood, in Chandavarkar's account, for instance, was shaped by the dynamics of industrial strikes. Rents and patterns of credit extended by shopkeepers in working-class localities have been viewed in terms of their contribution to the possibility of sustaining labour militancy. The more direct issues that arose from the commodification of urban space—high rents, the disappearance of urban commons, and so on—are rarely tackled. It is striking that there are few studies about protests over housing in the city.[26] The absence

(2001), *The Politics of the Urban Poor in Early Twentieth-Century India* (Cambridge: Cambridge University Press). More recently, Partha Chatterjee's influential formulation of political society seeks to capture some of the same sociological terrain. In his work, political society is contrasted with the more structured and law-bound politics of civil society. Partha Chatterjee (2004), *The Politics of the Governed: Reflections on Popular Politics in Most of the World* (New York: Columbia University Press). Anindita Ghosh explicitly draws on the continuities between these formulations. Ghosh, *Claiming the City*.

---

[25] Rajnarayan Chandavarkar (1994), *The Origins of Industrial Capitalism in India: Business Strategies and the Working Classes in Bombay, 1900–1940* (Cambridge: Cambridge University Press). Gooptu, *The Politics of the Urban Poor*. Chitra Joshi (2005), *Lost Worlds: Indian Labour and Its Forgotten Histories* (London: Anthem).

[26] A few works look at agitations about house tax. See Richard Heitler (1972), 'The Varanasi House Tax Hartal of 1810–11', *Indian Economic and Social History Review*, 9 (3), 239–57,

of such a perspective tends to reinforce the idea that Improvement Trusts and measures to provide subsidized housing in cities were outcomes solely of elite deliberations or benevolence. In fact, I demonstrate that the strength or weakness of struggles for housing played a crucial role in contributing to the creation of public housing.

A second body of work that has taken up mass politics in the city has dealt with communalism and riots in the city. Following Sandria Freitag's brilliant account of religious mobilizations in Benares, much of this writing attends to spatial configurations, and particularly those with rich symbolisms.[27] A related set of texts examines the symbolisms of religious clashes and riots. What each of these has demonstrated, in contrast to earlier explanations of communal clashes (for instance, in terms of factional interests), is a productive sense of the role of urban space as more than a mere location for religious conflict. However, perhaps wary of mechanistic accounts of communalism—as mere displacement of economic struggles —there has been little effort to link communal clashes with the political economy of urban space. Is it possible to navigate a different path between the Scylla of economism and Charybdis of an account of communal clashes solely rooted in symbolisms?

Jyoti Hosagrahar's work on the *haveli* (the 'traditional' courtyard house) is, perhaps, the best illustration of another way of thinking about the relationship between culture and space, closer to the perspectives which I adopt. This is the idea that quotidian spatial arrangements have a determinate impact on the cultural forms that emerge around them.[28] Thus, in Hosagrahar's account, between 1857 and 1920 the external life of the *haveli* went from forming the symbolic core of entire neighbourhoods to representing rational

Gupta, *Delhi Between Two Empires*. For a work largely focused on post-colonial agitations about agrarian commons in Delhi's periurban fringes, see Minoti Chakravarty-Kaul (1996), *Common Lands and Customary Law: Institutional Change in North India over the Past Two Centuries* (Delhi: Oxford University Press). A recent exception is the important work of Vanessa Caru on Bombay. Vanessa Caru (2013), 'Circumstantial Adjustments: The Colonial State, the Nationalist Movement, and Rent Control Legislation (Bombay, 1918–1928)', *Le Mouvement Social* 242, 81–95.

---

27 Sandria B. Freitag (1989), *Collective Action and Community: Public Arenas and the Emergence of Communalism in North India* (Berkeley, CA: University of California Press).

28 Jyoti Hosagrahar (2005), *Indigenous Modernities: Negotiating Architecture and Urbanism* (London: Routledge), ch. 1. Chattopadhyay, discussing Calcutta, also develops this dimension of 'representational space' to great effect. Swati Chattopadhyay (2000), 'Blurring Boundaries: The Limits of "White Town" in Colonial Calcutta', *Journal of the Society of Architectural Historians*, 59 (2), 154–79.

and ordered 'modern' familial existence. Inside the sprawling eighteenth-century *haveli*, male–female segregation was originally mapped horizontally around distinct courtyards. With the subdivisions and sale of most portions of *havelis*, the 'modern' *haveli* came to map male–female segregation vertically around just one courtyard. In this account, complex social pressures—of the market and declining aristocratic incomes—interact dynamically with meanings and practices within the cultural sphere through the mediation of the built environment. It is possible, then, to come to non-mechanistic explanations of cultural change within the context of transformed social and spatial relationships.

In contrast to the literature just surveyed, two recent works, both about Bombay, have focused squarely on the question of urban property.[29] Mariam Dossal's study—spanning over three centuries—demonstrates the crucial importance of land at various stages in the history of the city. In particular, she outlines how the nineteenth-century conversion of a welter of tenures—in urban Bombay and its immediate suburbs—was considered necessary for planning and administering the city effectively. Processes of mapping and surveying the city were also closely tied to the market in urban land. Comprehensive planning in the city—envisioned often in its history but most elaborately in the twentieth century—was in large measure ineffectual. As Dossal points out, 'the state had never been dominant nor determined enough to ensure that planning initiatives were actually implemented.'[30] While her account is largely descriptive, she sketches a narrative of the continuous effort to recreate land in Mumbai as a more effective commodity. What emerges is a sense of the power that the property market was able to exert in the development of Mumbai and its imbrication in wider cycles of accumulation of capital.

Nikhil Rao's finely crafted portrait of the rise of a community-based form of suburban development in Matunga is a further demonstration of the value of historians 'spend[ing] more time with the evidence of land ownership and speculation'.[31] Rao's study traces the evolution of the apartment as the paradigmatic form of suburban living for upper-caste lower-middle-class groups in Mumbai from 1898 to 1964.

[29] Dossal, *Theatre of Conflict, City of Hope*. Rao, *House, but No Garden*.
[30] Dossal, *Theatre of Conflict, City of Hope*, p. 164.
[31] Here Rao is citing the American urban historian Sam Bass Warner. Rao, *House, but No Garden*, p. 10.

The first step in the process was, as we have seen in Dossal's work, to consolidate and homogenize the various forms of property holding in Bombay's hitherto agrarian suburbs. This commodification ensured that suburban land in Bombay was amenable to sale and purchase. Consequently, land would be sensitive to wider circuits of capital in the city. Indeed, the multi-apartment flat was not, Rao argues, a consequence of the shortage of land in Mumbai, as is commonly held. In fact, it appeared at a particular moment in the 1920s when economic activity in the city was depressed, and speculators who had purchased land during the preceding boom could not make a profit out of house-style or bungalow-style residential accommodation.[32] The fascinating connections between architectural form, commodification, and wider economic trends suggested in this instance characterizes much of this work, as does the running concern with cycles of accumulation in the property market. In another highly original section, Rao demonstrates that the identity of being 'south Indian' emerged at the intersection of pre-existing caste and cultural attributes and new forms of finance—the cooperative society in particular—that sprang up in the 1920s and 1930s.[33] Engaging with architecture, voluntary societies, caste institutions, and state action, he is able to develop a compelling account of the transformations involved at the level of land, dwellings, and communities. Rao's ability to suggest insightful links between the material, social, and cultural, mark his work as a significant departure within South Asian urban history.

These books demonstrate the importance of a history of urban property—to understand the urban built environment itself as well as to engage with more established historiographical themes within South Asian urban history—planning, mapping, architecture, community formation, and conflict. All this, however, is based on paying attention to what is happening in the property market. Demarcating periods of boom and bust, scrutinizing the practices through which commodification occurs, the forms of representation evolved, and being sensitive to ways in which finance, building activity, specialized knowledge, and cultural norms interact.

A current of Marxist theorizing deriving from the work of Henri Lefebvre, David Harvey, and Neil Smith is particularly important to this book. Of these, the most significant has been Harvey's account of the circulation of capital through urban space;—an issue which he has analysed over a large

[32] *Rao, House, but No Garden*, ch. 3.

[33] *Rao, House, but No Garden*, ch. 5.

and wide-ranging body of work.[34] Harvey suggests that cities have a particular salience in the capitalist search for a "'spatial fix"' to the recurring problem of overaccumulation. Overaccumulation, in Harvey's reading of Marx, occurs under capitalist social relations as a result of the fundamentally unbridgeable gap between production that is individual, and an aggregate social requirement that can only be known *ex post* through the market. Thus, individual acts of uncoordinated production constantly generate social imbalances. Financial instruments play a crucial role in coordinating capital—, switching it from less to more profitable sectors, initiating new ventures, and generally tiding over the temporal lag between production and the realization of profit. Overaccumulation in the realm of production sparks a search for profitable new avenues for investment. Under these conditions, finance will stream towards the "'secondary circuit"'—the creation of infrastructure—that can support and augment a new cycle of accumulation in production. This is the "'spatial fix"': the production of new configurations of space at particular conjunctures within cycles of accumulation. Land, therefore, plays a crucial role in the circulation of capital, b. But it can only do so when it circulates as a commodity, ; that isi.e. , as property. By becoming a commodity, it allows speculators to bet upon the future value of land. This, in turn, dictates the uses to which land can be put—, forcing it to be monetarily productive. In twentieth- century Delhi, there is much evidence for the presence of this set of pressures. As will be elaborated belowlater, the cycle of boom and bust and the reconfiguration of the property market operated in close connection with local finance. However, due attention must be paid to the form in which land was created as a commodity. As Harvey points out, unless land can be represented in certain forms it cannot circulate effectively. In order to elaborate what this could entail, it is useful to turn to one of the major sources of Harvey's theorizsations about space—: the work of the Marxist philosopher Henri Lefebvre.[35]

Lefebvre's critique is directed at the twin problems of treating space as a mere setting for the unfolding of events or as pure metaphor. In fact, for Lefebvre, space is produced within particular social relations and, in turn,

[34] David Harvey (1999), *The Limits to Capital*, new edn. (London: Verso); David Harvey (1989b), *The Urban Experience* (Oxford: Blackwell); David Harvey (2003), Paris, Capital of Modernity (New York, NY: Routledge); David Harvey (1989a), *The Condition of Postmodernity: An Enquiry into the Origins of Cultural Change* (Oxford, England; Cambridge, MA: Blackwell).

[35] Henri Lefebvre (1998), *The Production of Space*, trans. Donald Nicholson-Smith (Oxford: Blackwell).

helps to produce thesrelations. In order to capture this 'produced' nature of space, analysis must treat its perceived, conceived, and lived dimensions as a unified totality.[36] Furthrmore, this lso requires sensitivity to historical transformations in the production of space. Of particular importance for this study is his idea of abstract space. For Lefebvre, abstract space is a particular historical form of spatial production, in which space is conceived as as homogeneous, empty, and exchangeable. These attributes are achieved through the domnance of certain forms of knowledge about space (representations of space).[37] This is also a space within which violence, particularly that of the state, remains embedded 'sometimes latent, or preparing to explode; sometimes unleashed, and directed now against itself, now against the world [. . .]'.[38] While abstract space present itself as homogenus, it is, in its lived forms, hardly so. Abstraction is produced as a result of concrete processes which involve, amng other thigs, reductive violence.

There is a close relationship between the concept of abstraction used by Lefebvre, in the context of space, and that deployed by Marx in his analysis of abstract labour and the commodity form.[39] In both these instances, abstraction is not a mere philosophical proposition but is held to be the outcome of concrete social processes. Among other crucial processes—such as the emergence of certain kinds of political authority, the separation of town and countryside, and so on—the circuit of capital accumulation, and the ways in which it operates through space, generates abstract space. The abstract quality of abstract space cannot be understood solely on the basis of its forms of appearance, in its representation as geometric

[36] Perceived space refers to the elements of space as they are sensed by the body, manipulated with the hands and moved through 'the practical basis of the perception of the outside world'. Conceived space, in contrast, is the idea of space that derives from specialized knowledge. Lived space differs from both the perceived and the conceived. It takes up elements of each, but with the addition of affect and meaning it could either amplify or undermine each of the other two aspects. Henri Lefebvre (1998), *The Production of Space*, trans. Donald Nicholson-Smith (Oxford: Blackwell.

[37] Lefebvre suggests, for instance, that abstract space has a 'geometric formant'—the possibility of three-dimensionality being reduced to two-dimensionality—an 'optical formant'—the dominance of the visual, with non-optical impressions becoming mere precursors of the visual—and a 'phallic formant'—the effort to fill space with an 'objectal absolute'. Lefebvre, *The Production of Space*, pp. 285–87. A wide range of practices that emerged in the nineteenth-century colonial city—mapping, photography (as a primarily visual manner of relating to space) and the conceptualization of the public sphere as male—can be seen in these terms.

[38] Lefebvre, *The Production of Space*, p. 277.

[39] Lefebvre, *The Production of Space*, pp. 306–8.

relationships, or manifestation as a particular form of architecture—Le Corbusier's modernism, for instance. The process as a whole must be grasped.[40] Indeed, Lefebvre repeatedly highlights the social nature of the production of space. Thus he rejects any effort to classify modern spaces on the basis of mere appearance, insisting that they be grasped as part of a social process of abstraction. Abstraction is, in fact, an extremely dynamic process.[41]

The geographer Neil Smith's work *Uneven Development* can be seen as developing the implications of this proposition. Smith points out that tendencies internal to the spatial process of the circulation of capital generate a landscape characterized by opposed tendencies towards equalization and differentiation.[42] These derive from drives towards equilibrium states within capitalism and their constant disruption. Different spatial scales—the urban, the national, the provincial, and so on—display different forms and degrees of stability and instability. The scale of the urban, Smith suggests, is particularly fluid; new construction, suburban development, and inner-city redevelopment are all taken for granted. By comparison, the scale of the national has historically demonstrated greater stability; for example, with boundaries remaining the same over extended periods of time.[43]

Abstraction cannot be found simply by identifying repetitive patterns of space or by the appearance of centralized visions of planning. It is only by studying the movement of capital through the city that the particular forms and effects of abstraction can be discerned. There is also a subsidiary

[40] My use of the terms 'property', 'the property market', 'private enterprise', and 'property development' derive from this philosophical holism. On such a view, the legal–juridical form of property or its sale and purchase are simply individual facets of commodified urban space. Each of these must be accompanied by exploration of the connections between capital moving into construction and property development, and that which was available in other spheres of the local economy.

[41] The converse is also affirmed by Lefebvre; that is, the appearance of abstract space as homogenous is deceptive. It does not, for instance, manifest itself only in the form of indistinguishable organizations of space or uniform planning. 'Abstract space is not homogeneous; it simply has homogeneity as its goal, its orientation, its "lens". And, indeed, it renders homogeneous. But in itself it is multiform.' Lefebvre, *The Production of Space*, p. 287.

[42] As Ahuja points out in developing a similar set of ideas: '. . . processes of fragmentation are *constitutive* for processes of homogenization in modern societies such as, for instance, the social and spatial fragmentation of labour processes for the global proliferation of wage labour relations.' Ravi Ahuja (2009), *Pathways of Empire: Circulation, 'Public Works' and Social Space in Colonial Orissa, c.1780–1914* (Hyderabad: Orient BlackSwan).

[43] Neil Smith (2008), *Uneven Development: Nature, Capital and the Production of Space*, 3rd edn. (Athens, GA: University of Georgia Press).

implication: there is no single form taken by the practical struggles dealing with the impact of abstraction. These are inherently diverse. As will be elaborated in the latter part of this book, with respect to religious property in particular, the impact of abstract space in colonial Delhi was profoundly paradoxical.

These three insights—the circuit of capital through space, abstraction, and scalar unevenness developed within the tradition of thinking represented by Lefebvre, Harvey, and Smith—inflect the ways in which property is conceived in the chapters that follow. It is treated as a social relation, embracing both the particular forms in which urban property appeared as commodity and the social processes and struggles through which commodification was generated.

Plan of the Work

Three major aims are pursued over the seven chapters that follow. First, to illuminate the actual trends in the property market. What were its ups and downs? Who were the actors in the market, and how did they respond to its various perturbations? What were the mechanisms through which property circulated? A second theme that runs through the chapters is the relationship of the state to the property market in Delhi. Among other things, the nature of how the colonial state both embraced and was constrained by the commodification of land in the city is explored. Third, the impact of commodification on popular struggles in the city is examined. Repeatedly in those struggles, we find diverse articulations of the desire for spaces outside the process of commodification. These popular struggles shaped the city even as they were themselves shaped by the structure of property relations and state power.

Chapter 1 surveys the history of property in Delhi from 1860 to 1911. The period after the rebellion of 1857 has a strong claim to being the point at which new and more absolute forms of private property were first introduced in the city. I then trace the impact of two key spatial transformations between the 1860s and 1911. First, within the city itself, there was an effort to dismantle divided urban sovereignties and reduce the number and variety of overlapping administrative and economic designations of urban space. The second transformation was the repositioning of Delhi in the urban system of north India, most significantly as a result of the railways. By the turn of the century, as a result of these transformations, Delhi was already a city in which expansion was expected, and property sales occurred which were guided by this expectation.

Chapters 2 and 3 focus on the first of the overarching themes of this book, developing a picture of the trends in the property market. 'A Malleable Cityscape' reconstructs some of the major trends in the property market in the city based on a database of building permissions sanctioned by the Delhi Municipal Committee. It plots the trajectory of construction in the city, identifying a slump in the 1920s which ended around 1930, and explores the differences in patterns of construction in the areas within the city walls and those outside it. Relating this to other forms of investment in the city, the chapter suggests that significant amounts of capital in Delhi found their way from the city's pressured financial sector into real estate in the 1930s. The patterns of construction also suggest that land development by the state lagged behind investment by private capital. Chapter 3 elaborates the trends indicated in Chapter 2 by looking at the actors involved in the property market. Tracking a variety of participants in different parts of the city, it reinforces the proposition of a fundamental shift in the property market in the 1930s. The lack of long-term finance available in the city prompted the gradual emergence and eventual stabilization of larger firms engaged in the business of real estate. These firms, more focused on linking urban space and finance, represented one route out of the problems of the early 1930s. Another potential source of new finance was cooperative housing societies. Cooperative societies did not take off in Delhi during the period of this study, but the repeated efforts to establish them, through private efforts and public authority, indicate the salience of this manner of connecting land and finance.

Chapters 4 and 5 explore the relationship between the state and the property market. Chapter 4 examines four means of representing urban property: maps, leases, auctions, and advertisements. For each of these I tease out the ways in which they reflected and came to constitute temporal aspects of the circulation of property. The fact that the state was the repository for these representations of space was indispensable to the power that the state could exercise vis-à-vis the property market. Synthesizing the temporal aspect of these documents with the ability to collect them, the state could create narratives about the property market—efforts to grasp its shape and the pattern of its temporal changes. This was a form of power—the power to 'narrate' property—with respect to the market that the colonial state was more happy to exercise than other, more material, interventions such as subsidized housing. Chapter 5 argues that while the operations of the state and the property market were closely intertwined in the period of this study, different state agencies had different capacities to deal with the property market. Thus, New Delhi Municipal Committee (NDMC) areas saw greater curbs on the ways in which the property market could impact urban form. In contrast, DMC and DIT areas (those with which I am concerned) saw much greater sway of the market as the ultimate principle for construction. DMC and DIT registered the external impact of the property market through categories such as 'unearned increment', or even the most basic category to the sale and purchase of land: 'market value'. Arguments within the administration over what these terms meant and how they should be determined reflected the profound paradoxes generated by a state desirous of moulding urban space but equally committed to protecting private property.

If property relations led to widespread and crisis-ridden private construction, were there any efforts to rein in the effects of the property market? Chapter 6, entitled 'Lineages of the Housing Question', considers the particular combination of factors through which the idea of state-subsidized housing took shape in Delhi. The Delhi Improvement Trust, established in 1937, represented the first large-scale attempt to address the deficit of housing in the city. However, a number of different struggles—from those conducted by government clerks and sanitary discourse within the state, to caste and nationalist struggles outside of it—had already given shape to varieties of state-subsidized housing in the city. In a variety of idioms, all the discursive and agitational forces studied here decried the influence of the market and sought different forms of state intervention to correct them. Nevertheless, each struggle had a different diagnosis of the problems and ideas about the forms of state intervention apposite to addressing the housing question.

In Chapter 7, 'Grave Investments', I consider a different kind of mass politics. In an urban landscape marked by malleability, religious spaces acquired a new valence as sites beyond or outside the process of capital accumulation—places that could anchor a sense of belonging and community. Nevertheless, as urban spaces, religious sites were subjected to the same social forces as others in the city that sought to turn a profit. Consequently, when clashes over sacral sites in the city—graveyards, temples, and mosques—generated ideas of community, property relations had a novel and peculiar salience within these notions of community.

Conclusion

In emphasizing the centrality of property relations to the twentieth-century transformations of the city, this book argues for a larger shift in studies of the city. Much more attention should be paid to the ways in which urban property shaped urban space. The effects of the property market were far-reaching, and can be traced in places one would expect (housing) as well as those one might not expect (communal mobilization). Our picture of the role of state and community in South Asian urban history is incomplete without better accounts of the ways in which urban property relations shaped each of those actors.

1
Background
Property in Delhi, 1857–1911

In January 1867 Syed Moheeuddin Khan, like many of his compatriots in Delhi, was seeking to prove his loyalty to the British cause during the upheavals of 1857. Prominent among the documents he marshalled to demonstrate that even while the rebels controlled Delhi he had had the best interests of the British at heart, was an agreement he had executed in June 1857 with Lala Jumna Das Sahoo. The agreement hypothecated a number of properties he owned across the city in lieu of a loan. Khan claimed that this was proof positive of his fidelity, for the agreement made reference to the return of British rule:

> I am unable . . . to execute legal bonds in consequence of adequate stamped papers not being procurable. I therefore execute this deed of agreement on a stamped paper of 8 annas, which has been in my possession for the satisfaction of [Lala Jumna Das] Sahoo, covenanting that on the restoration of British rule, I will re-execute on stamped papers of full value a bond hypothecating the Mahomed Gunj shops . . . and a mortgage deed of the Moorgh Khana . . . [1]

An allegiance declared in the terms of a mortgage is a prosaic profession of loyalty indeed, but ultimately Khan's claim was not accepted.[2] I would argue, nevertheless, that a germ of insight is contained in Khan's intuition about this document. He correctly grasped that property was central to the post-1857 dispensation. For the colonial state, both legitimacy and effectiveness flowed from a functioning property market, and its actions were geared towards ensuring that property transactions were both frequent and smooth.

[1] DDA, DC Office, F. no. 2, 1867. Copy of an agreement dated 1 June 1857.

[2] Moheeuddin Khan's appeal was rejected by the Secretary of State for India, but not because they could not imagine a mortgage as a proof of loyalty. As the official investigating Khan's case pointed out: 'It is no doubt a clear proof of his creditor's belief in the . . . British Government . . . ' Report dated 12 July 1867.

Possessing the City: Property and Politics in Delhi, 1911–1947. Anish Vanaik, Oxford University Press (2020).

DOI: 10.1093/oso/9780198848752.001.0001

In doing so it set in train forces that came to play a critical role in moulding the property market in Delhi before 1911.

Two key transformations can be traced in Delhi over the second half of the nineteenth century that laid the grounds for the twentieth-century developments that this book explores. First, there was a shift away from the city of divided sovereignties: the characteristic north Indian urban form described so effectively by Christopher Bayly.[3] The pre-colonial north Indian city consisted of a welter of overlapping and cross-cutting claims to authority. *Mohalla*, *haveli*, *panchayat*, and *kotwal* could lay concurrent claim to shaping urban space across a variety of fields—from transport to law and order, from sanitation to symbolism. Pre-colonial urban government was not animated by the urge to distinguish and clarify the legitimate jurisdictions of these entities in the way that colonial urban administration, even when unsuccessful, came to be. Over the nineteenth century, *havelis*, *mohallas*, *panchayats*, and numerous other terms were retained as vestiges in the administrative manuals of Delhi officials. The arrangements to which they referred, however, were radically and irreversibly altered.

A second animating impulse emerged from the large-scale geographical transformations wrought by the colonial state. Well before Delhi was propelled to status of capital city of British India the more rhythmic hum of the railways had already repositioned the city within the colony. By the early twentieth century, intersecting railway lines—among the punitive measures imposed on the city in the aftermath of the rebellion of 1857—had recast Delhi. From being a Mughal seat with a notional sphere of influence it became the commercial entrepot for Punjab, the western United Provinces, and Rajputana. These large-scale reconfigurations of commercial and financial life could not but affect the nature, density, and political significance of transactions in the local property market.

The intersecting processes which physically transformed Delhi can be traced through a number of events between 1857 and 1911: the demolition and reconstruction of the city after the rebellion, the process of building the railways, administering garden lands around Delhi, and the economic activity that developed once the railways were built and the post-1857 regime set in place. An extended process of 'primitive accumulation' can be traced here. These were violent upheavals which revolutionized the ways in which claims to space were made in and around Delhi. The more clearly defined structure

[3] C. A. Bayly (2012), *Rulers, Townsmen, and Bazaars: North Indian Society in the Age of British Expansion, 1770–1870*, 3rd edn. (New Delhi: Oxford University Press).

of property which emerged over the late nineteenth century formed the twin basis for land to be treated as a commodity and the city to be governed in more singular fashion. The state steadily began to claim sole right to determine the nature of large-scale flows through the city—of traffic, water, waste, and fuel (electricity). At the same time, more absolute and more likely to be traded, land now lent itself to the kinds of serial transformation—now a garden, now used for housing, now a densely-built suburb—expected of a modern city. Older patterns of urban development and authority were shaken up. If a previous Delhi could be thought of as contained within walls—a clearly defined cultural, economic, and political sphere—the lines between city and countryside, intramural Delhi and its suburbs were, over the second half of the nineteenth century, steadily blurred.[4] The peculiarity of this set of transformations was, in miniature, encapsulated by the post-1857 dispensation in which Khan was seeking a place.

The Reveille and the Ledger

British revenge for the rebellion of 1857 was a particularly bloody one. Carnage, looting, and expulsions of residents set the tone for the recapture of the city. The built environment was also subject to a similar violence. Extensive demolitions and reconstructions were envisaged. In the north, a railway station was built to separate the European residents of the Civil Lines from the bulk of Delhi's population that would now remain to the south of Chandni Chowk. Daryaganj—a neighbourhood in the south east of the city—was to serve as an army cantonment, and the palace itself was to be turned into a garrison fort. According to one Gupta, the inhabitants of the city were now huddled into just two-thirds of the area that had previously be occupied by civilians, while the rest was destroyed, reconstructed, or made to house the army.[5] The scale of destruction of life and property was a direct consequence of the violent conquest of the city after 1857.

Given this sanguinary setting, in which the sovereign authority of the colonial state was near absolute, it is all the more surprising that a mundane register of property values shaped Delhi's urban reconstruction as much as military orders. In fact, the foundation of the reconstruction was laid by an

[4] Narayani Gupta (1981), *Delhi between Two Empires, 1803–1931: Society, Government and Urban Growth* (Delhi: Oxford University Press), p. 65.

[5] Gupta (1981), *Delhi between Two Empires*, p. 30.

almost obsessive drive to assign clear monetary value to all house property that was to be demolished. Delhi in the aftermath of 1857, however, was a city with a broken economy and little liquid cash. The determination to monetize and account, then, derived from a combination of a short-term desire to preserve British cash reserves and colonial catechism about the importance of secure property. The so-called Ticket System—the mechanism through which the large-scale demolition and rebuilding of the city was carried out in the aftermath of 1857—was an ad hoc arrangement with a far-reaching impact.

The Ticket System was deceptively simple. For those who were able to prove their loyalty to the British during the rebellion, but happened to reside in the areas marked for demolition, a 'ticket' recording the value of their property was issued. These tickets could be exchanged for houses confiscated from rebels in areas that were not to be demolished, that had been deemed to be of equivalent value. Narayani Gupta—author of the classic history of Delhi during this period—remarks that the flurry of speculation following these arrangements was one of 'bewildering complexity'.[6] If anything, this is an understatement.

From the outset there were obstacles and inconsistencies. To begin with, there were disputes about how to value the houses. In a city where few economic transactions were possible, there was little by way of a property market. Assigning house property a value in such a situation was a difficult task.[7] Even as a method of valuation was fixed, other problems cropped up. In 1859 the Deputy Commissioner of Delhi, much to the surprise of the Executive Engineer, decided that the state must not profit from any of the ongoing property transactions and that any profits must go towards a fund for Europeans who had suffered in the revolt.[8] This suggestion, received the support of the Commissioner before being eventually rejected by the Lieutenant Governor.[9] Not even the extent of the demolitions could

[6] Gupta, *Delhi between Two Empires*, pp. 28–9.

[7] See the consultations about possible ways of valuing house property and why the criterion ultimately selected—the market value of the house at the current moment—involved no little contortion. NAI, Foreign (Part A), June 1860, 123–5. From Commissioner, Delhi Division to Military Secretary, Government of Punjab, 21 March 1860. Alternative valuations of the property were also current, as can be inferred from the reference to higher valuations by local *Panchayats* in the proceedings around the acquisition of a mosque in 1864. DDA, Residency Records, Box no. 5, F. no. 85, 21 March 1864. DC, Delhi to Commissioner, Delhi Division.

[8] DDA, Residency Records, Box. No. 5, 'Clearance of Chandni Chowk', F. no. 12, 16 May 1859. Executive Engineer, Delhi Division to Commissioner, Delhi Division.

[9] DDA, Residency Records, Box. No. 5, 'Clearance of Chandni Chowk', F. no. 16, 1 July 1859. Officiating Military Secretary to the Government of Punjab to Chief Engineer, Punjab.

be expeditiously settled. Initially fixed at 500 yards, Hosagrahar has outlined the ways in which the wealthy Hindu merchants of Dariba Kalan were able to rescue their shops and houses from demolition.[10] These were just some of the complications before the tickets were even in circulation.

The tickets were speculative tender par excellence. Once they began to be issued in June–July 1860 they entered a process of furious circulation. Initially, at least, much of this was driven by the depressed state of the economy of Delhi. Many of those who had had no source of income for a number of months saw the tickets as a means to earn some hard cash, and practically any sum which could have been had in exchange for these tickets was welcomed; an official noted that initially some of them were discounted by as much as 75%.[11] However, after a period in which tickets were circulating at well below their face value their exchange value rose quite fast. This was partly a consequence of their use in the auctions and sales that were taking place, which brought about a question about what kind of document the tickets actually were. As mentioned previously, they had been sold by holders to people who offered them cash. Did this imply an effective transfer of house property? Officials claimed that the tickets could not be seen as a claim to property transfer and therefore a kind of title deed.[12] Nevertheless, given that tickets could only be exchanged for house property they were not a mere claim to a certain amount of money. The exchange value of the tickets was volatile because they could be exchanged for property whose values were likely to increase over time. Even more immediately, if the auctions fetched more than the value of tickets issued, the profits from the sales would be divided between the ticket holders. Because of the way in which officials had framed the transaction, the tickets became claims to appreciating revenues. The situation was ripe for speculation, and a tremendous amount of it duly occurred.

By the time that accounts were finally settled, a small group of wealthy Delhi residents and European speculators had accumulated huge monetary profits and physical holdings across the city.[13] In the process, these speculators had used their political clout to reduce their risks. When there was a

[10] Jyoti Hosagrahar (2005), *Indigenous Modernities: Negotiating Architecture and Urbanism* (London: Routledge, 2005), p. 93.

[11] DDA, Residency Records, Box no. 5, F. no. 78, 21 August 1863. Report of DC, Delhi to Commissioner, Delhi Divison, paragraph 18.

[12] DDA, Residency Records, Box No. 5, 'Clearance of Chandni Chowk', File no. 78, 21 August 1863. Report of DC, Delhi to Commissioner, Delhi Divison, paragraph 55.

[13] Gupta, *Delhi between Two Empires*, pp. 29–30.

fear of a loss being made at the auctions, they harangued colonial officials into guaranteeing their profit margins. Indeed, by the time the process concluded in 1864, officials were thrashing about for ways to draw a line below the seemingly boundless demands for larger payouts that came from these ticket-holders. In a paradoxical turn of events, the colonial state, at a moment of complete military dominance of Delhi, was overwhelmed by a wave of real-estate speculation.

The peculiar step of employing the Ticket System to organise the post-1857 demolitions, then, had a number of portentous consequences. For one, at this moment an alliance was ushered into being between the colonial regime, Delhi bankers and merchants (largely Hindu), and sections of the erstwhile Mughal nobility (largely Muslim).[14] They were to constitute the city's power structure until the 1920s, when the national movement and other socioeconomic transformations propelled new social constituencies to prominence. The Delhi Municipal Committee (DMC), brought into being in 1863, was one important arena that expressed this alliance (Figure 1.1).

A broader point about government was also enunciated through the ticket system: that the state was necessarily concerned with movement of the property market. To choose property valuation and a predictable speculative frenzy as the means for determining the fate of post-1857 Delhi's built environment was a demonstration of colonial statecraft. This, even as a

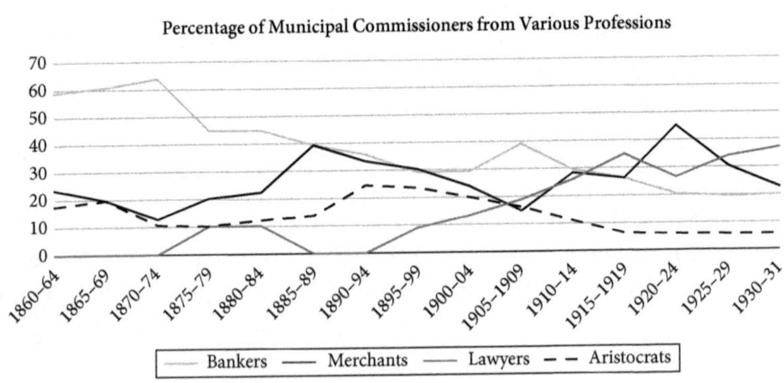

Figure 1.1. Percentage of Municipal Commissioners from various professions. (*Source*: Gupta, 1981.)

[14] 'In the ultimate analysis, therefore, in the counter-attack it was not the army or the civil authorities who really emerged as the gainers, but the new "Lalacracy".' Gupta, *Delhi between Two Empires*, p. 30. I would argue that this was not an outcome undesired by the colonial state.

properly sovereign power over life and death was exercised in other spheres. The state as tyrant and the state as book-keeper marched into the city in lockstep.

A third outcome of this moment was that the colonial state seized from its Mughal predecessor a large number of properties, in and around the city, that had hitherto been designated the personal property of the Mughal Emperor—so-called *nazul* properties. These were holdings that made the colonial state the largest single landholder in the city. The ways of using (and choosing not to use) *nazul* properties around the city over the twentieth century will be seen to have consequences of tremendous significance.[15]

The scarring of the political and cultural worlds of Delhi's residents by the events of 1857 has often been remarked upon. The passing of a world that twinned the *mehfil* and the *durbar*, however, was accomplished not simply through martial means. The vapid monotony of numbers in a ledger droned steadily alongside the insistent aggression of the reveille.

Simplifying Property

The ledger, however, depended for its transparency on the quality of the land record. Clarifying the latter was a challenge that occupied the colonial state in a variety of ways over the nineteenth century. In 1803, when they had first engaged with the administration in Delhi, two key terms were used to describe lands connected to the Mughal Court. *Nazul* lands were considered crown lands—that is, property of the state—while *taiool* lands were considered the personal possession of the Mughal Emperor. An extensive survey of *taiool* lands in and around Delhi in 1878, however, found that actual circumstances belied the earlier, seemingly clear, records.[16] G. Leslie Smith, Assistant Commissioner of Delhi, who was tasked with conducting a survey of land holding in Delhi found numerous irregularities, widespread lack of documentation, and general confusion about the categories of land holding in and around the city. His list of holdings requiring clarification of occupancy status ran into thousands of cases, recorded in no less than

[15] There was considerable confusion, eventually glossed over, about the legal basis on which the colonial state had claimed lands in Delhi after 1857. See the discussions of the question in 1869. DDA, Commissioner's Office, F no. 553, Vol. I, Box no. 44, 1868. Ibid. DC to Col. R. M. Best, Commanding at Delhi, dated 25 May 1869.

[16] DDA, Commissioner's Office, Serial no. 29-A, Box no. 27, 1878.

ten distinct classes of possession: *makbuza*, *sardarakhti*, non-occupancy tenants, *nazul* land, *abadi* lands, railway lands, canal lands, *nisf-ret* lands, perpetual *muafis*, and proprietary. The categories were deceptively distinct. In fact, both state practice and the transfers of these tenancies over the years had served to undercut the apparent solidity of these categories.

A typical example would be the *muafi* tenures. These were revenue-free grants of land in the area surrounding Delhi, ostensibly for charitable purposes. Smith, however, found numerous cases such as that of Kallan and Murad Bakhsh in Mouza Khandrat, who had purchased their *muafis* from Nur-nissa and went on to use the land to carry on their occupation of lime burning. Given that this was a business and not, therefore, a 'charitable' entity, Smith was inclined to recommend that suits be instituted against Kallan and Murad Bakhsh (and others like them) in order to recover revenue and incontestably establish state ownership of the land. Smith's immediate superior, the Deputy Commissioner of Delhi T. W. Smyth, demurred. Based on Smyth's own investigations he argued that the Assistant Commissioner had misunderstood the designation 'charitable purposes'. The term was simply a placeholder designed to bar any further inquiry by the state into the fate of such properties, and not, as Smith seemed to have assumed, a prescription of the use to which the lands ought to be put.[17] The Deputy Commissioner argued, in short, that anything classed as *muafi* ought to be considered property over which the state had abandoned its claims. In effect, these lands were to be reclassified quite simply as private property.[18] In the mid-1870s, local authorities set themselves the task of clarifying and simplifying the forms of property holding.

The reconstitution of fragmented property claims as more unitary ones is nowhere more evident than in *sardarakhti* holdings. Derived from *drakht*—the Urdu word for tree—these were usufruct rights to the trees upon the land. Most striking, however, was that the local administration had never laid out a clear definition of this category of tenure, while continuing to utilize the designation. R. B. Whitehead, in his 1910 *Report on the Administration of the Delhi Crown Lands*, described them as rights that were acquired by planters of trees. More crucially, he opined that they were 'not laid down in any statute, and are a legacy left to the British Government

[17] DDA, Commissioner's Office, S. no. 29-A, Carton Box no. 27, 1878. From Deputy Commissioner T. W. Smyth to Officiating Commissioner, Delhi Division, dated 13 August 1877.

[18] As it happened, the Deputy Commissioner's recommendation by and large carried the day.

from the times of the Kings of Delhi.'[19] Local practice, particularly during the construction of the railways in 1890, had been to treat *sardarakhti* as a full claim to property, and consequently entitled to full compensation. While horrified by this, Whitehead, in his final report, was forced to conclude that the best way of proceeding would be to simply continue local practice and recognize most *sardarakhti* tenures as ownership outright. What had emerged as de facto practice during the construction of the railways in the 1890s was now given the imprimatur of government policy: the recognition of *sardarakhti* right holders as full-fledged owners of the land.[20]

Within the city walls, the clarification of claims to urban land played out in a slightly different manner. Raghav Kishore traces the peculiar history of the *chabutra* (a platform built from the threshold of the shop to the edge of the street)—a quintessential architectural product of the negotiated claim to 'public' space that prevailed in pre-colonial Delhi. The Delhi Municipal Committee went from initially declaring these an illegal encroachment on public space, to demolishing *chabutras* of recent standing while allowing older ones to remain, to administering and claiming rent from these. In each of these instances, the claim of state ownership of public land was maintained.[21] In fact, this drive to more clearly demarcate and, in effect, restrict the rights of the residents of *mohallas* to shape the areas that they lived in was a repetitive motif in municipal administration. The recasting of sweepers and garbage collectors as municipal employees was accompanied by, on the one hand, a denial of neighbourhoods' rights to employ people conducting municipal work, and, on the other, by redefining nightsoil and other waste as municipal property.[22] Similarly, drains were to be built by the municipality and, as happened on occasion, if residents of a *mohalla* had one constructed it was only allowed to stand on the condition that the ownership

[19] Anonymous, 'Report on the Administration of the Delhi Crown Lands' (Lahore, 1910), pp. 10–11.

[20] By far the largest number of these cases arose in the suburb of Jehanuma. The net effect of Whitehead's recommendation was that from having approximately 230 acres of land under *sardarakhti tenure* there would remain only around 20 acres. For a different suburb, Sadhaura Kalan, Whitehead recommended delimiting and clarifying the tenurial rights involved. *Report on the Administration of the Delhi Crown Lands* (Lahore, 1910), pp. lxxvii, 11–12, and 22–5.

[21] Raghav Kishore (2015), 'Urban "Failures": Municipal Governance, Planning and Power in Colonial Delhi, 1863–1910', *Indian Economic and Social History Review*, 52 (4), 439–61.

[22] Vijay Prashad traces the history of these fascinating struggles. Prashad (2000), *Untouchable Freedom: A Social History of a Dalit Community* (Oxford: Oxford University Press).

of the Municipal Committee over the drain and the land it was built upon was acknowledged.[23]

This tendency towards the simplification of patterns of property holding around cities through the second half of the nineteenth century has been seen in other cities as well.[24] Whitehead's report on crown lands in 1910 represents just such a moment for Delhi.[25] His recommendation to collapse the two categories of crown lands (*nazul* and *taiool*) into each other symbolizes this trajectory very well. He pointed out that the retention of two terms had little meaning for administrative practice and that records could scarcely distinguish between what were *nazul* and what were *taiool* holdings. Crown lands in Delhi, after Whitehead's report, would simply be described as *nazul*.[26] This convergence was accompanied by a redefinition:

> The term *nazul* is restricted to those Crown lands within Municipal limits administered by the Delhi Municipality. Where *nazul* land is directly administered by Government in a Government Department, such as the Irrigation, Public Works, or the Railway Department, it will no longer be called *nazul*, but be treated as Government land pure and simple under departmental management.[27]

While the term *nazul* was retained here, it was now reinscribed in terms of the real difference between municipal management of land and the ways in which land was administered by Imperial authorities. Subsequent chapters will take up the disputes and contentions that accompanied *nazul* holdings over the twentieth century. Over the nineteenth century, however, the construction of the railways, and a series of official reports created a tendency towards simplification and clarification of rights to property in Delhi's vicinity.

One effect of the simplification of land tenures around Delhi was to dissolve the previous distinction, marked by the city wall, between the inside

[23] For two among numerous examples of small-scale changes conducted by residents of a *mohalla* which were disputed by DMC: TH, Proceedings of the Delhi Municipal Committee, Ordinary Meeting, 14 January 1908; TH, Proceedings of the Delhi Municipal Committee, Ordinary Meeting, 23 December 1907.

[24] Mariam Dossal (2010), *Theatre of Conflict, City of Hope: Mumbai, 1660 to Present Times* (New Delhi: Oxford University Press).

[25] 'If all property could be tidily classified then errant situations could be immediately identified and presumably rectified. Each owner could then go about developing their parcel to its fullest potential.' Hosagrahar, *Indigenous Modernities*, p. 137.

[26] *Report on the Administration of the Delhi Crown Lands*, p. 3.

[27] Ibid.

and outside of the city. The culture and economy of Shahjahanabad, since its inception, had been demarcated from that of its immediate vicinity. Leisure gardens and hunting to the west, and pilgrimages to shrines lying to the south of Shahjahanabad, were the major forms of intercourse between the walled city and the areas outside. The shrinking power of the Mughal emperors over the eighteenth and nineteenth centuries was, in fact, manifested in an increasingly fraught and perilous relationship between the Jat and Gujar farmers and pastoralists who roamed the plains around Delhi and also entered the city.[28] With the establishment of British power, these areas—some of which had already become market centres in the early nineteenth century—became suburbs of the city; a critical part of Delhi's built environment.

Four of these suburbs were particularly significant. To the north was the Civil Lines, where British civilians and Indian elites lived from 1857 onwards. This suburb, carefully tended by local authorities, housed a small proportion of the city's population even as it drew a large portion of its resources. To the west of the city lay the three suburbs of Sabzimandi, Sadar Bazar, and Paharganj. In the sixty years after the Uprising of 1857, these three suburbs were more organically connected to the city as commercial and industrial interests began to push outward from the constraining *karkhanas* of intramural Delhi. These became the great absorbers of the migrations to Delhi of Punjabi Muslim traders, Dalit landless labourers displaced by the Punjab Alienation of Land Act, and construction workers from Rajputana who built New Delhi. Land here—largely gardens or fields before 1857—was transformed by the redefinitions of tenures, the construction of the railways, the Jat agriculturists who owned it, and demographic booms into some of the most densely built-up areas of Delhi.

The gardens and small markets that lay to Delhi's west were already, in the early years of the twentieth century, being transformed. The announcement of Delhi as the capital in 1911, as we shall see, accelerated these nascent developments until by the 1940s these suburbs housed just under half the population of the city. No longer a garden or agrarian landscape, the general reinscription and simplification of tenures in Delhi had brought these suburbs within the purview of an urban economy pushing outwards.

[28] Gautam Bhadra (1988), 'Four Rebels of Eighteen-Fifty-Seven', in Ranajit Guha and Gayatri Chakravorty Spivak (eds.), *Selected Subaltern Studies* (Delhi: Oxford University Press), pp. 129–70.

Delhi's Economy

Between 1857 and 1911 Delhi's economic growth was sustained largely by commerce and finance. Its ability to do so was based not upon its preceding political eminence but rather the construction of railway lines in and around the city. Delhi was no exception to the transformations of economic and cultural geography of the subcontinent wrought by the railways.[29] As local mercantile fortunes flourished, the ribbons of track that stretched across the Gangetic plains also bound the financial fortunes of Delhi to wider spheres of capital within South Asia and, indeed, the globe as a whole.

The social group that benefited the most out of the post-1857 dispensation were the Hindu bankers and traders that Gupta terms the 'Lalacracy'.[30] The mainstay of their income was trade—wheat, cotton, and piecegoods were the most prominent commodities—and associated finance. The Punjabi Muslims constituted another trading group whose star rose from the 1860s.[31] Having found a foothold in the city, initially based on trade with the regions to the north-west, the Punjabis were quick to adjust to the ways in which the railways transformed Delhi's economic geography. Concentrating on trade in leather goods and wheat, Punjabi Muslims rose steadily in the city's pecking order, carving out a position of influence in a number of trades and even the Municipal Committee.

Financial fortunes were closely associated with the commercial activities outlined previously. In Delhi they circulated largely within the indigenous banking sector that Rajat Ray terms the 'bazaar'.[32] These were lines of credit, only partially connected to the official bank network, that enabled the great movements of agricultural commodities between city and countryside.

[29] Manu Goswami (2005), *Producing India: From Colonial Economy to National Space* (Delhi: Permanent Black).

[30] Gupta, *Delhi between Two Empires*.

[31] The discussion of Punjabi Muslims in this paragraph is, unless otherwise noted, based on Margrit Pernau's work. Her larger argument is that Punjabi Muslims were among the groups evolving an aesthetic, religious, and economic identity as middle class. Margrit Pernau (2013), *Ashraf into Middle Classes: Muslims in Nineteenth-Century Delhi* (Delhi: Oxford University Press).

[32] Rajat Kanta Ray (1988), 'The Bazaar: Changing Structural Characteristics of the Indigenous Section of the Indian Economy before and after the Great Depression', *Indian Economic and Social History Review*, 25 (3), 263–318. For a more extended discussion of the history of finance in the city, see Chapters 2 and 3.

As Moheeuddin Khan and Jumna Das Sahoo demonstrated, financiers had long used urban property as collateral. Over the nineteenth century, however, bazaar financiers concentrated on the money market and the movement of commodities rather than property speculation. Margrit Pernau points out that in the top three income brackets of the tax filings of 1870, only eighteen individuals earned income from property ownership or pensions.[33]

In contrast to commerce and finance there were relatively few large industrial enterprises in Delhi. It was only around the turn of the nineteenth century that large-scale industry began to emerge. Delhi Cloth Mills was floated in 1888 but did not commence operations until the 1890s, which was also when Krishna Mills was set up.[34] The more characteristic industrial activity in Delhi consisted of artisanal trades organized in the smaller *karkhanas* (workshops) scattered throughout the city. Particularly significant among the Delhi *karkhanas* were textile workshops and enterprises engaged in the working of precious metals and stones (especially gold and silver thread).

Wrecked in the traumatic aftermath of 1857, Delhi's economy began to thrive in the last two decades of the nineteenth century. Between the censuses of 1881 and 1901, for instance, the number of people involved in banking, money lending, and money exchange increased by 66%. This was matched by a 60% increase in the population engaged in the various forms of trade in the city. What impact did this boom have upon the urban fabric? Jyoti Hosagrahar has documented the connections between commerce and the planning of a suburb called Clarkeganj (Figure 1.2).[35]

The idea for this planned suburb combined the sanitary and commercial ideas that had pride of place in the colonial administration. The suburb would relieve congestion in the city and take advantage of businessmen seeking premises for their shops and warehouses. Hosagrahar's compelling reading of the plan argues that Clarkeganj was conceived as a modest endeavour, tinkering at the margins of the city rather than an audacious large-scale remodelling. It was hoped that the rationality of the plan, attractive

[33] Pernau, *Ashraf into Middle Classes: Muslims in Nineteenth-Century Delhi*. The one major exception to this relatively insignificant connection between finance and urban property in this period was, of course, the Ticket System.

[34] Arun Joshi (1975), *Lala Shri Ram: A Study in Entrepreneurship and Industrial Mananagement* (New Delhi: Orient Longman).

[35] My account of Clarkeganj is based on Hosagrahar's work, *Indigenous Modernities*, pp. 115–42.

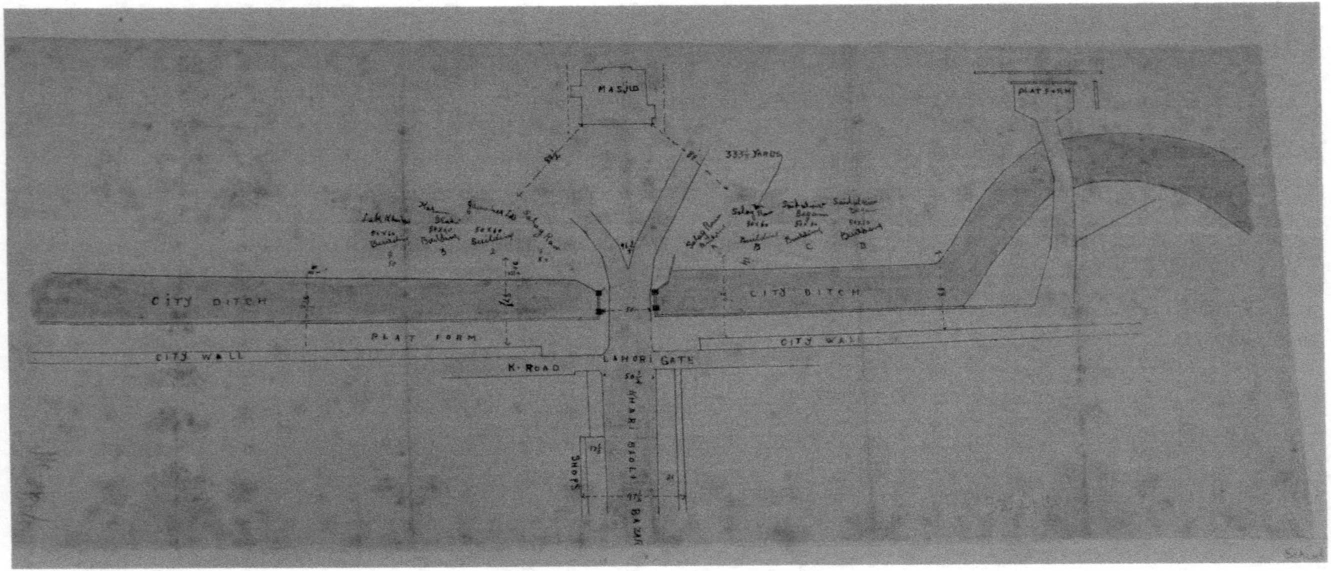

Figure 1.2. Map of the Clarkeganj Scheme.

Source: DDA, DCO, F no. 4, 1913: 'Site plan of Clarkeganj'

location, and its implicit tempering of commercialism by placing religious and public buildings at the heart of the layout would encourage steady emulation rather than dramatic and comprehensive reconstruction.[36] However, for a variety of reasons, including the construction of railways on part of its proposed site, Clarkeganj was left incomplete. Ironically, it is precisely this incompleteness that makes Clarkeganj all the more characteristic of colonial urban administration.

Mushrooming private construction in the suburbs to take advantage of the booming commerce in the city stood in stark contrast to the travails of state planning. The former contributed a greater portion of the urban fabric than any layout planned by the colonial state in this period. Increases in property values over the early twentieth century were an outcome of both this speculative construction and a spur to it. Between 1902 and 1908 there was a 700% increase in property values in Sadar Bazar, a 400% increase in Paharganj, and a 300% increase in Sabzimandi.[37]

A division of labour between the district administration and the Delhi Municipal Committee can be seen as partly driving this oscillation from sovereign power of the urban plan to laissez faire of private construction. The raison d'etre of the DMC was, within the colonial administration, only partly to do with the actual execution of urban plans. Indeed, over the nineteenth century DMC largely operated without the means to translate its plans into structures on the ground.[38] Far more significant was its function as a site to incorporate the local elite into the power structure of the colonial state. In many ways this elite was a direct beneficiary of the colonial state's commitment to the emergence of a market in urban land. We have seen that this was true of the auction of confiscated house property in the 1860s. I have argued elsewhere that the reluctance of the Municipal

[36] Hosagrahar points out that the seeming continuity with the existing cityscape created by Clarkeganj's mixed residential and commercial buildings was 'only a veneer'. Hosagrahar, *Indigenous Modernities*, p. 125. The connections between commerce, religion, and private and public life embedded in the plans were, in fact, starkly removed from those that operated in the rest of Delhi. For a contrasting urban intervention, see the discussion of the canal colonies in William J. Glover (2008), *Making Lahore Modern: Constructing and Imagining a Colonial City* (Minneapolis, MN: University of Minnesota Press).

[37] Hosagrahar, *Indigenous Modernities*, p. 133.

[38] Raghav Kishore argues that municipal failures were an outcome of the severely restricted ability to execute plans. Paradoxically, despite serial failures the committee's administrative apparatus and even the issues over which they claimed the power to exercise their power continued to expand. Thus, Kishore contends, 'failure' to implement plans meant only that municipal power expanded in unpredictable directions rather than well-laid out ones. Raghav Kishore (2015), 'Urban "Failures": Municipal Governance, Planning and Power in Colonial Delhi, 1863–1910', *Indian Economic and Social History Review*, 52 (4), 439–61.

Committee to enact building bye-laws, or (once they were set in place) to implement them, derived from these elites guarding their ability to build freely.[39]

Over the nineteenth century, then, a private market in property had emerged in Delhi. The city expanded in largely unplanned ways, driven by emergent connections between commerce, trade, and construction. These developments represent the beginning of connections between the circulation of capital in the city and the use of urban land that were to become decisive forces shaping Delhi in the twentieth century.

Conclusion

The post-1857 reconstruction, the redefinition of landed tenures, and the laying down of the railway lines each represented the exercise of state power in a consolidated form. These were acts that proceeded from, and were based upon, the principle that colonial plans could give decisive shape to urban space. Here is the extended form of primitive accumulation that characterized the second half of the nineteenth century. It incorporated the classic features of such a process: displacement of people, the creation of funds of wealth for future investment, and the employment of force to achieve this.[40] A crucial and less familiar aspect of the conceptualization of primitive accumulation seen in Delhi is the role played by the state in clarifying and simplifying property to ensure the greater legibility of land records. We shall see in a later chapter that this role played by the state—of shepherding accumulation by ensuring confidence in records of property—was a recurring one. Through the second half of the nineteenth century, then, the exercise of state power set in place the crucial preconditions for urban property relations to play a central role in Shahjahanabad.

[39] Anish Vanaik (2008), 'Changing the Plot: Property Relations in Delhi 1857–1920' (Jawaharlal Nehru University). For a reading that suggests that municipal councillors ignored 'illegal' activity because of the reconfiguration of traditional patron–client reciprocity, see Kishore, 'Urban "Failures"', p. 450.

[40] Much of the recent debate around primitive accumulation was inaugurated by David Harvey's book *The New Imperialism* and his development, within that work, of the idea of 'accumulation by dispossession'. David Harvey (2003), The New Imperialism (Oxford: Oxford University Press. Glassman provides a useful overview of the debates about primitive accumulation within Marxism, and points to the growing conceptualization of it as a continuous rather than one-off process. Jim Glassman (2006), 'Primitive Accumulation, Accumulation by Dispossession, Accumulation by "Extra-Economic" Means', *Progress in Human Geography*, 30 (5), 608–25.

The concentrated exercise of sovereign power in nineteenth-century colonial administration was leavened by an adherence to strictures about governmental action being directed towards enabling individual accumulation.[41] Already by the end of the nineteenth century, market forces were actively shaping urban space. The modest achievements of Clarkeganj—the largest state-driven urban intervention before 1911—were far exceeded by private construction in Delhi's exploding suburbs. Here, the redefinition of tenures generated patterns of boom and bust in the property market which, as will be argued in later chapters, shaped the actions of the colonial state rather than the other way around.

On the eve of the shift of the capital to Delhi in 1911, the railways, commerce, finance, and the actions of the colonial state had between them generated a cityscape in which properties were bought and sold and suburban land was being built over. What is traced over the subsequent chapters is not the creation of an urban property market, but a series of transformations within one that had already been created over the second half of the nineteenth century. In this new formation, each of the actors and processes outlined here—the state, the Delhi elite, and the local economy—took on strikingly novel contours.

[41] Hosagrahar, *Indigenous Modernities*, pp. 140–1.

2
A Malleable Cityscape

Shahjahanabad, which came to be known as 'Old Delhi' after 1911, with its monumental architecture cheek by jowl with genteel decay and outright poverty, was a cityscape eminently suited to being cast as picturesque and traditional. This was a characterization that no tourist guide to the city failed to adopt, and, indeed, continues to inflect popular accounts of Delhi's old city.[1] The easy freezing of Shahjahanabad's history as 'medieval' and picturesque obscures the veritable rollercoaster of boom and bust that took place in Delhi's property market between 1911 and 1947. Over this period the Building Sub-Committee of the Delhi Municipal Committee was the busiest of all the administrative organs of the city. The rise and fall in numbers of applications to build and alter houses reveal a dynamic space of construction and demolition. Indeed, the malleable quality of the 'Old' city—where changes to the built environment were probable rather than exceptional—was a sign of the growing sway and maturation of commoditized urban space that had been set in place over the nineteenth century. Delhi was very far from being a city conceived in the seventeenth century and preserved into the twentieth century.

In contrast to popular accounts of Delhi's history, academic approaches have argued that the city was transformed in many ways. In this literature, the key mechanisms driving urban transformation are typically identified as demography and (inadequate) colonial urban planning.[2] Undoubtedly a watershed in the demographic history of the city, the 1911 proclamation of Delhi as the future winter seat for the government of British India led a stream of people into the city, generating a readily identifiable locus for official intervention. This intervention was refracted through expert-led discourses (such as those about sanitation or the emerging discipline of urban planning) as well as the pervasive racism of the colonial state.

[1] William Dalrymple (1994), *City of Djinns: A Year in Delhi* (London: Flamingo); Malvika Singh (1994), *Perpetual City: A Short Biography of Delhi* (Delhi: Aleph).

[2] Stephen Legg (2007), *Spaces of Colonialism: Delhi's Urban Governmentalities* (Malden, MA; Oxford: Blackwell). Diya Mehra (2013), 'Planning Delhi ca. 1936–1959', *South Asia: Journal of South Asian Studies*, 36(3), 354–374.

Possessing the City: Property and Politics in Delhi, 1911–1947. Anish Vanaik, Oxford University Press (2020).

DOI: 10.1093/oso/9780198848752.001.0001

In metaphors like 'congestion', liberally employed by colonial authorities in the 1930s, both demography and urban planning were inseparably linked.[3] From these twin points of departure, scholarly accounts of Delhi's history have critiqued the alien conception, piecemeal execution, consistent under-funding, and invariably authoritarian planning efforts of colonial agencies to provide housing for the population that entered the city after 1911.

Problems remain, however, with approaches that locate urban change in terms of these two factors. For one, explanations that rely on demography and urban planning both ignore changes in local social structure as a possible source of transformations in the built environment. In general, explanations from demography replace social conflict and upheaval as the key drivers of change with sheer increase in numbers.[4] Similarly, viewing Delhi's development through the discourses of colonial planning reproduces a colonial/anti-colonial frame as the key means to understanding urban change over this period.[5] Aside from these more general objections, however, I would argue that neither of these explanatory mechanisms—demography or urban planning—provides a particularly complete account of the actual changes in Delhi's built environment over this period. Tellingly, scholars utilizing these approaches tend to rely on official testimony about the pace of urban development rather than an empirical examination of the patterns of construction in Shahjahanabad.[6] Studying the actual levels of construction casts 'old' Delhi in surprisingly new light.

Demographics and Construction

Perhaps more than most other cities in colonial India, the flow of urban developments in Delhi has been punctuated by political events laden with symbolism. The trend is striking: Shahjahanabad was a creation of Imperial

[3] Awadhendra B. Sharan (2014), *In the City, Out of Place: Nuisance, Pollution, and Dwelling in Delhi, c.1850–2000* (New Delhi: Oxford University Press).

[4] The general argument, in a very different context, is made by Robert Brenner in response to the work of M. M. Postan and others. Brenner (1976), 'Agrarian Class Structure and Economic Development in Pre-Industrial Europe', in T. H. Aston and C. H. E. Philpin (eds.), *The Brenner Debate* (Cambridge: Cambridge University Press), pp. 10–63.

[5] See Sumit Sarkar's brief but bracing call for greater attention to be paid to the ways in which fractures within Indian society might have shaped colonial-era social formations. Sumit Sarkar (2004), *Beyond Nationalist Frames: Relocating Postmodernism, Hindutva, History* (Delhi: Permanent Black).

[6] This is true of the empirical sources utilized by accounts as diverse in theoretical approaches as those of Narayani Gupta, Stephen Legg, Jyoti Hosagrahar, and Awadhendra Sharan.

Mughal diktat; the imperious actions of the colonial state after 1857 have already been discussed; in 1877 and 1903 Delhi was selected to be the site for Durbars to mark Imperial celebrations.[7] The 1911 Coronation Durbar, with the Emperor and Empress present, was the third and most elaborate version of Imperial congregation held in the city. During the course of the festivities, Delhi was proclaimed the future capital of British India.[8] As capital and symbolic centre of British India, the proclamation generated expectations that had real effects on the city. These ranged from a heightened concern for urban aesthetics to an effort to control press perceptions of the city, from the whimsies of Viceregal 'tours' of the city to the redoubtable organized agitations of the lower orders of Imperial administration. The most commonly remarked upon impact, however, was that of sheer numbers.

Each of the Durbars had had a telling effect on the dynamics of property in the city. Large contingents of wealthy nobles, officials, and their employees would pour into the city. The influx of money and population would bring in its wake, temporary but extreme, upward revisions of rents and commodity prices, prompting spurts of building in anticipation and leaving a city awash with capital as the flood of notables receded. The announcement of 1911, however, meant that these shifts of population were to become regular and institutionalized aspects of the Delhi landscape. As the seat of Imperial government each winter, Delhi would play host to large numbers of state functionaries and visitors. What analytical weight should be accorded

[7] Jyoti Hosagrahar (1992), 'City as Durbar: Theater and Power in Imperial Delhi', in Nezar Alsayyad (ed.), *Forms of Dominance: On the Architecture and Urbanism of the Colonial Enterprise* (Aldershot: Avebury); Alan Trevithick (1990), 'Some Structural and Sequential Aspects of the British Imperial Assemblages at Delhi: 1877–1911', *Modern Asian Studies*, 24 (3), 561–78; Bernard S. Cohn (1992), 'Representing Authority in Victorian India', in E. J. Hobsbawm and T. O. Ranger (eds.), *The Invention of Tradition* (Cambridge: Cambridge University Press), pp. 165–209; R. E. Frykenberg (1993), 'The Coronation Durbar of 1911', in R. E. Frykenberg (ed.), *Delhi through the Ages: Selected Essays in Urban History, Culture and Society* (Delhi: Oxford University Press), pp. 225–46; Julie Codell (2018), 'On the Delhi Coronation Durbars, 1877, 1903, 1911', *BRANCH: Britain, Representation and Nineteenth-Century History* (accessed 11 Novermber 2018). The 1877 event is usually referred to as an Assemblage rather than a Durbar. Many of the substantive symbolisms were, however, shared between the three. I therefore use the term 'Durbar' as representative of all of them.

[8] The plan for this had been a relatively well-guarded secret within the upper echelons of the administration Robert Grant Irving (1991), *Indian Summer: Lutyens, Baker, and Imperial Delhi* (New Haven, CT: Yale University Press). The terms in which the *Comrade*—a newspaper that favoured the shift—describes the announcement conveys some of the shock: 'Once out, the news travelled like wildfire and, while it occasioned both joy and sadness, the most predominant effect was the shock of surprise. An edict of the Emperor of China could not have been more sudden, a ukase of the Czar of all the Russias could not have been more despotic.' 'The Announcement', *Comrade*, 16 December 1911.

to these and other demographic upheavals that followed the announcement of Delhi as capital?

The only way for Delhi to accommodate the population that would inevitably follow from its new status was through expanded construction. Not all of this construction took place on the grand symbolic scale that was planned and executed in New Delhi by Edwin Lutyens, Herbert Baker, and the Imperial Delhi Committee. Building activity was also boosted in the neighbourhoods and streets of the older parts of the city. The fact that Lutyens' and Baker's plans were unable to house even the entire complement of the Imperial administration only underlines the importance of construction in other parts of the city.[9]

Table 2.1 shows the explosion in the decadal rate of increase in population after 1911.[10] In just the first decade after the announcement of Delhi as capital, the decadal rate of population growth tripled. The subsequent decade (1921–31) saw a further acceleration in the rate of growth of population. In particular, the areas of Delhi municipality saw a population increase of almost 40% over the previous decade. Even in the midst of the dislocations of World War II, population growth in Delhi continued to accelerate.

The built fabric of the city, according to official accounts, was strained, and visibly deteriorated under the pressure of these levels of increase. For nearly anyone who had an opinion about Delhi's housing—health officials, municipal commissioners, and Indian Civil Service administrators—Delhi's problems were invariably linked to population. Architectural historian Jyoti Hosagrahar provides a neat statement of this perspective:

> The creation of a land market combined with demographic changes to create an upsurge in the value of real estate in the city. The result ... was that landlords frequently added to existing buildings without due consideration to the health or safety of the inhabitants or the neighbours.[11]

[9] Stephen Legg points to an almost systematic policy of under-building in New Delhi. Legg, *Spaces of Colonialism*, pp. 62–6.

[10] It is also worth noting that the 1931 census identified Delhi as having one of the densest spatial distributions of population in the country, eclipsing larger metropolises such as Calcutta and Bombay in this regard. *Census of India, 1931, Vol. XVI: Delhi: Reports and Tables* (1933) (Lahore: Civil and Military Gazette Press), p. 12.

[11] Jyoti Hosagrahar (2005), *Indigenous Modernities: Negotiating Architecture and Urbanism* (London: Routledge), p. 152.

Table 2.1. Trends in the Population of Delhi, 1901–41.

Year	Population							
	Delhi municipality	Decadal increase (%)	Civil Lines	New Delhi municipality	Old Cantt.	New Cantt.	Total	Decadal increase (%)
1901	206,534	x	X	X	2041	X	208,575	X
1911	229,144	10.9	X	X	3693	X	232,837	11.6
1921	248,259	8.3	17,306	31,456	1127	6272	304,420	30.7
1931	347,539	39.9	16,347	64,855	1641	8798	439,180	44.2
1941	521,849	50.1	19,395	93,733	1740	23,140	659,857	50.2

Source: Census of India, 1921, 1931 and 1941

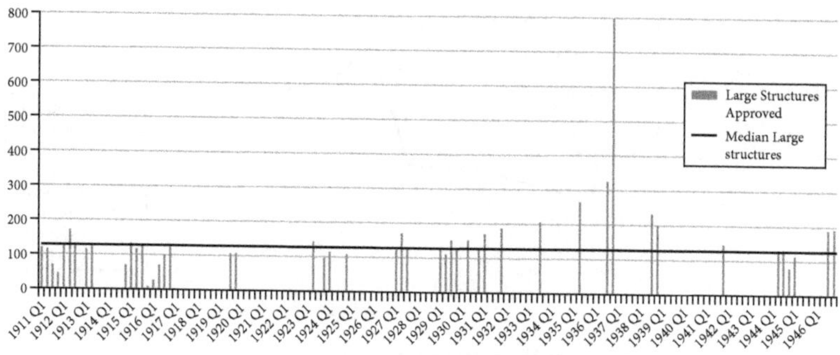

Figure 2.1. Sanctioned building applications for 'large structures'.

The mechanisms which Hosagrahar outlines here seem intuitively true. Population increases create higher demand. The raised demand raises prices, and people build houses (of good or, more frequently, bad quality) to take advantage of these higher prices. Can this argument from demography be substantiated by the empirical evidence about construction in the city?[12]

Figure 2.1 shows the number of applications to build 'large structures' that were sanctioned by the Delhi Municipal Committee.[13] The chart suggests a pattern of construction over the period. Between 1919 and 1929 in only two quarters (out of the ten for which information is available) did the number of applications exceed the median number of applications for the period as a whole.[14] In contrast, during the previous period (1911–19), six out of eighteen quarters saw applications above the median number. Or again, between 1929 and 1939, fourteen quarters out of fifteen saw more than the median number of applications. This last period can readily be

[12] I arrive at trends in construction by using building applications sanctioned by the Delhi Municipal Committee over forty-nine quarters between 1911 and 1946. From these (more than 15,000 individual applications) I have recorded information about who is applying, what kinds of building were being applied for, which of these were being sanctioned, and in what parts of the city they were located. A fuller account of the method of collection and analysis is provided in the Appendix.

[13] As outlined in the Appendix, 'large structure' refers to applications to build what were described as 'buildings': houses, shops, godowns, *katras*, temples, or mosques. There is no differentiation of how large these were, ranging from structures of one storey to as many as five storeys. The main purpose of the classification is to set these off from applications to build 'small structures' which include a variety of architectural elements: verandahs, storeys, rooms, *saibans*, and so on.

[14] All counts in this paragraph relate to the number of quarters for which information is available. In aggregate I have information relating to just over a third of the quarters over the whole period.

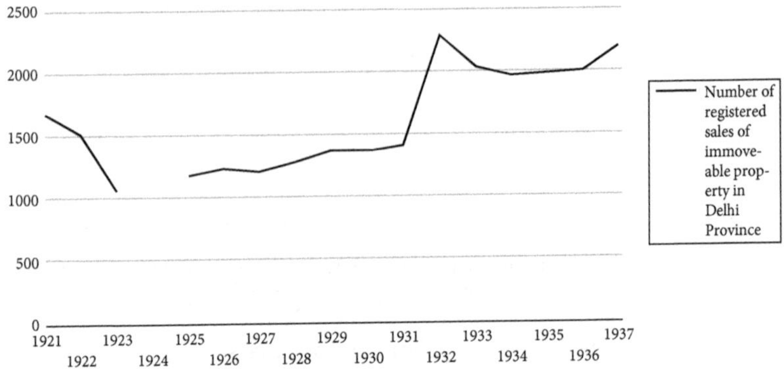

Figure 2.2. Registered sales of property in Delhi. (Data compiled from *Report on the Administration of the Delhi Province*, various volumes from 1921 to 1939).[15]

identified as a period of boom in construction—one that reached a pinnacle in the mid-1930s.[16] By comparison, the decade between 1919 and 1929 seems to have seen a slump in the amount of large-scale construction. The same basic trend—a slump in the 1920s and boom in the 1930s—can be seen in the number of registered sales of property in Delhi Province (Figure 2.2).

This pattern of fall and rise does not correspond in a straightforward fashion with population which saw an accelerating rise over the entire period (Figure 2.3). Juxtaposed in this manner, the demographic argument is less persuasive. Between 1921 and 1931, for instance, a period over which population growth was much higher than during 1911–21, construction was much lower. Again, population growth was sustained until well into the 1940s, where construction began to slow down from the mid-1930s onwards. This suggests that attributing levels of construction simply to the rise of population is unsatisfactory. Population change did play a role, but only when refracted through other social processes and economic circuits. I would argue that a more persuasive explanation for the pattern of

[15] A couple of points ought to be noted about these registered sales. First, the Delhi Province included the rural areas of Delhi. I have only fragmentary reference to the links between urban and rural property transactions in the Delhi province. It is difficult, therefore, to note anything beyond the coincidence in the patterns for each of these numbers. Second, the information relates to the number of sales rather than their value. Thus, a sale of 1 acre would be registered as one transaction, as would a sale of 100 acres.

[16] The enormous number of applications in late 1936 can be partially ignored as being skewed because of a very large number of applications from poor people rehabilitated en masse by a scheme for city improvement in that year.

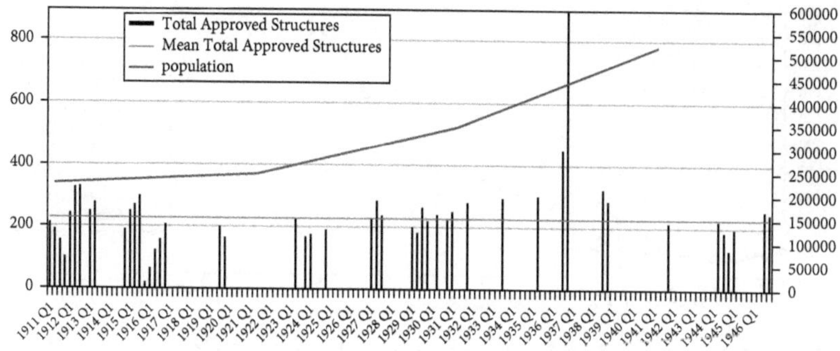

Figure 2.3. Building applications sanctioned and the population in Delhi, 1911–46. (*Census of India*).[17]

construction in Delhi is provided by the connections between real estate and Delhi's economy over this period.

Real Estate, Manufacturing, and Finance

The mainstay of the Delhi economy, as has been pointed out earlier, was the trade in piecegoods and agricultural commodities. The immediate post-war period saw a boom in local businesses. However, from around 1920, beginning with a series of droughts, there was a serious depression in Delhi's trade and industry.[18] The period saw volumes of trade shrink dramatically, particularly in piecegoods—the single largest segment of the Delhi market. Annual administrative reports from this period note the tightening credit in the city—an unsurprising outcome given the close interconnection between the Delhi money market and the movement of commodities through the city. The squeeze on incomes and credit in the 1920s supply a plausible explanation for the slump in construction during that decade. The precipitous decline in local commerce led to a drop in financial incomes and a greater degree of caution among financiers. In such circumstances, construction also slumped.

[17] Source for population is the relevant volumes of the *Census of India*.

[18] The pattern is widely attested to. The *Annual Report on the Administration of Delhi Province* of 1921–22 makes note of this and every year thereafter until 1934–35. The 1931 census report, with a few caveats, also reports this to be the economic trend of the decade.

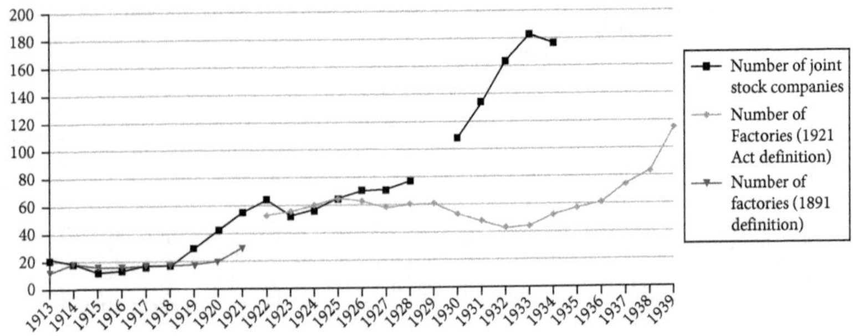

Figure 2.4. Indices of economic activity in Delhi, 1913–39.[19]

But what accounts for the boom in construction of the 1930s? Figure 2.4 shows two other indices of economic activity in the city: the number of joint stock companies and the number of factories in the city.[20]

The pattern of property construction in Delhi, slack in the 1920s and buoyant in the 1930s, is usefully contrasted with the course of industrial development, as revealed by the number of factories. The number of factories from 1913 to 1921 exhibits a steady trend moving upwards towards the end of the period.[21] Through the 1920s, the number of factories remained more or less constant. In the 1930s, however, when sales of land and levels of construction were rising, the number of factories fell, with many winding up or scaling back their operations. The basic cause of industrial difficulties and (though not to the same extent) commercial strife, was that demand for goods remained weak. More significantly, however, between the 1920s and the mid-1930s numerous reports suggest that credit on reasonable terms was hard to obtain for industrial and commercial outfits. Indeed, in the early 1930s the asphyxiating effect of tight money on trade and industry across India was recognized even by the Imperial authorities. Between December 1931 and August 1932 the interest rate of the Imperial Bank was slashed four

[19] Administration of the Delhi Province reports.

[20] Official reports through the 1920s explicitly linked the slump in sales of commodities in Delhi to the depression. *Report on the Administration of the Delhi Province, 1926–27* (Simla: Government of India Press, 1928), p. 15; *Report on the Administration of the Delhi Province, 1925–26* (Simla: Government of India Press, 1927), p. 11; *Report on the Administration of the Delhi Province, 1923–24* (Simla: Government of India Press, 1925) p. 13.

[21] The 1921 Act introduced a new definition of 'factory' dramatically increasing the number of enterprises that would qualify. Under the terms of the 1891 Act, enterprises employing more than fifty persons were classified as factories. The 1921 Act reduced the number of workers necessary for the definition to twenty.

times to reduce it from 8% to 4%.[22] The recovery of industrial production, from the mid-1930s onwards, was ultimately sustained by the production needs of World War II. We have, then, a clear divergence in the pattern of construction and the health of industrial enterprises in Delhi: when the number of industries rose in the late 1930s, levels of construction activity seem to have fallen.

What of the number of joint stock companies in the city? At first glance it would appear that the numbers of joint stock companies more or less follows the pattern of sales of land and construction activity—a lower level in the 1920s than in the 1930s. In other words, the number of joint stock companies rose at the same time as did activity in the urban land market. How should this convergence be understood?

Joint stock companies represented a segment of firms in Delhi which operated at the apex of the market. For instance, at least thrity-nine companies out of 284 floated in this period had authorized capital of over 5 lakhs.[23] The fact that, compared to the late 1910s, both the 1920s and the 1930s showed an increase in the number of joint stock companies, just at the time when trade and industry were bemoaning a lack of credit, suggests that, for larger enterprises, capital and credit could indeed be raised even during the depression.

Factories, in comparison to joint stock companies, were more heterogeneous. A few firms straddled both the worlds of factory production and joint stock companies. Thus in 1932 the family of Lala Sri Ram, owners of the Delhi Cloth and General Mills (one of the biggest factories in Delhi), floated a joint stock company called Madan Mohan Lal Sri Ram Ltd, with authorized capital of Rs. 50 lakhs.[24] But most factories were much smaller enterprises. There were, for instance, a large number of enterprises that employed between twenty and fifty persons, as was indicated by the rise in the number of factories between 1921 and 1922. Similarly, ten of the eighteen factories that were struck off the list between 1931 and 1934 had shrunk the number of employees below the minimum to qualify as a factory rather than winding up completely.[25]

[22] 'Trade and Industry in Delhi', *HT*, 24 February 1932; 'Trade and Industrial Conditions in Delhi', *HT*, 24 April 1932; 'Delhi's Trade during May,' *HT*, 23 June 1932; 'Trade and Industry in Delhi', *HT*, 19 August 1932. The bank rate was further cut in 1933 by 0.5% in 1933 and then again by 0.5% in late 1935. 'Depression in Textile Trade', *HT*, 20 April 1933;'Textiles and Piecegoods Section—Only Dark Spots', *HT*, 21 February 1936.

[23] Compiled from various editions of the annual *Report on the Administration of Delhi Province* between 1916 and 1936. Seven of these had authorized capital of more than 50 lakhs.

[24] *Report on the Administration of Delhi Province, 1932–33* (Delhi: Government of India Press, 1934), p. 64. Lala Madan Mohan Lal was Lala Shri Ram's father.

[25] The relevant editions of the *Report on the Administration of Delhi Province.*

It might be conjectured, then, that the property boom of the late 1920s and early 1930s was financed primarily from the same sources as those that funded the smaller firms—commercial and industrial—that were being squeezed by depressed demand for goods, while larger pools of financial investment continued to seek out joint stock companies. The worlds of property speculation and joint stock companies were not entirely separate; some joint stock companies registered in Delhi must certainly have been involved in the property business.[26] Indeed, the increasing importance of these larger property firms in the 1930s will be remarked upon in Chapter 3. However, it is more plausible to suggest that in the 1930s, rather than invest in risky industrial production or even trade, smaller firms fuelled the construction boom of the late 1920 to early 1930s. Subsequently, as industrial production picked up, levels of construction seem to have fallen off and the number of property sales plateaued. In an intriguing convergence, both Nandini Gooptu for UP towns and Nikhil Rao for Bombay find similar patterns of construction: a brief boom just after World War I followed by a slump in the 1920s and another boom in construction in the late 1920s and early 1930s.[27] Whether this points towards the prevalence of all-India forces having some effect on construction in larger cities is a question that deserves further investigation.

The account of construction offered here diverges from official explanations. The latter cited 'congestion' as explanation for the increased construction activity noted in the early 1930s. Thus, one official report could state:

> The remarkable increase in the registration of documents relating to immovable property is reported to be due to the increasing sales of land in the suburbs for residential building. The congested state of the city proper results in a keen demand for building sites outside the city walls.[28]

[26] Certainly some out of the following companies: Savaria Construction Ltd (authorized capital, 15 Lakhs, floated in 1924, liquidated in 1933); Land Development and Engineering Company Ltd (authorized capital, 5 lakhs, floated in 1931); Colonization Ltd (authorized capital, 5 lakhs, floated in 1932), New Delhi Improvement Trust (authorized capital, 1 crore, floated in 1928). Compiled from the relevant editions of the annual *Report on the Administration of Delhi Province*. See also Chapter 3.

[27] Nandini Gooptu (2001), *The Politics of the Urban Poor in Early Twentieth-Century India* (Cambridge: Cambridge University Press), pp. 94–5; Nikhil Rao (2013), *House, but No Garden: Apartment Living in Bombay's Suburbs, 1898–1964* (Minneapolis, MN: University of Minnesota Press), pp. 103–9.

[28] *Report on the Administration of Delhi Province, 1932–33* (Delhi: Government of India Press, 1934), p. 32.

In locating a problematic of congestion at the heart of the question of housing in Delhi, much historiography has followed the colonial state's narrative.[29] The narrative also suggests a corresponding analytical viewpoint: that of sanitation, planning, and governmentality. The upshot is a reification of a discursive investment of the colonial state: presenting native (supposedly) insanitary habits and its own executive capacities as problem and solution, respectively. While interesting at the discursive level, this pattern of argument fails to provide explanations of either the timing or the particular pattern of the building boom. Arguably, it situates key problems of Delhi's built environment away from where its centre of gravity ought to lie: in the wider circles of economic life in Delhi.

There is yet another important implication that follows from the patterns outlined previously: that finance in Delhi was coordinating the movement of capital and spatial arrangements in the city. If capital streamed into construction and property in the 1930s, it seems to have headed in the direction of manufacture in the late 1930s and 1940s. In Chapter 3 I explore these connections more closely through the firms that emerged in Delhi over this period.

Finally, the argument outlined here suggests that there was a significant reorientation in the historic connections between finance and urban land. A relatively passive relationship between the two was characteristic of the late nineteenth century: urban land only appearing as collateral in credit arrangements, while investment in property was not a mainstay in commercial and financial circles. In response to the crisis of the 1920s a more active connection emerged, with pools of capital—large and small—seeking out of opportunities to invest in urban land and real-estate markets.

The Suburbs and the City Centre

This pattern of boom and bust in the property market also shaped the relationship between Delhi's suburbs and centre. The most readily evident trend from the data seems to be the differences between intramural and extramural parts of the city. Figure 2.5 shows two clear divergences. First, the timing of periods of boom and slump was quite different in Delhi's intramural and extramural areas. In the intramural wards, the boom of large-scale construction in the early 1930s was more muted: while the number

[29] Legg, *Spaces of Colonialism*; Diya Mehra (2013), 'Planning Delhi *ca.*1936–1959', *South Asia: Journal of South Asian Studies*, 36 (3), 354–74.

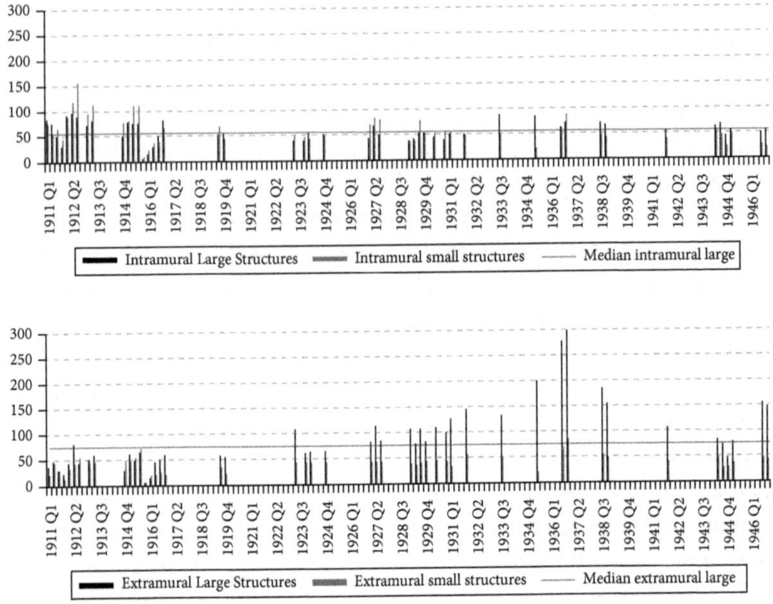

Figure 2.5. Building applications sanctioned in intramural and extramural Delhi, 1911–46.

of applications rose in the 1930s, it was nowhere near as pronounced as for the city as a whole. More significant was the rise in the number of applications to build in the early period from 1911 to 1917 when the maximum amount of large construction seems to have taken place. (See also Table 2.1 showing the population rate.[30]) In contrast, the extramural areas show a quite different pattern of construction. Compared to the city as a whole, the boom in number of sanctioned applications to build large structures seems to have begun even earlier (from the late 1920s), while the period until the 1920s saw very small numbers of applications to build large structures in the extramural wards.

Again, demographics only partly explains the phenomenon. Table 2.2 shows the relative decennial growth rates for intramural and extramural areas. Even though the rate of population growth of the suburbs during 1911–21 was higher than that for the inner city, rates of construction in the latter outstrip the former. From the mid-1920s suburban Delhi was the site

[30] This was a period over which there was a fall in the rate of population increase for these parts of the city compared to 1901–11.

Table 2.2. Intramural and extramural population, 1911–31.[31]

Date	Intramural Wards		Extramural Wards	
	Population	Growth rate	Population	Growth rate
1911	143,449	–	82,122	–
1921	152,661	6.4%	94,326	14.8%
1931	193,887	27%	153,705	62.9%

for investment in construction. Conversely, the most dramatic changes in the suburban landscape also date to this period.

The other notable difference between intramural and extramural areas is in the kind of construction being undertaken. Until the 1940s, intramural wards tended to have greater numbers of sanctioned applications to build 'small structures' than large ones. This is in notable contrast to the wards outside the city walls, where permission was usually sought to construct large structures.

The Intramural House and Street

"'Small structures' were either modifications of spatial configurations within a house or of the relationship between the house and the street. If we further disaggregate the type of 'small structure' in question, the five most common small structures in the intramural area (in order of frequency) were described as 'portion', '*saiban*', 'room', '*chajja* verandah', and 'storey'. Most of these (portion, room, storey, and *saiban*) refer to reconfigurations of space within the house, creating more space within an existing plan. Inevitably this would have meant either subdividing existing spatial layouts or covering up hitherto open areas within a given layout. Whether built for living—as most storeys probably were—or storage—the *saiban* was a shed, sometimes a temporary one, placed in an open part of the house—these structures speak to the emergence of additional demands upon an existing urban fabric. Between them, construction of 'portions' of a house, storeys, and rooms accounted for well over a third of the total number of 'small structures'.[32] Jyoti Hosagrahar's

[31] *Census of India*, 1911, 1921, 1931.

[32] Broadly speaking, constructions designated 'portions' involved building of multiple rooms. Other kinds of small-scale construction might include verandahs, latrines, and *chajjas* (eaves).

compelling discussion of the subdivision of the archetypal *haveli* seems well borne out by this evidence.[33]

The *chajja* verandah refers to a different process. This was a kind of balcony constructed along an eave and can be seen as modifying the relationship between the house and the street. Swati Chattopadhyay has shown, for Calcutta, that the *baithak* (a receiving room often left open to the street) was closely integrated into patterns of fluid interaction between the house, the neighbourhood, and the street.[34] Raghav Kishore has also chronicled the ambivalent success of the nineteenth-century push to redefine the *chabutra* (a platform running along the front of the house) as an encroachment on public land.[35] These two architectural elements, both located at street level, traditionally formed the membrane between the house and the street, across which people and conversation would move between inner and outer realms. Municipal records, however, indicate that applications to build these were much more infrequent than those for *chajja* verandahs. Elevated from street level, the noticeable increase in applications to build *chajja* verandahs over this period would seem to herald markedly new forms of concourse between the street and the house.[36]

But 'small structures' were far from being the only kinds of construction in the intramural wards. The applications to the Municipal Committee, in fact, suggest that there was a significant amount of 'large structure' construction in the old city as well (see Table 2.3). In half the intramural wards, more large than small structures were sanctioned.[37] Although the overall number of 'large structures' being built in intramural wards was smaller than in the suburbs, the area over which the construction was taking place was also more constrained. Doubly so, since most building was in the parts to the south of Chandni Chowk, away from the areas rebuilt by the colonial

[33] Hosagrahar, *Indigenous Modernities*, ch. 2.

[34] Swati Chattopadhyay (2005), *Representing Calcutta: Modernity, Nationalism and the Colonial Uncanny* (London: Routledge), ch. 4.

[35] Raghav Kishore (2015), 'Urban "Failures": Municipal Governance, Planning and Power in Colonial Delhi, 1863–1910', *Indian Economic and Social History Review*, 52 (4), 439–61. Kishore's discussion deals largely with *chabutras* in front of shops.

[36] Hosagrahar points to the conversion of a horizontal separation of male and female quarters of the traditional haveli into a vertical separation, with upper floors being occupied by the women. This is precisely where the *chajja* verandah was located. This conjunction, then, opens up intriguing avenues for future research into the gendered interaction between street and home in twentieth-century Delhi.

[37] Daryaganj is a bit of an exception to the general consideration of the antiquity of the intramural wards. Occupied by the army from 1858 until the first decade of the twentieth century, it was extensively redeveloped from 1914 onwards. The preponderance of 'large structures' in that ward, then, is no surprise.

Table 2.3. Ward-wise distribution of 'large' and 'small' structures sanctioned, 1911–46.

Ward number/area	Number of 'large' structures sanctioned	Number of 'small' structures sanctioned
Ward 1: Kashmere Gate	150	184
Ward 2: Katra Nil	98	166
Ward 3: Khari Baoli	302	273
Ward 4: Dariba Kalan	103	204
Ward 5: Nai Sarak	132	209
Ward 6: Ballimaran	363	435
Ward 7: Farashkhana	389	352
Ward 8: Kucha Pati Ram	298	272
Ward 9: Bhojla Pahari	352	340
Ward 10: Turkman Gate	239	168
Ward 11: Daryaganj	438	332
Total Intramural wards	2,864	2,935
Ward 12: Sabzimandi	931	348
Sadar North	643	324
Sadar South	649	337
Paharganj	974	360
Ward 16: Karol Bagh	1152	120
Total Extramural wards	4,349	1,489

state after 1857 (wards 1 and 2). As such, this is construction which would have entailed tearing down existing structures to rebuild *in situ,* as well building in parts of the city that were hitherto free of constructions.

Construction in Shahjahanabad was both widespread and extremely significant. Nor can it be argued that the basic form of construction in this period followed medieval architectural principles. Whether through more permanent structures such as *chajja* verandahs, or more temporary ones such as the *saibans,* the architecture of the old city emerged in dynamic interaction, with economic upheavals, municipal by-laws, and changing urban sensibilities.

Suburban Development

Turning to the suburbs, the graphs make it clear that at some point in the mid-1920s the sheer volume of construction in these parts of the city began to dominate construction in the city as a whole. It is striking that the state-planned new layouts in the suburbs began largely in the early 1930s and really took shape in the latter half of that decade (Table 2.4). The Delhi

Table 2.4. Major city extension and slum clearance schemes, 1911–47.

Date of sanction	Scheme	Intramural/ extramural
1912	Western Extension Area	Extramural
1913	Burn Bastion Road Scheme	Intramural and extramural
1914	Daryaganj South Scheme	Intramural
1914	Garstin Bastion Road Scheme, Jhandewalan Road Scheme, Idgah Road	Extramural
1915	Idgah Road Extension, Mondhewalan Road	Extramural
1930	Basti Harphool Singh Slum Clearance	Extramural
1931	Karol Bagh Scheme	Extramural
1936	Northern City Extension Scheme no. 1	Extramural
1937	Daryaganj South	Intramural
1937	Paharganj Fuel Market, Andha Mughal, Western Extension, Mondhewalan Road Development	Extramural
1938	Garstin Bastion Road	Intramural
1938	Paharganj Original Road	Extramural
1939	Faiz Bazar Police Station Plot development	Intramural
1939	Qutab Road Plots Development, Roshanara Extension, Northern City Extension no. 2, Basti Ara Kashan Clearance	Extramural
1940	Ramnagar Plots, Ahata Kidara Slum Clearance, Hathi Khana Slum Clearance Scheme, Industrial Area Part 1	Extramural
1941	Paharganj Circus Slum Clearance Scheme	Extramural
1942	New Delhi Northern City Extension	Extramural
1945	Western Yamuna Canal Clearance Scheme	Extramural
1946	Gilheri Bagh Development, Yamuna Village and Slum Clearance Scheme, Delhi Ajmere Gate Slum Clearance Scheme, Sarai Purani Idgah Slum Clearance Scheme	Extramural

Improvement Trust (DIT), set up in 1937, also saw its major spurt of construction activity in the period up to the 1940s. In short, the upward trend in construction shown in the graphs precedes the major interventions planned by the local administration. Similarly, the peak of construction activity (even barring the anomalous 1936 numbers) were reached slightly before the setting up of the Delhi Improvement Trust.[38] In short, construction in the suburbs usually preceded planned schemes.

[38] It should be noted that these figures do not include construction taking place in areas administered by the DIT, but would include areas around it. It would also include construction that took place after an area was handed back to the Municipality by the DIT.

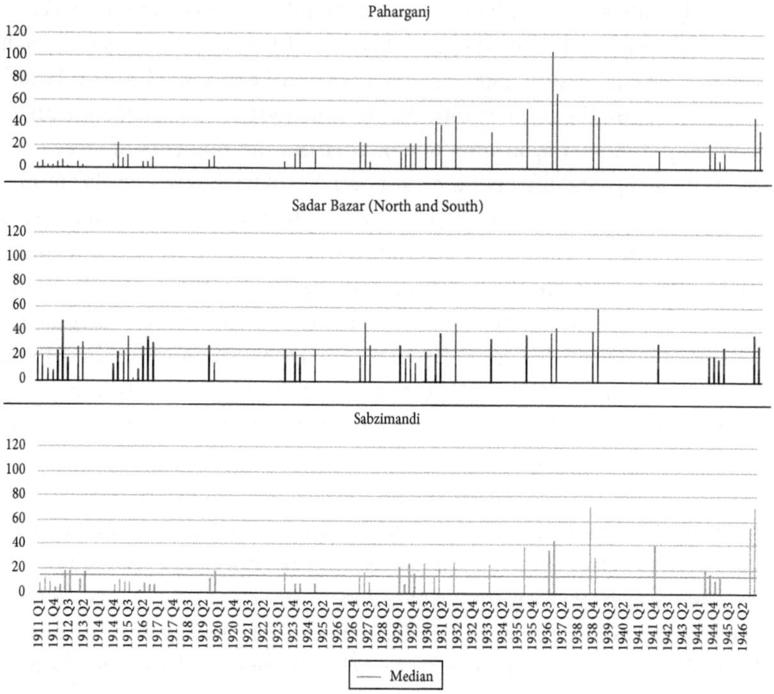

Figure 2.6. Building applications sanctioned: large structures in extramural wards, 1911–46.

The four suburban wards have so far been discussed in more or less homogeneous terms, but it is striking that Sabzimandi, Sadar Bazar North, Sadar Bazar South, and Paharganj do not all display the same pattern of development (Figure 2.6). Paharganj and Sabzimandi—the northern and southern suburbs which adjoined the Civil Lines and New Delhi respectively—were built up at around the same time. Most of the large-scale construction in these two areas took place between 1929 and 1946. Paharganj in particular shows large amounts of construction in the mid-1930s, while building in Sabzimandi reached its peak a few years later. Sadar Bazar (North and South combined) had a far higher number of buildings sanctioned over the period as a whole than either of the other two areas. However, in this ward construction was steady and dispersed over the period as a whole rather than being concentrated in the 1930s. Thus, even within the suburbs the patterns in which construction occurred varied.

Two localities planned by state authorities illustrate yet another striking aspect of construction in the city. Between 1923 and 1935, Karol Bagh (where a layout of sorts but few amenities were established in the 1920s) was consistently the locality with the most large-structure building activity in the city.[39] However, in only one quarter did the numbers of large constructions go beyond fifty. For the most part, Karol Bagh saw a steady amount of construction over the whole period rather than a spurt in a compressed period of time. This is in sharp contrast to Rehgarpura, a resettlement neighbourhood, which saw a clear rise for a few years in the mid-1930s and very little construction either before or in the 1940s. The implication of such a pattern is that even where state layouts created the conditions for the settling of an area, it was not always the case that a rush of investments in building followed automatically. In fact, the rhythms of urban development in state layouts were also governed by other factors.

Taken together, these patterns point towards the significance and rapidity of private developments on urban land. On this account, public interventions often seem to follow in the wake of preceding private initiatives. Sometimes, as in Karol Bagh, extensive planning by the state was little more than recognition of transformations that had already occurred. At other points, as during the mid-1930s, the plans of state agencies—layouts and the provision of amenities—might buttress a pre-existing trend in the property market. To see planned interventions in the cityscape as the primary loci of urban development, then, is to underestimate the degree to which city development, based on a commodification of urban land, was already tied up with patterns and cycles of accumulation in other sectors of the economy.

Conclusion

This chapter has argued for a reassessment of the role of the property market in generating Delhi's landscape. Even as New Delhi was erected under Imperial diktat and the watchful eye of its planners, its neighbour to the north was also being transformed. The spectacular colonial architecture of the former (celebrated in contemporary postcards even while it was a

[39] In 1936, A. P. Hume noted that the population in this area were living in much discomfort owing to the lack of essential services. *Report on the Relief of Congestion in Delhi*, vol. 1, p. 10.

construction site),[40] should not be allowed to obscure our view of the more anarchic and less harmonized stylings of the latter.

If ruler and pencil, allocation of funds, and availability of materials determined the pace and design of Imperial Delhi, a more complex assemblage of forces was brought to bear on Shahjahanabad. I suggest that the patterns of construction in the Old city must be understood bearing in mind the emergence of a set of connections between urban land, finance, and the rhythms of economic life in the city.

Rather than explain Delhi's transformations through demographics or view it through the lens of the urban plans, looking at construction in the city itself reveals a very different pattern. The slump of the 1920s and the recovery from the late 1930s did not simply restore traditional economic activity in the city. The prevailing connections between industry, commerce, and urban land were, in fact, transformed in passing through the bust and boom. The fact that financial flows could shift capital between urban construction (or land purchases) and industry (in the 1940s), or between commerce and real estate (in the 1930s), represents the emergence of circuits of capital in the city that have not been fully appreciated in the South Asian context.[41] While suburb and city centre responded to these forces in different fashion, the operation of similar forces across these areas is remarkable. Even though the winding *galis* and *kuchas* of Delhi seemed to resemble those of long ago, the forces that pulsed beneath the opaque surface were modern ones of profit and accumulation.

[40] See various postcards in H. A. Mirza and Sons album in the Alkazi Collection of Photography.

[41] David Harvey's work has highlighted the importance of the spatial fix—that profitable accumulation in moments of crisis might require a move of investment into the built environment from other circuits of capital. David Harvey (1999), *The Limits to Capital*, new edn. (London: Verso).

3

Landlords, Tenants, and Real Estate Firms

The cycles of boom and bust, graphs of property construction, and tables of population growth that we have encountered so far have sketched the outlines of Delhi's urban expansion in the twentieth century. Filling in this picture demands a closer investigation of the ways in which Delhi's denizens engaged with the property market. Tracking these everyday processes, of seeking out places to live, renting out structures, and buying and selling land, opens up a much finer-grained view of the operations of the property market than the graphs and figures in Chapter 2.

This chapter considers the people who constituted the urban property market. It examines a number of different levels: the poor, the suburban ex-farmer, women, and the wide variety of intermediate groups, from petty traders to the emerging professional middle classes. The incomes and activities of this latter class in particular are of considerable interest and arguably lay at the heart of the torsions in the property market from 1920 to 1940. Already by the late 1920s, the professional middle classes were being identified by officials as a target for new institutional financial arrangements that might address the slump in the housing market. However, a more diverse swathe of intermediate groups—small traders and erstwhile agriculturalists—were also using urban property to consolidate their incomes. Simultaneously, a larger scale of operations was also emerging within the property market. This was represented in the mid-1930s by (often short-lived) joint stock firms that speculated in property, placing land and finance at the centre of their operations.

Economic activities relating to urban land, however, also involved the use of violence, power, and influence. The collection of rent was not automatic, the construction of new houses was not always by the book, and property deals often had more to them than met the eye. Real estate fortunes were always constituted in close association with other forms of power and influence in the city. This was a circuit that the crisis of the 1920s did not disturb: coercion, corruption, and other supposed illegalities characterized

Possessing the City: Property and Politics in Delhi, 1911–1947. Anish Vanaik, Oxford University Press (2020).

DOI: 10.1093/oso/9780198848752.001.0001

relationships between landlords and tenants as well as between landlords and colonial officials.

Housing the Poor

A large portion of those who were beginning to swell Delhi's population so dramatically over this period was constituted by poor migrants. They came as construction workers for the new capital, as unskilled labourers who carted goods between the railway stations and the godowns that dotted Delhi and as workers in the few industries that sprang up in Delhi over this period. State-planned and subsidized housing for the poor was, however, a measure that was sometimes considered and rarely delivered. How, then, were Delhi's urban poor housed?

The spaces in which Delhi's urban poor found housing were quite different in the intramural and suburban areas. From the 1900s, market gardeners and suburban agriculturists in the areas adjoining the city were converting their lands into settlements. The *basti* (settlement) of *chappars* (huts with thatched roofs) was the form of collective dwelling that began to dot the outskirts of the city. The iconic instance of this in Delhi was Basti Harphool Singh, a vast area of makeshift housing which by the mid-1920s was condemned by officials and Congress nationalists alike as the most execrable slum in the city. Situated in the heart of the busy commercial, industrial, and retail suburb of Sadar Bazar, the land on which it was situated belonged to the eponymous Jat landlord Chaudhari Harphool Singh.[1] Basti Harphool Singh was not the only one of its kind. In Abadi Pulewalan, not far from Basti Harphool Singh, about one hundred huts were occupied 'by low class people' on private land.[2] Similarly, Abadi Chamaran in the same ward had 125 huts occupied by around 300 people.[3] While there were some instances of settlements like these springing up on public lands, a large proportion were situated on privately owned lands.

Within the city walls, the equivalent to the *basti* was the *katra*. At its most basic, the *katra* was a building or series of buildings that consisted of structures built around a central courtyard that opened onto the street.

[1] Jats are an agrarian community found across many parts of north India, including much of the countryside in which Delhi is located.

[2] TH, DMC Progs, Sanitary Sub-Committee meeting (Sany SCM) of 16 March, confirmed at Ordinary Meeting (OM) of 30 March 1915, prog. no. 4.

[3] TH, DMC Progs, Sany SCM of 30 March confirmed at OM of 20 April 1915, prog. no. 2.

Not all, nor even most, *katras* in Delhi were inhabited by the poor; many were markets, and others housed tenants that were more comfortably off. A significant number of *katras*, however, often because of dilapidation, were occupied by the urban poor. As with the land on which *basti*s arose, most *katras* were privately owned; some even by the city's elite. Thus, Rai Bahadur Lala Sheo Prasad CIE owned *katras* in two localities which were inhabited by 'the humble and menial classes'.[4] By building their own structures and long occupation, in many instances tenants acquired rights to reside in these structures, leaving reluctant owners unable to move them.[5]

Neither *katras* nor *bastis* were planned layouts; they often lacked even the most basic sanitary facilities, and owners had no interest in providing them. The Municipal Committee, for instance, had to demand that the owners of the land and huts in both Abadi Pulewalan and Abadi Chamaran, as well as RB Sheo Prasad, provide drainage and latrine arrangements and employ sweepers to clean the area.[6] The Rai Bahadur's response was to ask that the tenants be compelled by the Municipal Committee to build the required latrines and drains. Pershottam Das, another owner of property on which numerous poor families were housed, stated that although he owned the land he received a very small amount of rent from the tenants. He suggested that the tenants be asked to construct the drains, or else the municipality ought to issue notices to the plot and he would have the land cleared out.[7] Apart from other ways in which sanitary discourse could be deployed against the poor—as during plague measures or the use of nuisance laws[8]—this points to yet another situation in which elites were eager to use rules regarding sanitation as a weapon against the poor.

Rent collection in *bastis* and *katras* was often subcontracted. Mohammad Saddiq and Mussammat Akhtarzamani Begam owned vacant pieces of land in the vicinity of the market of Ajmeri Gate which they leased to Bhima and Husain Ali respectively, who in turn sub-let plots to vegetable and leather

[4] The two localities were Chah Indara and Aqab Kalan Masjid. TH, DMC Progs, Sany SCM, 11 May confirmed, at OM of 25 May 1913, prog. no. 1, and Sany SCM, 11 May 1915, confirmed at OM of 25 May 1915, prog. no. 9.

[5] TH, DMC Progs, Sany SCM, confirmed at OM of 7 September 1915, prog. No. 2.

[6] TH, DMC Progs, Sany SCM of 16 March, confirmed at OM of 30 March 1915, prog. no. 4, Sany SCM confirmed at OM 27 May 1913, prog. no. 1, and Sany SCM of 30 March, confirmed at OM of 20 April 1915, prog. no. 2.

[7] TH, DMC Progs, Sany SCM confirmed at OM 4 June 1913, prog no. 2.

[8] M. R. Anderson (1992), 'Public Nuisance and Private Purpose', *SOAS Law Department Working Paper 1* (Law School of Oriental and African Studies); Rajnarayan Chandavarkar (1998), *Imperial Power and Popular Politics: Class, Resistance and the State in India, c.1850–1950* (Cambridge: Cambridge University Press).

sellers.[9] Sheikh Mohammed Rafi from Gali Hinga Beg installed a contractor to live in his *Katra* and collect rent. The contractor, a dental surgeon, paid Rs. 435 per month to Rafi. He also ran his surgery out of a set of rooms valued at Rs. 115 per month, and collected Rs. 385 from the other tenants of the structure.[10] In other *bastis* we hear of the presence of 'Chaudharies'—figures who assumed responsibility for a group of inhabitants of the *basti.* Thus, when Lala Sheo Prasad's tenants at Aqab Kalan Masjid were asked to build facilities for sanitary needs on the premises, the Municipal Committee isolated Chaudharies to be 'called upon to induce the rest of the tenants to build the required drains, sanitary privies, and urinals.'[11] For the poor, then, a favoured means of rent collection adopted by their landlords was to farm out the responsibility and deal with them as a collective.

Particularly in the early years after Delhi became the capital city there were analogous transformations in the *bastis* and *katras* of the suburban and intramural parts of the city respectively. For one, it was the same class of people—the working poor—who streamed into the *bastis* and *katras* around the city. But another shared peculiarity was that influential elites in these localities were renting property to some of the poorest residents of Delhi. There is, however, a significant difference in the role that such properties played for owners in intramural and suburban areas respectively. Many of the intramural owners were more or less established within the city's power structure, occupying positions in DMC and, as with Lala Sheo Prasad, on the colonial honours list. To them, *katra* dwellers were often a nuisance—to be evicted if possible. For those in the extramural areas, settlement by the urban poor was often the moment in which their lands entered into the urban property market. This was, therefore, a more consequential occupation of land.

Many of the agrarian tracts that surrounded Delhi were owned by members of the Jat community. Property speculation and renting, often initially to the urban poor, provided a material basis for the claim of Jat landowners to positions of influence in the urban power structure.[12]

[9] TH, DMC Progs, Sany. SCM 2 March, confirmed at OM 16 March 1915.

[10] TH, DMC Progs, SM 10 July 1929 and SM of 14 August 1929.

[11] TH, DMC Progs, Sany SCM, confirmed at OM of 7 September 1915, prog. No. 2.

[12] Historians have suggested that participation in communal riots (for instance, around cow slaughter in the mid-1920s) was a means by which these Jat landowners sought incorporation into the symbolic world of (Hindu) urban society. Awadhendra B. Sharan (2014), *In the City, Out of Place: Nuisance, Pollution, and Dwelling in Delhi, c.1850–2000* (New Delhi: Oxford University Press); Narayani Gupta (1981), *Delhi between Two Empires, 1803–1931: Society, Government and Urban Growth* (Delhi: Oxford University Press), pp. 218–19.

Chaudhari Harphool Singh's trajectory illustrates this well. The eventual acquisition by the Municipal Committee of the land on which the *basti* bearing his name stood yielded a sum of Rs. 2.40 lakhs as compensation in 1929.[13] Some of this money went back into purchasing a market in the Sabzimandi ward. By the 1940s, Chaudhari Harphool Singh was acknowledged as one of two influential Jat leaders in Sadar Bazar South ward. It was inevitable, therefore, that when the colonial state was looking to appoint *Mir Mohallas*[14] to the Pahari Dhiraj-Jatwara locality they would select Chaudhari Hari Singh, Harphool Singh's younger brother (whose own properties yielded over Rs. 1000 per month in rent).[15] Hari Singh had been selected over Chaudhari Harnarain, who owed allegiance to Harphool Singh's major rival, Chaudhari Umrao Singh.[16] Perhaps to re-establish balance, a relative of Umrao Singh, his nephew, was selected to be *Mir Mohalla* from a neighbouring locality in ward 14.[17] Such was the power of the Jat landlords in this ward that even the two Brahmin candidates from the nearby Gali Lallu Missar locality were divided into pro- and anti-Umrao Singh camps.[18] For groups like the Jats, not traditionally counted among the Delhi elites, property ownership in the outskirts and conversion of suburban lands into urban localities were often initial stepping stones towards acquiring both wealth and political influence in the city.[19]

Consolidating real estate in order to cement upward mobility was not, however, restricted to erstwhile agrarian groups. Sections of subaltern

[13] DDA, CC records, Education, F no. 4(36), 1930, DMC to DC 18 December 1929 indicates that Harphool Singh received the rent from the tenants of the *basti*. DDA, CC Records, Eduction, F. no. 4(141), 1935 DC to CC 18 July 1935 records that the owners had agreed to receive Rs. 2,40,000 for the land.

[14] This was a novel petty-administrative post designated by an ostentatiously traditional title. *Mohalla* was the local term for neighbourhood, and *Mir* is an honorific of leadership. The responsibilities of the *Mir Mohallas*, in fact, were far from traditional. Their major roles appear to have involved the stamping of ration cards and helping the police with investigations in their areas. DDA, DC, F no. 151, 1941. The scheme itself was short-lived and does not seem to have survived more than a few years. They open an interesting window onto the social structure of these localities and have been used, in what follows, for this purpose.

[15] DDA, DC Records, F no. 381, 1944.

[16] Chaudhari Harnarain reportedly received Rs. 300 per month from rent.

[17] He was found to earn Rs. 150 per month as rent from properties registered in his own name. DDA, DC Records, F no. 379, 1944.

[18] In comparison to the Jat owners, however, their incomes from rents were, respectively, Rs. 50 and Rs. 100 per month. DDA, DC Records, F no. 384, 1944. Another case was Chaudhari Ghasi Ram from Jatwara, made *Mir Mohalla* for Teliwara area. Also a Jat of long-standing residence in the area, his property holdings were valued in excess of Rs. 10,000. DDA, DC Records, F no. 363, 1944.

[19] This is a trajectory that can be seen as initiating a template for urban growth that has been repeated on numerous occasions in Delhi down to the contemporary period.

groups[20] within the city also seem to have used property for this purpose. Thus, among the weaver caste that lived in Basti Julahan was one individual who worked as a broker and owned two houses (which together yielded Rs. 40 per month as rent), and another who owned a house valued at Rs. 6,000.[21] From among the Ahirs (an agrarian caste) of Basti Ahiran, three residents were identified as candidates for *Mir Mohalla*-ship.[22] Each of them owned property, the 'most' influential of them with holdings valued at Rs. 1 lakh. The 'least' influential of the three being considered worked as an agent to a local cloth merchant at a salary of Rs. 99 per month, and owned property that yielded a further Rs. 60 per month. Among the Qassais (traditionally butchers) of Qassabpura, Badruddin, and Bashiruddin, both stated their primary occupations as dealers in meat (mutton and beef respectively). But they also earned Rs. 125 and Rs. 100 per month respectively from rents.[23] Haji Alimuddin of the lime burner community—a migrant who had arrived in Delhi as a young child—was entirely dependent for his income on property, and received Rs. 300 per month.[24] All the cases discussed so far were located in the suburbs. Within the city too, Haji Ghaffor-ud-din, also a Qassai, was no longer involved in the meat trade and depended solely on his property, valued at Rs. 20,000,[25] for his income.

We see here evidence for the existence, if not extent, of processes of social differentiation within poor communities. The examples cited here are not representative of wider trajectories of upward mobility, and most members of these communities did not own property.[26] Nor is it possible to trace how many individuals from these neighbourhoods were property owners. Nevertheless, from the mix of occupations that are recorded it is safe to conclude that for a section of the intermediate castes in the less affluent areas around Delhi, including those who were in or just beginning to move out of their traditional occupations, property and rental income was an important way of consolidating and augmenting their income from other sources.

[20] I use the term 'subaltern' here consciously to designate a range of groups that were not counted among the traditional elite. As becomes evident, there was significant differentiation within them.

[21] DDA, DC Records, F. no. 380. The weavers are recorded as for the most part having taken to the occupation of plying carts.

[22] DDA, DC Records, F no. 393, 1944.

[23] DDA, DC Records, F. no. 394, 1944.

[24] DDA, DC Records, F. no. 421, 1944.

[25] DDA, DC Records, F. no. 367, 1944. The locality is recorded as being dominated by qassais (butchers), ghosis (cattle rearers), and Rajputs.

[26] The previous discussion is based on investigations carried out by colonial officials seeking candidates for *Mir Mohalla*. Thus, by virtue of the fact that officials were seeking neighbourhood leaders, these examples were not representative of the locality as a whole.

Even as they were largely excluded from property ownership, the relationship of the urban poor to the property market was variegated. The living conditions afforded them in Delhi were usually terrible. For a select few among the poor and (more often) for their landlords, rentals in these *bastis* and *katras* could become sources of upward mobility. Indeed, particularly in the suburbs, the poor can be thought of as establishing a kind of 'urban frontier', the monetary benefits of which were reaped by erstwhile agriculturists. Delhi's unplanned development, then, did not lack in opportunities to turn a profit.

The Intermediate Classes

If sections of subaltern groups cemented upward mobility by acquiring and renting property, this was also the case for numerous other groups in the city. Table 3.1 lists, in descending order, the professions with the highest number of unique advertisements[27] that appeared in the local English-language daily *Hindustan Times*.[28] On the lists there are a number of professions which might be expected—in particular, those related to finance

Table 3.1. Professions of people or companies advertising property rentals in *Hindustan Times*.

S no.	1924–29	1930–34	1935–39	1940–44	Overall
1	Banking	Banking	Insurance	Banking	Banking
2	Law	Automobiles	Government Employee	Insurance	Automobiles
3	Automobiles	Cabinet maker	Builder	Builder	Builder
4	Government employee	Law	Property, estate agents	Property, estate agents	Law
5	Doctor	Contractors	Rais	Automobiles	Insurance

[27] For the purposes of this Table, repetitions of the advertisement (thats is, the same advertisement appearing more than once in a given year) are not counted. All the statistics about advertisements use this way of counting, without taking into consideration the number of times an advertisement repeated in a year.

[28] This is based on a comprehensive compilation of classified advertisements from the extant issues of the *Hindustan Times* available at the Centre for South Asian Studies at Cambridge. The run is from late 1924 onwards, and I was able to look at every available issue up to the end of November 1946.

(banking and insurance), and building and property dealership. Some of the other professions that appear here refer to another sphere which burgeoned in post-1911 Delhi. Automobile dealers, cabinet makers, estate agents, and contractors were all part of the segment that catered to the colonial officials and princes who frequented Imperial Delhi. Apart from those specializing in property transactions and those catering primarily to the sphere of colonial elites, a third category of advertisers is also in evidence. Sections of the local commercial classes—iron merchants, pharmacists, watchmakers, and gramophone dealers—also rented out properties, as did professionals—doctors, lawyers, and government employees. This describes a wide section of intermediate classes.

Further evidence that the intermediate classes were involved in property rentals is borne out by disaggregating the spatial pattern indicated in the advertisements. Most of the structures let out for rent were located in New Delhi. This is not surprising for an English language daily during this period. However, the single largest chunk of advertisers was based in the intramural parts of Delhi (Table 3.2). Among the advertisers from Delhi, the localities of Kashmere Gate, Chandni Chowk, and Daryaganj between them account for just over half the advertisements. These were areas that in this period were more Anglicised (Kashmere Gate) or inhabited by the native elite (Daryaganj and Chandni Chowk). However, a significant number of advertisements were issued by people based in other areas—Katra Nil, Nai Sarak, Dharampura and Fatehpuri—neighbourhoods in which the intermediate segments of the retail and wholesale trade of the city were concentrated.

Other more anecdotal evidence (from the information compiled for the *Mir Mohallas*) also attests to property ownership by wide segments of the intermediate classes. Individuals from various professional classes (doctors, lawyers, government employees, and those who were otherwise salaried or had retired from these sorts of occupation) constituted almost a quarter of those considered for appointment as *Mir Mohallas*. Most of these were

Table 3.2. Location of rental structures and advertisers.

Location	Structures advertised	Advertisers
Old Delhi	235	258
New Delhi	312	168
Suburbs	76	46
Civil Lines	111	29

propertied to various degrees.[29] Another significant chunk of individuals was involved in small trades of various sorts (cloth, boots and shoes, jewellery, sundries, hosiery, and contractors).[30] This set of intermediate classes—professional and small-trade based—is likely to have been the source of much of the building in Delhi of the 1930s. Property put out on rent was a viable supplement to other incomes until 1942. The introduction of rent control in that year, however, had a sharply negative impact on the rental market. The number of advertisements for rental properties declined, and at around the same time the number of advertisements for property sales registered a steep rise.

This latter sphere—of property sales—is more difficult to track. As Table 3.3 shows, the immediate agency for most sales tended to be auctioneers, property dealers, and the state. While lawyers and doctors are present at times, they are markedly less frequent than in rental advertisements. There are a number of other differences between the market for sales and the market for rents. For instance, the number of advertisements for rentals issued by individuals is greater than those issued by firms, while the opposite is true in the case of advertisements for sales of property.[31]

Table 3.3. Professions of organizations and people advertising property sales in *Hindustan Times*.

S no.	1924–29	1930–34	1935–39	1940–44	Overall
1	Law	Property	Auctioneers	Property	Auctioneers
2	Auctioneers	Auctioneers	State	State	Property
3	State (including princely states)	Engineers	Trade	Auctioneers	State
4	Banking	Doctors	Property	Automobiles	Law
5	Retail	State	Insurance	Contractors	Trade

[29] Among those who owned property and whose valuations are mentioned, the smallest amount mentioned is a rental income of Rs. 50 per month. The largest owned property worth Rs. 1,40,000, with the largest number concentrated in a property valuation of between 10,000 and 30,0000.

[30] The largest of these had property worth Rs. 2,00,000, and the smallest rental income mentioned was Rs. 250–300 per month.

[31] In both instances—for rentals and for sales—this is based on instances where a decision can be made one way or another about whether it is an individual or a firm issuing the advertisement (374/576 discrete advertisements in the case of sales, and 538/786 in the case of rentals).

Advertisements placed in an English-language newspaper (albeit a nationalist one) over this period would have been aimed at the elite sections of the city. The fact that advertisers for rentals are a fairly heterogeneous group—not concentrated among those operating in large-scale finance or specifically the property business—is therefore significant. Having said this, a relatively small proportion of the rental business in the old city is likely to have been conducted through the newspaper.[32] Nevertheless, there is evidence for a very wide base of participation in the rental property market among intermediate classes in Delhi.

Women and Property

Advertisements in the newspaper, however, can tell us little about the ways in which women were active in the property market. Only seven of around 327 rental advertisements seem to have been placed by women.[33] If we return to the building statistics used in the Chapter 2, however, a more substantial picture can be compiled. Around one tenth of the total number of approved structures, large and small, in the city as whole were applied for by women. Since owners applied to construct structures, large or small, this evidence is a reasonable approximation of women's nominal ownership of property in Delhi over this period. Seen in this way, the picture of women being excluded from property by the laws of inheritance set in place under colonial rule seems well borne out for Delhi.

Disaggregated further, a more novel finding can be offered. When broken down by religion, there is a stark difference in the extent to which Hindu and Muslim women could nominally control property. Considered as a whole (including men and women), the amount of construction applied for by the two communities is more or less equal.[34] However, Muslim women constructed almost two-and-a-half times as many structures as Hindu women. Muslim women's ability to control urban property, if only nominally, appears to have been significantly greater than those of their Hindu counterparts.

[32] Much more significant are likely to have been oral networks of local knowledge for which evidence is hard to come by.

[33] In terms of advertisements for sales, three women can be identified out of 116.

[34] Muslims constituted more than 40% of the population of the municipal area, and Hindus just over 50% over most of this period. Muslim construction, then, was slightly higher than its proportion of the population.

Another interesting result emerges when we look at the contribution of women to construction in different wards. It will be recalled that, particularly after the mid-1920s, the volume of construction in suburban areas—Paharganj, Karol Bagh, Sabzimandi and Sadar Bazar—dwarfed the amount of construction in the intramural parts of the city. Table 3.4 lists side by side the top five wards by volume of overall construction and women's contribution to overall construction.

The difference between the two lists is striking. Apart from Sabzimandi, all the other wards with a high proportion of construction by women were in intramural portions of the city. The mixture of wards is also striking. The suburbs of Paharganj and Karol Bagh (the latter had a distinctly large number of residents of the professional classes) were among the wards with the lowest proportion of construction applied for by women. The wards in which women's construction was relatively substantial are a motley collection. Daryaganj, as a more recently reconstructed locality, was distinctly elite. Turkman Gate, Farashkhana, and Bhojla Pahari were wards with large Muslim populations, but also had concentrations of the urban poor. In general, however, as intramural wards these were portions of the city with older histories of settlement and longstanding local traditions.

It is not surprising to find that women's control of property was rare. It is clear, however, that there were stark differences between the abilities of Muslim and Hindu women to control property. It is also striking to find that over this period it was in the older parts of the city that women's ability to control property was most marked. This was unaffected by the patterns of boom and bust for the city as a whole. Figure 3.1 also shows that construction by women in Delhi mirrors overall trends in construction: a slump in

Table 3.4. Comparison of wards by construction, and women's contribution to construction.

Top five wards by volume of construction	Top five wards by proportion of construction by women
Paharganj	Sabzimandi
Sabzimandi	Ward 7: Farashkhana
Karol Bagh	Ward 11: Daryaganj
Sadar South	Ward 9: Bhojla Pahari
Sadar North	Ward 10: Turkman Gate

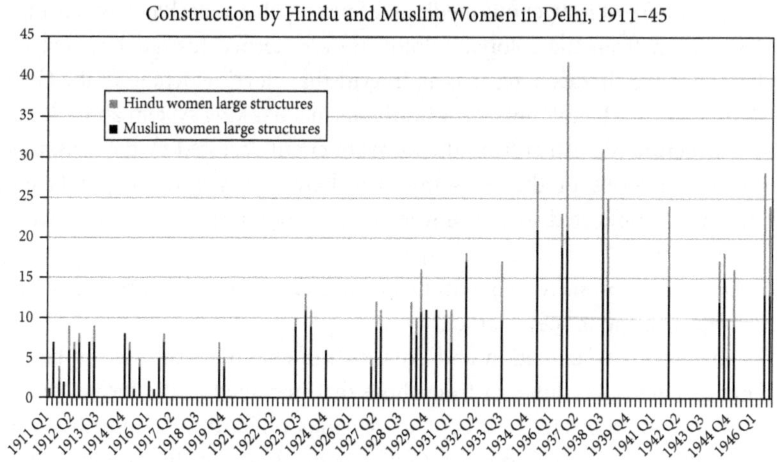

Figure 3.1. Sanctioned applications to build made by women.

the 1920s followed by a boom in the 1930s into the early 1940s. The fact that women's construction follows the pattern of construction in the city as a whole suggests that economic cycles of boom and bust did little to change the patterns of property-holding by women in Delhi.

Crisis and Recovery, 1920–40

So far we have seen that the property market in Delhi was fairly broad-based. A crucial new conjuncture was initiated by the period of crisis of the 1920s and the boom in construction that followed it. The links between finance and real estate for this period are particularly important, because both the roots of the crisis and the ways of emerging from it were moulded by these connections.

Finance and the Property Market

Delhi was one of the largest centres of finance in colonial India, ranking behind the port cities of Bombay and Calcutta. Financial firms located in Delhi included the highest echelons of the 'modern' banking system: joint stock, and exchange banks. Delhi was also, however, an important location for the sphere of indigenous credit and finance. Historian Rajat Ray, using a designation from the colonial administration, terms this latter sphere the 'bazaar'.[35] He characterizes it as an intermediate level which, until the Great Depression, had weak linkages with the formal banking system above it and was structurally distinct from the forms of credit accessed by the peasant at the lowest levels of the economy. The bazaar was also, he points out, intimately connected to the movement of goods (especially grain) across the interiors of India. It is not surprising, then, that much economic activity in Delhi, for reasons rooted in its historical and commercial importance, was tied up with the money market.

The culture of operation and even instruments of credit used in bazaar finance were quite different from those that prevailed in the formal sector. Family reputation and traditions of religious philanthropy contributed to the credit actors could command quite as much as did the rumours about their solvency. Ray points out, however, that it is a mistake to see the bazaar as representing some kind of static remnant, reflective of South Asian *gemeinschaft* which was passively overtaken and subsumed by Western *gesellschaft*.[36] On the contrary, the bazaar had a dynamic history of interaction with the formal structures of colonial finance, commerce, and industry. Ray's account of the bazaar concentrates on its role as a driver of trade and seed bed from which the indigenous industrial bourgeoisie grew. The relationship of finance to urban property, however, is left without remark in his account.

In Delhi, from the turn of the century a number of developments transformed the links between finance and urban property. The Punjab Alienation of Land Act, legislated in 1900, had an impact on the structure of credit in the rural parts of Delhi's hinterland.[37] The Act designated agriculturist and non-agriculturist castes and restricted transfers from the former to the latter. One of the outcomes of this change was that money lenders (largely belonging to trading castes) were unable to accept land as collateral for loans to peasants. Many of them sought to withdraw from

[35] Rajat Kanta Ray (1988), 'The Bazaar: Changing Structural Characteristics of the Indigenous Section of the Indian Economy before and after the Great Depression', *Indian Economic and Social History Review*, 25 (3), 263–318, p. 263.

[36] Rajat Kanta Ray (1995), 'Asian Capital in the Age of European Domination: The Rise of the Bazaar, 1800–1914', *Modern Asian Studies*, 29 (3), 449–54.

[37] The act stipulated that agricultural land could only be alienated to persons of designated agricultural castes. Most moneylenders in the villages and cities of Punjab were not members of these castes.

the business of agricultural loans altogether and instead invest in the city.[38] In contrast, property in urban areas, given the increase in prices until around 1919, remained a safe investment. As was pointed out in the *Report of the Banking Enquiry Committee for Centrally Administered Areas* (*BECCAA*) carried out in 1929–30: 'In the urban areas [. . .] it is a common thing in prosperous years for a merchant or even a banker to invest heavily in house property.'[39]

From the early 1920s, however, the situation began to change. Delhi went through a period of agricultural and trade depression. Historically linked to the movement of grain and piece goods in (and through) Delhi, the bazaar was also hit. Credit on offer in the city began to seize up. An already teetering financial sector was tipped over into meltdown by the emergence of new financial actors—in particular, cooperative and joint stock banks—that were receiving state support.[40] With access to cheaper credit from the Imperial Bank (which was established in 1921), the rates they were able to offer stiffened competition with indigenous bankers. As a result, whereas around 1910 there were as many as 200 indigenous bankers regularly dealing in *hundis*,[41] loans, and deposits, by 1930 only forty-three family firms were recognized as *shroffs*, and for each of them banking was a 'side-line in their main business'.[42] The amount of loan and deposit business transacted by indigeneous firms also shrank substantially, with the discounting of *hundis* becoming the sole activity of any scale that they pursued. These multiple strands of crisis in the bazaar transformed what began as a trade and agrarian crisis in the 1920s into a credit crisis in the urban economy.

One reaction to this shakeup of the financial market in the 1920s appears to have been that many of the largest indigenous bankers replaced their banking operations with property concerns. Thus, of the seven major family banking firms mentioned in the Delhi District Gazetteer of 1913, only one remained in the banking business in any appreciable sense by the late 1920s: the Dhuliawalas, whose patriarch Minamal Somany also had large property

[38] *Banking Enquiry Committee for the Centrally Administered Areas, 1929–30* (Calcutta: Government of India, Central Publication Branch, 1930), p. 165.

[39] Ibid., p. 315.

[40] Nandini Gooptu also points to a similar process in UP in the 1920s. Nandini Gooptu (2001), *The Politics of the Urban Poor in Early Twentieth-Century India* (Cambridge: Cambridge University Press), pp. 94–5.

[41] An indigenous financial instrument, some versions of which were similar to bills of exchange. These were used to extend credit and to transfer funds from one location to another.

[42] *Banking Enquiry Committee for the Centrally Administered Areas, 1929–30*', pp. 338–40.

holdings in the city.[43] Among the others, RB Madho Parshad, an active member of the Municipal Committee and chronicler of its activities,[44] had wound up the banking business, now solely concentrating on rentals of property. Property also formed the mainstay of another former banking firm: that of Gulabrai Meharchand.

The contraction of credit on offer in the city was reflected in the property market. As has been pointed out, urban property had been a way for firms of all kinds to secure their profits and secure future returns. In the 1920s the ability to access credit through mortgaging house property was severely attenuated. While joint stock banks had initially been happy to advance loans against mortgage of immovable property, by 1930 they had sharply curtailed the amount of longer-term credit offered against property.[45] More generally, as the Banking Enquiry Committee noted:

> Well known commercial firms have sometimes been obliged to go into liquidation not because the normal values of their assets locked up in immovable property are insufficient for the discharge of their debts, but only because no adequate banking facilities are available for the purpose of fairly long-period loans on the security of immovable property.[46]

There were also other manifestations of the crisis in the relationship between credit and the property markets over this period. *BECCAA* suggested that a large swathe of the middle classes had had to sell their house property in the city over this period, since they could not access credit.[47]

Respondents to *BECCAA* pointed to a number of factors that had contributed to the disturbing severing of links between credit and urban property. For one, they attributed the breakdown to the ambiguities of title that persisted in most Indian cities. Without clear up-to-date surveys and accurate records it was often difficult to establish clear legal title to urban land,[48] and the situation was complicated by a second factor: the nature of

[43] Ibid., p. 340. We shall encounter some of the properties of Lala Minamal Somany in Chapter 4.

[44] Rai Sahib Madho Pershad (1921), *The History of the Delhi Municipality, 1863–1921* (Allahabad: The Pioneer Press).

[45] *Banking Enquiry Committee for the Centrally Administered Areas, 1929–30*, p. 371.

[46] Ibid. p. 315.

[47] Ibid., p. 286., Ibid., vol. 2, p. 90 (evidence of Mr Radhika Narain, Lecturer in Economics, Hindu College, Delhi).

[48] Ibid. p. 312.

Mitakshara family law.[49] Since under this code property was jointly owned, it could only be alienated in the interests of the family as a whole. What such interest might be was frequently a point of dispute, and challenges subsequent to sales were quite common.[50] A third complaint related to the long and disputatious procedures in the courts.[51] Property cases, it was alleged, moved too slowly for it to be profitable to advance credit with real estate as security.[52] Reform along these three lines were, according to *BECCAA*, the key to restoring credit markets hit by crisis.

Each of these three issues is significant and revelatory of the specific difficulties of creating capitalist financial institutions while operating in the situated context of the Hindu family firm.[53] Nevertheless, these explanations were all long-term issues that were being brought up in the context of a conjunctural problem. In the run-up to the crisis of the 1920s (and after the 1930s), sales had been carried on at higher volumes, credit had been extended against property, and mortgage loans were on offer. All these activities occurred, even with questions relating to the family structure and clear title not having been satisfactorily resolved. Instead of explaining this particular crisis, the findings of *BECCAA* are better understood as relating to the clarification and refinement of the representations of property—deeds, leases—and processes that guaranteed their authenticity (court cases). This was indeed an important task, as without clarity and efficiency in procedures for generating and enforcing representations of space as commodity, effective circulation was made difficult. (This is discussed further in Chapter 4.) Nevertheless, the Banking Enquiry Committee seems to have had little to say about the moment in which it was convened and the more conjunctural scarcity of long-term credit in the city.

[49] Mitakshara was one of the two major streams of personal law that applied to Hindus in the colonial period.

[50] *Banking Enquiry Committee for the Centrally Administered Areas, 1929–30*, and vol. 2, p. 5 (evidence of Mohd Aminuddin Malik, Pleader and Notary Public, Delhi). Challenges to sales were so common that the standard deed of sale included a clause stating that if any new disputation or claimant to the property were to arise after the sale was completed, the responsibility for conducting (and payment for) any court procedures would lie with the seller and no expenses would have to be borne by the buyer: for example, DDA, Private Collection no. 30, Lala Jhabban Lal Collection, Sale deed from Bishamber Nath to Lala Mathra Das, 2 September 1905; sale deed from Abdulla to Mazharul Haq, 14 August 1915.

[51] *Banking Enquiry Committee for the Centrally Administered Areas, 1929–30*, vol. 2, p. 247 (evidence of L. Janki Pershad, Munim of RB Sultan Singh).

[52] *Banking Enquiry Committee for the Centrally Administered Areas, 1929–30*, pp. 313–14.

[53] On this, see also Ritu Birla (2009), *Stages of Capital: Law, Culture, and Market Governance in Late Colonial India* (Durham, NC: Duke University Press).

As numerous metrics explored here have shown, the 1930s saw the revival of activity in the property market. Over this period, new formations emerged—larger organizations that came to constitute a distinct real estate segment. In what ways were these developments linked to finance? Ray argues that the interwar period saw Indian capital move out of the bazaar and towards industrial investment.[54] This was achieved, at least partially, through the greater integration and expansion of the bazaar sector as the exchange banks began to withdraw their inland branches and concentrate on business in the port cities.[55]

Ray's concentration on trade and industry occludes the role that other elements of the economy might have played with respect to capital circulating in the bazaar. As we have seen previously, while the number of joint stock companies and property-related transactions increased in 1930s Delhi, the same cannot be said for the number of factories in Delhi. In fact, production of urban space was an important means for the revival of the credit market itself. We have already seen that numerous banking families in Delhi moved into property in the 1920s. Somewhat lagging behind buoyant private construction, the state also began to announce significant initiatives of construction with the DMC in the 1930s and the Delhi Improvement Trust (DIT) in 1937. Two other ways in which finance and real estate were woven together, however, were housing cooperatives and joint stock real estate companies. These remained incipient but important developments throughout the 1930s.

Housing Cooperatives

Within the problem of creating long-term credit in the city was nested yet another issue: who was to be offered the credit? *BECCAA* unearthed much about the ways in which the urban poor accessed credit. Nevertheless, the core of its recommendations with respect to expanding the credit market in cities was centred on the middle classes.

> Special credit facilities seem to be required also for the solution of some of the most urgent problems in the city of Delhi, *viz.* the problem of

[54] Ray, 'The Bazaar: Changing Structural Characteristics of the Indigenous Section of the Indian Economy before and after the Great Depression', 264–67.

[55] Ibid., 289–91.

> congestion and that of its milk supply. There appears to be considerable scope for cooperative housing societies in Delhi and we commend to the notice of the Local Governments and the Government of India the view taken by the Madras Government that financial help from Government to housing societies in the shape of loans is not only essential but also proper as representing a legitimate contribution by Government towards the solution of the housing problem and the relief of congestion in towns.[56]

The idea of cooperatives, particularly agrarian cooperatives, had preceded this judgement by a couple of decades. Thus far, however, cooperative institutions in Delhi had been restricted to rural areas. *BECCAA* proposed that the 1930s were a moment when this ought to be extended to the urban classes. Salaried classes—in particular, government and municipal clerks—were identified as the most important constituency for cooperative societies. More familiar than most with official procedure and paperwork, it is not surprising to find that they were enthusiastic adopters of the cooperative creed.

The earliest instance of a cooperative housing society in Delhi was registered in 1927. The Cooperative House Building Society was constituted by twenty members who described themselves as 'low paid clerks receiving from Rs. 50/- to Rs. 100/- per mensem.'[57] In 1930 they applied to the Delhi administration for a loan at a low rate and land to build houses at a nominal premium. In a motif that was to recur, the Chief Commissioner (CC) was disinclined to extend credit or land since he was sceptical of the financial viability of the cooperative.[58] T. K. Roychowdhury, an engineer who had expressed interest in the formation of a cooperative building society as early as 1930, finally succeeded in establishing one in 1933 called Cooperative Land and Building Society.[59] Neither of these two societies, however, was able to create any actual housing—a markedly lacklustre inauguration.

More propitious ground would seem to have been laid with the establishment of the DIT. As Stephen Legg has argued, the DIT operated within a discursive space in which it became acceptable to suggest that the state

[56] Ibid., 289.

[57] DDA, DC Records, F no. 112, 'from G. S. Mathur, Hony. Secy proposed Cooperative House-building society to CC', 20 February 1930.

[58] DDA, DC Records, F no. 112, 'CC to DC', 23 June 1930.

[59] 'Co-operative Building Society, *HT*, 31 January 1930. DDA, DC Records, F no. 112, 'Extract from *Statesman*', 13 January 1933.

prioritize the decongestion of Delhi over the dictate to turn a profit.[60] If housing the urban poor was supposed to be the mainstay of DIT's operations, one of its subsidiary impacts was to give a fillip to cooperatives as a way of accommodating the middle classes.

The story, however, was more complicated. The Krishna Cooperative Housing Society Ltd (KCHS), registered in 1937 at around the same time as the DIT itself came into existence, offers an interesting window into this moment. In its correspondence with the Delhi administration, KCHS constantly invoked the basic principles on which DIT was founded. Thus, they could aver that:

> (a) The Trust was constituted to remove congestion in the Delhi City. Congestion resulted from men who had not the means sufficient enough either to own a house or to pay exorbitant rents charged by landlords, and such men formed 90% of the City population.
>
> (b) The Krishna Cooperative Housing Society Ltd, Delhi, is composed of men of middle class and sundry other folks who earn their living by labour, clerical or otherwise, in Government or other private institutions. Their means are limited and savings practically nil in the majority of cases. They have, moreover, no credit in the market.[61]

KCHS petitioned the DIT to offer land at nominal rates. DIT, however, consistently resisted this proposition, offering land at Rs. 6 per sq. yd, where KCHS expected that land would be assigned at prices of around Rs. 2 to 3 per sq. yd. to cooperatives. Nevertheless, they wrote, they were prepared to pay this rate as long the land was provided on a freehold basis. DIT responded that, as a matter of policy, it was opposed to alienating land permanently. KCHS countered that exceptions to the policy had in the past been made for wealthy individuals and that it was apposite that a cooperative society like their own, claiming 200 members, be considered for such a grant.[62]

KCHS's insistence derived from a combination of a sense of entitlement to state subsidy and an understanding of middle-class respectability. They put it to the DIT chairman that a lessee's

[60] Stephen Legg (2007), *Spaces of Colonialism: Delhi's Urban Governmentalities* (Malden, MA; Oxford: Blackwell).

[61] DDA, CC Records, LSG-LB, F no. 1(61), 1939, 'J. D. Sharma, Secy of the Krishna Cooperative Housing Society Ltd. To CC, Delhi', 25 March 1939.

[62] DDA, CC Records, LSG-LB, F no. 1(41), 1940, 'J. D. Sharma, Secy of the Krishna Cooperative Housing Society Ltd. To Chairman, DIT', 25 January 1940.

> position is lowered contemptuously as soon as the man in the street comes to know that they have their houses on lands of 90 years' lease with an enormous amount of rent payable thereon yearly. Generally he is inclined to think that after lapse of the stipulated period, nay even during the currency of the covenant, they are liable to be turned out and their houses confiscated. Rightly or wrongly such a feeling does exist in the minds of the public and I hope you will recognize it.[63]

Here KCHS presented themselves, on the one hand, as persecuted: 'the actual sufferers of exorbitant rents and congestion in thc city.'[64] On the other hand, as a reliable bet for the extension of credit—salaried, with a keen sense of honour, 'men of decent orders and manners'.[65] In a pithy statement, they claimed an important position in contemporary Delhi society: the 'average middle-class man'.[66] The kind of middle-class identity that emerges from the correspondence of the KCHS mixes an appeal to the state with a sense of class position. In the KCHS correspondence there is constant reference to not just the language of the state, but to its stated goals and intentions. From these goals there is a determined effort to present themselves—respectable and educated—as deserving recipients of the state's largesse.

Two other clues to the worldview of the promoters of KCHS can be found in their choice of antagonists. First, their correspondence contains pervasive reference to a class of wealthy people that were undeserving of state patronage but in receipt of it nonetheless. They repeatedly point out that the purposes of the Trust—with respect to reducing congestion—would not be solved by helping people who were already comfortably off: the 'fat salaried and moneyed persons and landlords'.[67] These landlords, who looked solely to make profits from the sale of lands and property in the city, were painted as clearly undeserving of state support based on its own stated aims. One of their more damning indictments of the DIT was that the Trust often behaved much as one of these landlords. In fact, when it became clear that the cooperative was likely to be wound up, KCHS bitterly denounced the

[63] DDA, CC Records, LSG-LB, F no. 1(61), 1939, 'Secy The Krishna Cooperative Housing Society Ltd. To A. P. Hume, Chairman DIT', 26 September 1939.

[64] Ibid., 'Secy The Krishna Cooperative Housing Society Ltd. To CC, Delhi', 25 March 1939.

[65] Ibid., 'Secy The Krishna Cooperative Housing Society Ltd. To A. P. Hume, Chairman DIT', 26 June 1939.

[66] DDA, CC Records, LSG-LB, F no. 1(41), 1940, 'Secy The Krishna Cooperative Housing Society Ltd. To CC Delhi', 22 July 1940.

[67] Ibid.

'officers who wield some power and authority in the administration of the locality.'[68] They had suborned the state's largesse to particularistic interests.

The second element of the KCHS worldview was the emergence of an anti-colonial tone. The Secretary of KCHS had, early on, placed the Delhi administration's actions in a comparative framework, contrasting its actions with those of foreign governments that had encouraged cooperative societies. The implication was that it was because India was a colony that cooperative housing initiatives did not receive greater support. In that instance, he had softened the comparison by pointing to the few cooperative schemes—in Madras and Bombay—that had been supported by the colonial state.[69] In the 1940 correspondence prior to the dissolution of the KCHS, however, a sharper formulation was arrived at:

> In fact the Trust wants to keep everyone under perpetual subjection and control and at its mercy. It cannot tolerate to allow even cooperative Housing societies to grow and flourish as the Governments of other countries do. So if the Krishna Housing Society dissolves, it is not because it wishes to be dissolved but because, rather too, the circumstances over which the society has not control [*sic*] force it to do so, much against its will.[70]

On this occasion, the comparison between nations was posed in the course of an explicit discussion of themes of subjection and coercion. This was an unusually bold formulation for state employees. KCHS's claims here demonstrate the flip side of the state-directedness of the middle class identity being forged. KCHS appealed to the state in terms of the aims voiced by the state itself. The premise was that these were aims best served when they—middle-class honourable citizens—received attention. If this attention were to continue to be directed elsewhere—towards the rich or high-ranking

[68] Ibid.

[69] DDA, CC Records, LSG-LB, F no. 1(61), 'Secy The Krishna Cooperative Housing Society Ltd. To CC, Delhi', 25 March 1939. Incidentally, in much of the official correspondence relating to housing cooperatives here and elsewhere, Madras Presidency and Bombay, where Nikhil Rao has studied the emergence of a middle-class identity based around cooperative finance, are both mentioned. Nikhil Rao (2013), *House, but No Garden: Apartment Living in Bombay's Suburbs, 1898–1964* (Minneapolis: University of Minnesota Press). For Ahmedabad, which saw great success in setting up housing cooperatives, Abigail Mcgowan (2013), 'Ahmedabad's Home Remedies: Housing in the Re-Making of an Industrial City, 1920–1960', *South Asia: Journal of South Asian Studies*, 36 (3), 397–414.

[70] DDA, CC Records, LSG-LB, F no. 1(41), 1940, 'Secy The Krishna Cooperative Housing Society Ltd. To CC Delhi', 22 July 1940.

administrative officials—this was a perversion of the proper conduct of state activity. This was the precise point at which they brought up the themes of subjugation and coercion, and placed the colonial state in international comparison. Housing, and cooperatives more specifically, appear here to be one of the incubators of middle-class claims upon the state.

The DIT, never particularly enamoured by the clamours of the clerks of KCHS, set about establishing its own system of cooperatives in 1940. The vision articulated was a more expansive one—a system of individual project-based Cooperative House building societies that would be unified under a Delhi Cooperative House Building Union. In turn, the Cooperative Union's finances would be guaranteed by the state. The target remained the large chunk of 'intermediate classes', but the scope of operations would be restricted specifically to the areas of the DIT.[71] A. P. Hume welcomed this structure of cooperative housing, contrasting it with initiatives like the KCHS.

> There are several so-called housing and cooperative societies in Delhi, some of these have from time to time approached the Trust. They always repeat the monotonous request for land at much less than market value and I have not found that they add any substantial contribution to the real principles of cooperative building societies.[72]

Hume's professions of support notwithstanding, the DIT's ambitious scheme joined KCHS and the other cooperatives mentioned so far in failing to get off the ground. While elaborate plans were drawn up, none of these were actually created until well after 1947.

The burgeoning of proposals for cooperative housing societies in the 1930s was a consequence of the key fault line of this moment: the difficulty of accessing long-term credit. Cooperatives had a troubled initiation in Delhi. The tepid response of local authorities to the housing cooperative was the typical reception of the idea until the early 1950s: much faith placed in cooperatives as an easy solution to the problem of housing the middle classes, and little by way of practical assistance.[73] Where real support to

71 DDA, CC Records, LSG-LB, F no. 1(71), 1940, 'CC to Registrar Cooperative Societies, Punjab', 21 May 1940.

72 Ibid., 'Chairman of DIT to CC', 30 November 1940.

73 *Report of the Delhi Improvement Trust Enquiry Committee 1951*, vol. 2 (Delhi: Government of India Press). See pp. 168–75 for evidence of the difficulties faced by housing cooperatives in Delhi. None are referred to as having successfully created housing on public lands.

cooperative societies was endlessly deferred, a different solution to the issue of accessing long-term credit for housing was also emerging among private developers.

A Real Estate Segment?

The lineaments of a new sector of the property market can be discerned from the 1930s onwards. We can see this in a number of different areas. Only relatively large operators could have been repeatedly involved in both rental and sales of property. Table 3.5 is a list of all the firms that placed, more than one rental and sales advertisement in *Hindustan Times*. These firms can be divided into a number of categories. We have already encountered those whose business catered for the colonial elite. Among these were firms like that of L. Gopinath—an auctioneer, commission agent, cabinet maker, and coach and pram builder.[74] The world evoked in this portfolio of activities refers to mobility, temporariness, and opulence that characterized Delhi, when the Imperial administration was quartered there for six months every year. Capital Estate Agency, with concerns in Simla and Delhi, as well

Table 3.5. Firms that placed advertisements for rentals and sales in *Hindustan Times*.

S no.	Name of company	Date of first rental appearance	Date of last rental appearance	Date of first sales appearance	Date of last sales appearance	
1	Sanon Bros.	1930	1939	1940	1942	Colonial sphere
2	Capital Estate Agency	1938	1941	1939	1939	
3	L. Gopinath	1929	1929	1927	1927	
4	Haji Ali Jan Traders	1929	1935	1931	1931	Commercial origins
5	Reliance Trading Co.	1928	1928	1929	1936	
6	Colonization Ltd.	1933	1941	1933	1943	Property specialists
7	Ravi Bros.	1934	1942	1936	1940	

[74] Their telegraph address was 'FURNITURE DELHI': *HT*, 25 February 1927.

as Sanon Bros, based out of Lahore with branches in Mussoorie and Dehra Dun, catered for a similar clientele. All the properties these concerns offered for sale or rent were located in New Delhi. The other four companies, however, were of a different order. Each of these was located in Old Delhi and offered up properties for sale in Old Delhi or the newly emerging suburbs around Delhi.[75]

Of the four based out of Old Delhi, two seem to have had their major stakes in commerce (Reliance Trading Co and Haji Ali Jan Traders). The other two companies—Ravi Bros and The Colonization Ltd—point towards the emergence of a sector of the Delhi economy that was beginning to specialize in property dealings. Table 3.6 puts together some of the firms that constituted this 'real estate' segment. Tellingly, none of them was in operation before 1933. Versions of 'housing', 'building', and 'real estate' came to be associated with these firms only around the mid-1930s. Again, judging by the period over which the advertisements appeared, there seems to have been a certain amount of instability in the segment: firms issuing advertisements and then disappearing, often quite quickly.[76] Nevertheless, a series of these continued to appear in rapid succession over the period.

The key question for the firms emerging in the mid-1930s was finance. Thus, the Prudential Housing Corporation touted the easy terms on which it offered loans for housing. Housing and General Finance indicated the importance of the question in the name itself. The Delhi Housing Corporation, apart from issuing an advertisement in the 1940s about a sale of property, also placed an advertisement asking for a financier to join the 'profitable scheme relating to property'.[77] Although the earliest advertisements referring to the buying and selling of properties as investments date from around 1930, from the mid-1930s they became decidedly more common. Percentages of return and comparisons with other investments started to appear:

> Valuable New Delhi Residential Property: Why run after investment in 3% Bonds and court disappointment? Here is a guaranteed return of 5% from enviable New Delhi property (already on long lease)—as good as gilt-edged

[75] The partial exception here was Ravi Bros. who were estate agents and spanned the worlds of colonial circulation—houses and other services for princely visitors to Delhi and New Delhi—as well as properties in other parts of the city.

[76] The disappearance might indicate either failure of the enterprise or relocation of the project away from Delhi.

[77] *HT*, 10 November 1940.

Table 3.6. The real-estate segment.

S. no.	Name of company	First appearance of advertisement	Last appearance of advertisement	Approximate number of years of operation
1	Land and Development Syndicate	1932	1932	<1
2	Colonization Ltd.	1933	1943	10
3	Ravi Bros.	1934	1942	8
4	Land Development Association	1935	1935	<1
5	Real Estates Corporation	1936	1936	<1
6	Hindustan Housing Co.	1937	1937	<1
7	Model Building Corporation	1938	1938	<1
8	Prudential Housing Corporation[a]	1938	?	?
9	Associated Traders (describing themselves as land and property dealers)	1940	1942	2
10	Housing and General Finance	1940	?[β]	<11
11	Delhi Housing Corporation	1940	1940	<1
12	Modern Housing corporation	1940	1940	<1
13	Land and Trade Corporation[a]	1945	?	?

[a] Evidence for the existence of these companies comes from records in the Delhi Archives rather than *Hindustan Times*; [β]mentioned in *Report of the Delhi Improvement Trust Enquiry Committee, 1951*, vol. 1.

> securities! Only those prepared to invest Rs. 85,000 or more need apply in the first instance.[78]

Most of these companies operated in the area outside that controlled by DIT. Nevertheless, the DIT's installation of infrastructure in large swathes of

78 *HT*, 8 August 1938. See also 25 February 1937, 12 June 1940, and 21 July 1940. For an isolated early instance claiming to offer 12% interest, see 29 December 1930.

the city certainly contributed to the milieu which generated these larger conglomerations of capital.

Two further aspects of these firms might be remarked on. First, their orientation towards the middle classes. The Housing and General Finance Company bought up land in Dilshad Gardens, across the Yamuna, where they were planning a middle-class suburb.[79] They were also trying to solve some of the same dilemmas over credit for the middle classes that we have seen previouly. The Prudential Housing Corporation, for instance, stated in their literature that middle-class people were prevented from buying houses and land because 'The money market in India is too shy and tight to provide these people with any reasonable facility to obtain money cheaply.'[80] Their own hire purchase scheme was designed to allow people with regular salaries to end up owning their houses after twenty years of payments that were not much more than the average rental of a comparable structure.[81]

Second, and related to the previous example, these were firms that vigorously advertised their modernity—in operational terms as well as in the actual physical developments. They claimed to have clear title deeds, and offered ownership that would be free of challenges. Financial statements were presented as transparent—through floating shares and conducting audits—and building based on plans prepared by professional architects. No surprise, then, that they were proposing urban developments in areas near Delhi but which had little history of urban occupation. These were real estate firms pushing into the urban periphery. In a number ways, then, from the amounts of capital they commanded to the practices of construction, they presented themselves as departures from traditions within the Delhi property market.

The two decades of the 1920s and 1940s were each marked by a crisis and its resolution. Connections between finance, property, and the urban economy lay at the heart of the process. The contraction of credit was caused by a trade depression and changes in the conditions under which the bazaar operated: the rise of joint stock, and cooperative banking backed by the state. In this circumstance, new formations appeared in

[79] DDA, CC Records, LSG, F no. 10(101), 1940, 'Letter of 5 October 1940 from Superintendent of Industries, Delhi to DC, Delhi'.

[80] DDA, CC records, LSG-LB, F no. 1432, 1938, 'A few facts why the Delhi Government, the Delhi Improvement Trust and the Various Local Bodies should help the Prudential Housing Corporation Ltd.'

[81] Ibid., 'Brochure of Prudential Housing Corporation Ltd.' p. 7.

Delhi's real estate markets: real estate companies and cooperative house building societies. Neither of these were roaring successes over the period of this study. Both faced stumbling blocks—not least the high cost of land and continuing volatility in credit markets. Their significance lies not in the amount of actual housing that they were able to build, but the way ahead to which they pointed. Of the two, it was real estate companies that were beginning to establish themselves by the end of the period. By 1947, Housing and General Finance was still in the process of laying out its planned suburb in Dishad Garden. Its ranks, however, had been joined in 1946 by a new firm which went on to have a much longer history: Delhi Land and Finance. Known to most present-day Delhiites simply by its seemingly omnipresent acronym DLF, it was established in 1946, a product of the many reconfigurations of this turbulent period.

Coercion, Corruption, and Power

While the transformations in the local property market over the 1930s were momentous, how did this affect the operations of power in the property market? The question can be addressed at two distinct levels. There was, first, the operations of power within the rental relationship; that is, between landlords and tenants. Second was the relationship between large property owners and the local administration. For both these levels, however, the legally stipulated relationship—between landlord and tenant and between citizen and administrator—is an inadequate guide to the actual operations of power. Coercion, including the use of violence, was a routine fact in the relationship between landlords and tenants. Manifested most spectacularly in the period during which rent control was introduced in Delhi, traces of the role that violence played in everyday rental relationships can be found throughout this period.

The most obvious place in which violence was manifested with respect to property was rent collection. We have seen that the collection of dues was often farmed out. This was the case particularly when there were a large number of tenants who, individually, paid only small amounts of rent. In itself this points towards the possibility that rent collection was not a smooth operation free of hassle or effort. That this might have also entailed violence is hinted at in an episode narrated by Brij Kishen Chandiwala, scion of an important trading family in Delhi, in his memoirs. Chandiwala describes a loyal family retainer called Thakur Murali Singh who specialized in collecting rent from the many properties owned by the Chandiwala clan.[82] He recounts an occasion on which there was a dispute over a wall being built by their neighbours. In the course of an argument about the matter, Murali Singh brought out a gun from his room and fired on the people building the wall, killing one of the workers.[83] It is possible to infer that the characteristics reflected in this story—aggression, access to arms, and a willingness to use them—were not unrelated to his role as rent collector for the Chandiwalas.

More direct evidence of physical violence playing a seminal role comes from another segment of the property market. The Colonization Ltd was one among the growing cohort of firms that accumulated property in the outskirts of the city. Its owner, Lala Raj Kishen Jain, was a 40-year-old Jain residing in Daryaganj South, a locality described as 'inhabited by the educated class of people'. He was recorded as owning landed property worth Rs. 50,000.[84] His name was the only one initially put up for consideration as *Mir Mohalla* for Daryaganj South. The Deputy Commissioner rejected this recommendation out of hand, stating:

> I am afraid it will be useless to try to persuade me. I convicted two of Raj Kishen's hired assassins to three years under 307 for [beating?] a man and they were lucky not to be [?] under 302.[85]

In a sense, it is not surprising to find instances of coercion and violence in a city undergoing a boom in property speculation, nor yet to find its deployment by a company that operated in the semi-agrarian lands on the outskirts of the city. The structural role that such violence played can be seen as an extension of the role of violence and intimidation in the credit market, particularly concerning loan activity in its lower strata.

BECCAA suggests that *Rahti* loans, for instance, were offered to workers, and even some penurious clerks, at extortionate rates—usually around 37.5% per annum—for short periods. Itinerant trans-border money lenders, the so-called Kabuli lenders, also offered short-term loans at similar rates of interest. The success of these groups in the realization of these rates from

[82] NMML, Manuscript Section, Individual Collections, B. K. Chandiwala, Instalment II–III, F no. 6, 'Family History of Chandiwala Family' p. 49.

[83] Singh was arrested and sent to jail, where he met Chandiwala. The latter—by this time a devoted follower of Gandhi—was in jail for his participation in the 1930 non-violent *satyagraha*.

[84] DDA, DC Records, F no. 369, 1944, 'Report of the Inspector of Shops and Commercial Establishments', 20 November 1944.

[85] DDA, DC Records, F no. 369, 1944, DC note, n.d.

people who had little or no collateral to offer was based on methods of recovery that were described by *BECCAA* as 'more or less high-handed'.[86] A more vivid description comes from the *Hindustan Times.*

> On 26th morning two Kabuli money lenders caught hold of an old Parsi gentleman [...] and threateningly asked him to pay the sum of Rs. 300, which he owed them. The Kabulies had *lathies* with them and had come, it was clear, with the intention to intimidate the gentleman.[87]

Violence in these settings overlapped with class. Money lenders and landlords who entered into credit and rental agreements with the poor took on the risk of defaulting on loans or rent. Physical force and extortion were characteristic elements of these kinds of arrangement almost everywhere, and late colonial Delhi was no exception.

In relationships among elites and intermediate classes, other forms of illegality were more typical. Violations of the building codes were routine. The sheer regularity of it might be confirmed by a glance at the relative number of resolutions that the Building Sub-Committee spent on building permission violations as compared to sanctioning new buildings. To select three random sittings spread across the period, the Building Sub-Committee's meeting on 8 November 1919 considered twenty-two applications to build and twelve reports about building code violations; on 20 September 1930 the sub-committee considered forty-two applications to build and thirty reports about violations of building codes; and on 18 September 1944 it considered twenty-four applications to build and five violations of building code. The violations range from petty ones that might be overlooked—minor discrepancies in the size of built rooms compared to the plans submitted–to ones that were prosecuted with greater alacrity (projections over public land were a common example of the latter).

More generally, however, the building department of DMC appears to have had a poor reputation. A vigilance sub-committee report from 1925 noted that there were persistent reports about irregularities in the building department.[88] One of the cases highlighted was that of Lala Nanak Chand, a jeweller who in 1919 was found during routine inspections to have been building a two-storey house without municipal permission. His retrospective

86 *Banking Enquiry Committee for the Centrally Administered Areas, 1929–30*, vol. 1, p. 172.
87 *HT*, 28 December 1924, 'Kabuli Zulum in Delhi'.
88 TH, DMC Progs, E&FSC, 22 December 1925, prog no. 19.

application for permission to build was rejected, and after exhaustion of the appeals process a demolition order was issued in September 1921. Ghulam Bari, the Building Jamadar, was the municipal functionary in charge of reporting on compliance with the demolition order. Bari stated that the order had been carried out, but he did not send the file to the official record room until 1923. In 1925, the building was found to be standing just as it had been constructed in 1920. The allegation made at this point was that Rs. 400 had been paid to Ghulam Bari for his part in enabling the building to remain standing. After investigation of the case by the municipality, Ghulam Bari was dismissed from municipal employment.[89]

The previous incident occurred at a relatively low rung of the municipal ladder. In 1937, however, the very highest levels of the municipal hierarchy were accused of inappropriate benefits and favouritism . In the course of the municipal acquisition of Kolhapur House it was discovered that the Secretary of the Delhi Municipal Committee had been registered as the owner of the property in the recent past. These events throw light on the connections between operatives of the state and wealthy private interests.

According to the Secretary's own account of the events, he had met Sumair Chand of the British Motor Car Co at a Club.[90] After a few too many drinks, the latter told him about falling out with his friend Shanker Lal. Shanker Lal was the younger brother of Lala Shri Ram, one of the richest men in Delhi and proprietor of the Delhi Cloth Mills. Shanker Lal, for his part, was in a dispute with his brother and was looking to make some money 'for himself by stealth.'[91] The stumbling block was that Lala Shri Ram was the head of a joint family, and consequently Shanker Lal was debarred from selling property on his own account. The latter was forced, therefore, to use some money he had made on the side to purchase property in the name of his (then) friend Sumair Chand. Chand told the Secretary that he now planned to defraud Shanker Lal of his property, by selling it and keeping the profits for himself. When the Secretary conveyed this to Shanker Lal, the latter was concerned. He was keen to ensure two things: that Lala Shri Ram did not find out about these transactions, and that he be able to retrieve the property from Sumair Chand. During a prolonged absence from Delhi, Sumair Chand had given power of attorney to Lala Hanuman Pershad

[89] TH, DMC Progs, E&FSC, 22 October 1925, prog no. 19.

[90] DDA, CC Confidential, Education, F no. 10, 1937, 'Note of explanation by Sohan Lal', 28 August 1937. The following account is based entirely on this written submission by Sohan Lal, secretary of the Delhi Municipal Committee.

[91] Ibid.

(among other things, a municipal commissioner). Shanker Lal hoped to retrieve his property through Hanuman Pershad during the absence of Chand. In order to achieve this, however, he required another person in whose name the transaction could be conducted. Lala Shanker Lal proposed that the Secretary stand in this capacity, but the Secretary claimed to have consistently opposed such a course. He claimed that it was against his firm protestations, and that it was through a combination of deception and misunderstanding that his name was stated as purchaser of the property. Six months later, however, Lala Shri Ram, Shanker Lal's elder brother, found out about the transactions and forced Shanker Lal to sell the property immediately. It was soon after these transactions that it came to light that the Secretary's name had been entered as owner of the property.

Regardless of the legitimacy of the Secretary's eventual exoneration, these transactions reveal the subversion of a variety of stipulations of the law.[92] To begin with, the role of the Secretary in these developments—conveying stories from one person to the other and being present at transactions he knew to be of dubious legality—was, as he himself admitted, amenable to uncharitable interpretations. At any rate, the sphere of socializing—moving between the club and various other members of elite circles of Delhi, of which the Secretary seems to have been considered a natural member—created opportunities for these kinds of deal to be struck. There are, however, a number of other suspicious transactions. The routineness of what were called *benami* transactions—conducted by parties under false or substitute names—represents another instance of dubious legality. Finally, we should also take note of Hanuman Pershad's role. He was quite prepared to utilize the power of attorney he held from Sumair Chand for the benefit of Lala Shanker Lal. Bending and twisting the law along these lines appears to have drawn little comment from the local administration.

The various forms of coercion and corruption explored in this section are useful reminders that beneath the modern property market there remained a subterranean bed of violence and extralegal transactions.[93] Administrative structures like the Delhi Municipal Committee were deeply mired in this generalized state of illegalities. Other forms of violence and intimidation

[92] More precisely, they were described as 'serious irregularities' that were an outcome of 'thoughtlessness and indiscretion rather than of dishonesty.' DDA, CC Confidential Records, 1938, F no. 33, 'DC to CC', 28 March 1938.

[93] Vivek Chibber (2013), *Postcolonial Theory and the Specter of Capital* (London: Verso).

were characteristic accompaniments of the very process of extracting interest or rent at an everyday level. As much as other structural elements—the rise of real estate firms, and the extension of credit to the middle classes—these forms of violence and coercion were a crucial substratum of the operation of the modern property market.

Conclusions

Delhi's property market embraced a fairly wide swathc of its intermediate classes, and these continued to be active within it: small traders from the old parts of Delhi, pharmacists, gramophone dealers, iron merchants, booksellers, and government servants. Joining them after 1911 in particular were people who catered for the needs of the colonial sphere: furniture producers, estate agents, and military contractors. On the outskirts of the city, which were rapidly becoming its suburbs, agrarian groups charted paths into the urban elite that began from unplanned slums. Even within those slums, however, upwardly mobile sections of subaltern groups favoured property as a form of investment and security.

The period between 1920 and 1940 changed many things about Delhi's property market. There remained, however, aspects on which it had little impact. Women's participation in the property market, for instance, remained more or less the same. Various forms of back-stage dealing and even violence and coercion also continued to accompany the operations of the property market throughout this period. If anything, various forms of illegality played an even larger role in the property boom of the 1930s, as we have seen in the cases of The Colonization Ltd and the Secretary of DMC. Despite these continuities, many of the new organizational forms that sprang up in this period continued to have an impact on the city over a long stretch of time.

At a more structural level two incipient formations emerged to address the general problem of accessing long-term credit in the city. As industry and trade suffered, property speculation was on the rise. Taking note of the need for new financial arrangements apposite to the changing urban landscape, officials spent much time touting cooperative housing societies. The talk translated into little action. More successful, however, were the new real estate firms that represented the maturation of the property segment of the local economy. Both the more abstract view of Delhi's property market and the close-up that has been explored in this chapter reveal a dynamic cityscape which was tied into the local economy. Within this dynamism, however, we have also encountered long-term structural issues that were seen as retarding the operations of the property market. *BECAA*, for instance, referred to the difficulties in establishing titles and the inadequacy of cadastral surveys of the city. It is to this sphere of the 'representation of space' that we now turn.

4

Representing Commodified Space

Maps, Auctions, Leases, and 'Narration' of Property

Introduction

> Doubts about title . . . to landed property even in the city are not a little responsible for the unwillingness of bankers and other lenders of money to advance amounts against mortgage of property.
>
> *Banking Enquiry Committee for the Centrally Administered Areas*, 1929–30, vol. 1, p. 312.

The sense of crisis about the lack of secure land titles expressed in the epigraph to this chapter underlines the importance of the instruments through which property could circulate as a commodity. Without accurate maps, leases, deeds, or a secure monetary value, no market in property could exist at all. Equally, the particular characteristics taken on by the ways of representing property can tell us a lot about the nature of the property market in Delhi.

Urban theorist Henri Lefebvre argues that ways of conceiving space, of representing space in particular conceptual categories, are a fundamental constituent of the production of space.[1] Conceptions of space that emphasize visual, mathematical, and financial aspects, for instance, by suggesting that space is homogenized and comparable, are associated with the production of the abstract space of modern capitalism. Indeed, the very ways in which such conceptions encourage the utilization of, and dwelling in, space are part of what makes that space abstract. Lefebvre's theoretical formulations

[1] Henri Lefebvre (1998), *The Production of Space*, trans. Donald Nicholson-Smith (Oxford: Blackwell).

Possessing the City: Property and Politics in Delhi, 1911–1947. Anish Vanaik, Oxford University Press (2020).

DOI: 10.1093/oso/9780198848752.001.0001

highlight the broad significance of paying close attention to the particularities of the domain of representations which form the subject of this chapter.[2]

I examine four ways of representing space which played a determinate role in the circulation of property in Delhi at this time: maps, deeds and leases, auctions, and advertisements. Each of these are related to the circulation of urban land as property in distinct ways, and I examine both the form of these documents/activities as well as their concrete linkages with the cycles of accumulation in the property market. Despite their specific differences, I argue that each of these representations of space necessarily described two relationships: between space and time, and between space and the state. The latter, in particular, derived from the state's role as guarantor of the regime of property. This dual reference of each representation of space—to time and the state—was used by administrative authorities to generate regular reports about the property market. In turn, these 'narratives' of property anchored the interventions of the state in the property market. In studying these representations of space, therefore, we are inevitably confronting one of the key pillars upon which the relationship between the state and space as a commodity was based.

Maps

Of all the representations of space that I discuss subsequently, the map is the most widely analysed in the South Asian context. Much of the analysis of maps has concentrated on broad and epochal transformations of consciousness that large-scale maps were able to effect.[3] Maps, however, also

[2] Lefebvre argues that space is always conceived but is also perceived and lived. As with much of Lefebvre's oeuvre, of course, the point of distinguishing between these categories was to reassemble them into a more holistic view of space, one that would constitute a critique of the compartmentalization and separation of these ways of viewing space as apposite, for instance, to the planner, the worker, and the artist.

[3] Matthew Edney's work, which looks at the Great Trigonometric Survey, is the paradigmatic instance of the discussion of large-scale maps. While some studies refer to the deployment of maps in non-state everyday contexts (Ramaswamy in terms of images, Goswami as textbooks, and Barrow as tourist guides), these are often divorced from analysis of the ways in which their *use* became part of daily life. The map of India with Bharat Mata superimposed circulated widely, generating potent symbolisms. These were not, however, circulating in utilitarian contexts. One aim of the following discussion of mapping and its relationship to commoditized space is to highlight this dimension of everyday circulation for use. Ian J. Barrow (2003), *Making History, Drawing Territory: British Mapping in India, c.1756–1905* (New Delhi: Oxford University Press); Sumathi Ramaswamy (2001), 'Maps and Mother Goddesses in Modern India', *Imago Mundi*, 53, 97–114; Manu Goswami (2004), *Producing India: From Colonial*

circulated in contexts freighted with less symbolism. These were, after all, designed to be representations of actual space, markers of the footprint of the built environment of the city. This, more utility-oriented aspect of maps is relatively underexplored in the South Asian context.

From the 1900s or so, maps were increasingly reproduced for the purpose of governance in the city. Stephen Legg has pointed to the diffusion of a logic of visualization in a range of administrative contexts over this period—from the police, to the Delhi Improvement Trust (DIT).[4] Even though the map had long been a point of reference for administration in the city, actual maps were not plentiful. The contrast between the near absence of maps in the local administration records of the nineteenth century and their routine presence in those of the twentieth century is striking. Overwhelmingly, however, the form in which the map entered the twentieth century administrative archive was as the partial map, describing a circumscribed area under discussion. The increasing reproducibility of maps (on a variety of scales), the deployment of their ability to offer up dissected and fragmented images of the city, and the ubiquity of the map as an element of governmental practice, in fact, increased in lockstep.

Temporalities

If maps became central to colonial administration, however, they also required actual processes of mapping. By around 1900 the maps being used in Delhi were considered woefully inadequate because there had been no recent full-scale surveys of the city. These maps were based on a Public Works Department survey in 1865–66 and corrected up to 1873.[5] The late nineteenth century, as has been outlined in Chapter 1, was a period of steady but significant changes in the landscape of Delhi. The suburbs, in particular, had been transformed beyond recognition. From small, largely rural outposts,

Economy to National Space (Delhi: Permanent Black); Matthew H. Edney (1998), *Mapping an Empire: The Geographical Construction of British India, 1765–1843* (Chicago, IL: University of Chicago Press).

4 Stephen Legg (2007), *Spaces of Colonialism: Delhi's Urban Governmentalities* (Malden, MA; Oxford: Blackwell), p. 214.

5 DDA, DC Office, F. No. 23, 1910. From E. Burdon, Municipal Secretary, to C. A Barron, Deputy Commissioner of Delhi, 22 February 1910.

Sabzimandi, Sadar Bazar, and Paharganj had, by 1910, grown into settlements that housed a significant proportion of Delhi's population. Existing maps, officials complained, were simply not useful any more.

One of the problems with the existing suburban maps derived precisely from the difference between spatial representations considered adequate for rural areas and those necessary for urban areas. Delhi's suburbs had only been mapped in the course of revenue settlements, and therefore, as was normal with respect to agricultural areas, employed the scale of 16 inches to the mile.[6] At this scale, very little of the official work for which maps were needed in urban areas—fixing property lines, straightening roads, adjudicating encroachment, and so on—could be carried on. As part of a wider concern with the status of *nazul* property in the area around Delhi, officials demanded that a new and up-to-date map and record of rights be commissioned. The moment was thought particularly opportune given that around the same time a revenue settlement was also in progress in the areas surrounding Delhi. Thus, beginning in 1908, G. T. Hall, a retired Extra Deputy Secretary of the Survey of India, was commissioned to put together a series of maps that would accompany a report about the condition of *nazul* lands in Delhi by Assistant Commissioner R. B. Whitehead.

At around the same time, the Delhi Municipal Committee (DMC) passed a resolution demanding a new map of the city. The chairman of the committee (who was also Deputy Commissioner of Delhi), C. A. Barron, remarked about the transformations that the city had undergone.

> The matter has been in my mind ever since I took charge of the district eleven months ago, for I at once found myself hampered in all directions owing to the absence of an up-to-date map of the important suburban area to the west and north west of the City Wall. This neighbourhood is, as you are aware, utterly unrecognizable in its present state on any map of Delhi that we possess.[7]

Nor were the transformations restricted to the suburbs. Within the city walls too, the old plan was 'though occasionally useful [. . .] of course very out of

[6] DDA, Commissioner's Office, F. no. 13, Vol. I, Box. No. 64, 1908. From E. R. Abbott, Senior Secretary to the Financial Commissioner of Punjab, to W. S. Hamilton, Secretary to the Government of Punjab, 25 November 1908.

[7] DDA, DC Office, F. No. 23, 1910. From C. A. Barron, Deputy Commissioner, to Commissioner, Delhi Division, 20 March 1910.

date and inaccurate in places'.[8] Delhi, quite simply, had no usable maps. As Barron pointed out:

> [...] I have watched with something akin to despair the appalling waste of time and trouble in the Municipal Office caused by there being no reliable large-scale plan of the land outside the city walls. I should think that at least three-fourths of the contentious business connected with buildings and encroachments would disappear if the municipality had such a map or plan and a properly attached khasra of ownership and measurements attached to it.[9]

A direct consequence of this was that in 1910 A. U. Wilson was contracted by DMC to draw up a map.[10]

We see here that after almost thirty-seven years of using a set of maps, two partially independent sources within the state felt the need to survey and map the city. The Municipal Committee needed one to conduct everyday business around the whole city. The district and provincial authorities were keen to have one to arrive at a clearer picture of the value of state holdings in the suburbs of Delhi. The demand for maps at this particular conjuncture in Delhi was a response to the evolving situation of property in the city.[11] Planning was impossible without maps, and with the city perceptibly on the verge of a take-off, administrators were eager to anticipate the areas of development.

> The directions in which extension must take place are well known and it is essential that it should be foreseen as far as possible and guided and regulated. The areas which will be absorbed into the city during the next twenty or thirty years ought now to be mapped and definite conclusions arrived at as to the alignment of the principal roads and streets.[12]

Arguments about maps being either emanations of colonial state discourse or technologies of governmentality, in different ways make mapping

[8] Ibid. [9] Ibid.

[10] Apart from Delhi, in these early decades of the twentieth century both Shimla and Lahore had had maps along with records of rights prepared.

[11] Whitehead noted: 'I understand that all the districts of British India come within the scope of the operations of the Indian Survey in rotation. But such a large and important city as Delhi, which has expanded so greatly within recent years, should be treated as a special case.' *Report on the Administration of the Delhi Crown Lands* (1910) (Lahore: Civil and Military Gazette Press), p. 7.

[12] DDA, Commissioner's Office, F. no. 13, Vol. no. 1, Box No. 64, 1908. R. Humphreys, Deputy Commissioner, to A Meredith, Commissioner, 14 August 1908.

inevitable correlates of the colonial state. Peculiarly, both formulations make the chronologies of mapping almost incidental, ignoring the dynamic relationship between these representations of space and social processes of commodification and abstraction. One of the ways in which the passage of time and the effects of cycles of accumulation were registered by the state was through the need to generate representations of space that kept track of a changing landscape.

Wilson's survey was the magisterial instance of mapping Delhi over this period. Conducted at the enormous scale of 50 feet to 1 inch, and done with widely attested accuracy, the resultant map became the main point of reference for urban administration for many years to come. Yet such was the acceleration in urban transformation that, even as Wilson's survey established the accuracy of Delhi's maps, the shifting spatial coordinates of the city were already a source of concern for authorities.[13] In 1939, when the Sabzimandi Extension area was to be incorporated into the municipal boundaries, it was found impossible to notify it because there were no physical features of a permanent nature to which it could refer.[14] In fact, the superintending engineer had to insert a steel crowbar into a concrete block at the intersection of the Malkaganj and Roshanara roads, to accurately carry out the survey for notification.[15]

While this was a more fastidiously technical solution to the issue of a shifting cityscape, other modes of resolution can be traced. When preparing for the census of 1931, local officials were already finding that the map was out of date, since 'several vacant plots had since been built upon…' To solve the problem, 'local knowledge and personal inspection thus became necessary'.[16]

Ironically enough, then, representations of space that were presented as being objective reflections could have substantial amounts of subjective human mediation. Maps were therefore caught up in the temporalities of the city's development. As a direct consequence, the representations of space that emerged carried traces of both technical and non-technical inputs into urban mapping: the most up-to-date survey methods and local knowledge.

[13] The earliest reference to Wilson's surveys being outdated can be found as early as 1929. TH, DMC Progs., OM, prog. no. 6, 20 March 1929.

[14] DDA, CC Records, LSG-LB, F no. 5(45), 1939. CC to Suptdg Engr, 11 September 1939.

[15] Ibid. Suptdg Engr to CC, 10 October 1939.

[16] *Report on the Administration of the Delhi Municipality in the Year 1930–31, Vol. I General Administration* (1931) (Delhi: Municipal Press) p. 68.

Abstraction

Maps were the official representation of space that circulated most comprehensively in contexts within and beyond the state. More often than the map of the entire city, maps that zeroed in on particular parts of the city were the most frequent. This ability to focus on particular areas exploited two capacities of maps that were a direct outcome of the abstract quality of these representations. First, the ability of the map to convey information about an area without reference to its individual particularities: structural elements of the built environment were blank spaces on the map. And second, the ability to separate the part from the whole. Crucially, the partial map was able to do this while maintaining reference back to the larger whole. In Figure 4.1, for instance, without showing the whole of Paharganj or Qadam Sharif, the map indicates their existence while zooming in on the details of the portion situated at their junction. Familiarity with these visual conventions accompanied their greater circulation.

These visual conventions also operated in other documents. At the microlevel of the house, the plan for construction plays a similar role. Although driven by different rules, there was also an increased circulation

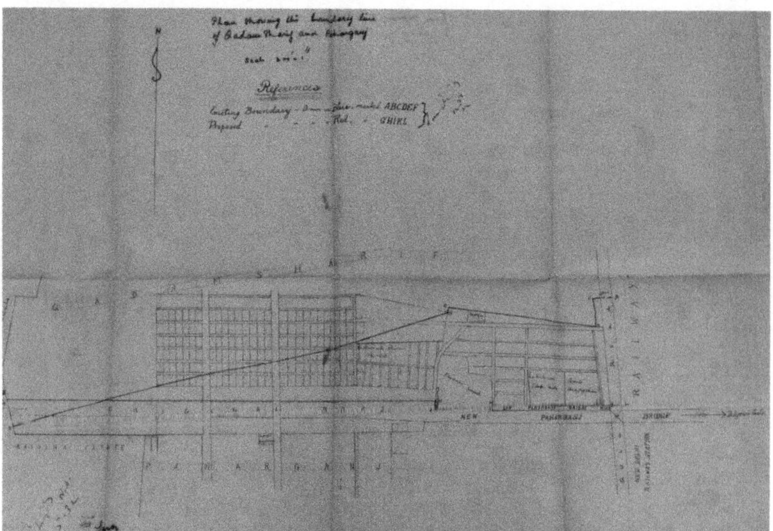

Figure 4.1. Map showing the boundary between Paharganj and Qadam Sharif. (DDA, CC Records, Revenue and Agriculture, F. no. 88, 1932.)

of building plans in Delhi. The requirement that a plan be submitted along with every application to build was only introduced by the Delhi Municipal Committee in 1915.[17] Once introduced, however, it was enforced. The proceedings of the Building Sub-Committee (BSC) of DMC contain numerous instances of applications to build that were rejected because they included plans that were not drawn up in the correct fashion. Figure 4.2 shows an example of an application to build a property on Chandni Chowk in 1933. Figures 4.1 and 4.2 quite evidently share much in terms of the raw material out of which meaning is created in them. In both, it is the intersection of straight lines through which information is conveyed; in both, the straight lines are understood as bearing a mathematical relationship to elements of the real world; and so on. Crucially, both also share the two elements of abstraction discussed previously: the ability to visually ignore

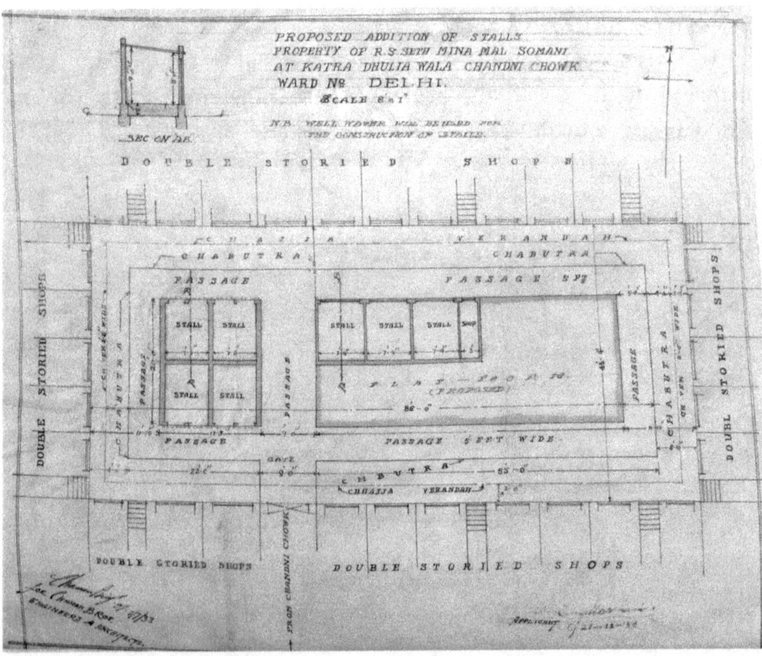

Figure 4.2. Building plans for additional stalls at a Katra in Chandni Chowk. (DDA, Private Collections, Minamal Somany Collection no. 86.)

[17] Anish Vanaik (2008), 'Changing the Plot: Property Relations in Delhi 1857–1920', (Jawaharlal Nehru University), pp. 132–6.

materiality and over-generalization and to dissect parts while maintaining reference to the whole.

Abstraction, then, was a powerful tool for the operations of the state, allowing both erasure and precision. Unsurprisingly, the state itself was an active promoter of the visual conventions of abstraction in the city.

Truth

In common with the other forms of representing space discussed subsequently, the effectiveness of maps was based on the possibility of connecting them with other documents. For instance, one of the desired attributes of a map of *nazul* lands in Delhi was that 'each separate block could be placed accurately on the existing large-scale topographical map of the city of Delhi and its environs, and on the village maps to be prepared by the Revenue patwaris.'[18] In other words, maps had to be compatible with other maps.[19] Wilson's survey too was a link in a more far-reaching chain of records. As Barron outlined: 'Along with the map a *khasra* will be prepared containing a few simple entries showing the area ownership, tenancy, &c. of each plot given a separate survey no.'[20]

As has been mentioned previously, Wilson's map of Delhi became the most significant point of reference for administrative action in the city. Paradoxically, however, its own status was far from secure. On commissioning the survey, the Municipal Committee was keen that 'some sort of authority should attach to the map and connected record of ownership &c., so that they shall be accepted in courts of Law as presumptive evidence of the truth of the facts shown in them.'[21] It was suggested that, since the Municipal Act empowered the Municipal Committee to survey and the Evidence Act attached the presumption of truth to maps made with the authority of government, a legal basis existed for official authority to attach to the map. It turned out, however, that this supposition would not hold water, and DMC's appeal for the presumption of truth was dismissed.

[18] *Report on the Administration of the Delhi Crown Lands*, p. 6.

[19] In the event, this proved impossible. As Whitehead pointed out, 'it was impossible to place each separate block on the existing large-scale map of Delhi because the latter was found to be incorrect.'

[20] DDA, DC Office, F. No. 23, 1910. From C. A. Barron, Deputy Commissioner, to Commissioner, Delhi Division, 20 March 1910.

[21] Ibid.

Undeterred, the proposal was revived a little later in the year when discussing amendments to the Punjab Municipal Bill. The Home Department suggested that a clause be inserted to empower municipalities with the authority of the Land Revenue Act for the purposes of preparing records of rights.[22] This was important, precisely because, in contrast to areas from which no land revenue was extracted (such as cities), records prepared by government for areas from which revenue was to be extracted carried the legal presumption of accuracy.

Once again, the response from the department of Revenue and Agriculture was negative. One official from that department noted:

> A municipality is concerned with occupancy and has no authority to settle matters of right. That is a matter for the civil courts and the state to control by law and executive order…
>
> Their enquiries should be embodied in a 'register of occupancy' and not in a 'record of rights'. A 'record of rights' is a sort of insurance against litigation and is no concern of a semi-private body such as a municipality, but is a matter for the state.[23]

The crux of the matter did not lie in the technical accuracy of the record that the municipality was capable of making. The municipalities of Lahore and Shimla had already produced maps of this kind, and it was well established that municipalities could create accurate maps and records of rights. Even officials in the recalcitrant Land and Revenue Department were prepared to accept as much. Furthermore, as mentioned previously, Wilson's survey maps were used in a number of situations where accuracy, without the need for authority, were required.[24] Accuracy, however, was not the key question when it came to which maps ought to be presumed true.

[22] NAI, Home (Municipalities), A Progs, August 1910, No. 22.

[23] Ibid. Note of H. B. Holmes, 21 July 1910.

[24] The proposal for presumption of legal accuracy was ultimately dropped. The other grounds for rejection included worries about the excessive increase in powers that some of the penal provisions enshrined in the Land Revenue Act might give to the Municipal Committee, and also that there were 'strong objections of principle in applying to municipal areas the provisions of an Act drawn up for another purpose and admittedly and obviously requiring alteration and modification before they could be put in force in a municipality.' Ibid., from H. G. Stokes, Deputy Secretary to Government of India to Secretary to the Government of Punjab, Boards and Committees Department, 13 August 1910.

The debate over the record of rights helps situate the question of the truth of representations of property more precisely. We have seen already that the temporality of urban construction and demolition meant that maps and plans needed non-technical human inputs based on experience and particularistic knowledge. In symmetrical fashion, technical accuracy did not automatically come to be accepted as true. Truth in the representations of space was constructed out of a hybrid mix of technical and non-technical elements. The *sine qua non* of this process, however, was the authoritative pronouncement of the state.

Historians have studied the circulation of maps through their association with emotive images such as *Bharat Mata* or the text of events surrounding the 'Black Hole' incident in Calcutta.[25] What we see in these quotidian interactions with maps was the stabilization of a different nexus of forces: the authoritative pronouncements of the state, the use of abstract visual conventions of representing space, and the operations of the market. Time, objectivity, and the legal authority of the state were being closely connected in the everyday use and circulation of maps.

Leases

Leases (or *kirayanamas* as they were called in Delhi) are documents generated out of the most elemental level of the property market: the relationship between landlord and tenant. In their repetitive and formulaic clauses, leases record the prevailing view on what constitutes a fair relationship between the two parties. The lease also, however, presents the landlord–tenant microdrama as necessarily mediated by the state. The state is an implicit party to the agreement and, through the courts, its guarantor. Within the lease, then, can be found reflections of relations between landlord and tenant, the place of the state within the rental market, and a general view of the rights and obligations of tenants and landlords. The keyhole view of the landlord–tenant relationship offered by the lease opens onto an unexpectedly expansive landscape.

As early as the nineteenth century, Delhi officials recognized that the central issue of the lease was the relationship between time and the economic activity to which the property was put. One of the most significant

[25] Barrow, *Making History*; Ramaswamy, 'Maps and Mother Goddesses in Modern India'.

recommendations of the 1910 *Report on the Administration of the Delhi Crown Lands* (*RADCL*) was precisely the suggestion that DMC, in its role as caretaker of *nazul* property, be allowed to lease lands on a variety of timescales. The author of the report, R. B. Whitehead, stated that 'existing forms of *nazul* lease were drawn up in a haphazard manner, and it is now impossible to trace their development, and the authorities under which they were framed.'[26] Under existing statutes, the different demands for the use of *nazul* property could not be adequately met. The committee could not, without recourse to higher authorities, lease land to build on for more than ten years or for non-agricultural purposes without informing higher authorities.[27] In practice, however, DMC had allowed long-term leases by presenting them as 'yearly leases which, as they [were] never revised and [were] allowed to run on indefinitely, act[ed] as if they were leases in perpetuity.'[28] Whitehead suggested that DMC be empowered to draw up three kinds of lease. The first was a building lease which allowed for renewals up to ninety years. The periodical revision of ground rent was to be every ten years with a maximum increment in rent of 25% each time. The second was a monthly lease 'to be used for such purposes as the erection of thatched huts, lime-burning, brick-making, the storage of grass, sleepers, fuel.'[29] The third was a form to let out agricultural lands on the edge of the city for a period of around five years.

Whitehead's three leases were designed to be sensitive to the turnover times of the various kinds of productive activity. The time required for realization of the value produced in agriculture and temporary activities such as lime-burning, and so on, was relatively short.[30] On the other hand, the extremely complex process of realization of the value embedded in more durable structures such as buildings necessitated a longer period of predictable returns to rent.[31] Even thirty years after *RADCL*, the same basic considerations were at work in the stipulations about leases drawn up by DIT in 1939. The Trust could issue leases for (i) a month, (ii) a year (for temporary building and cultivation), (iii) thirty years (with revision every fifteen years), (iv) ninety years (four points of revision), (v) for any period up

[26] *Report on the Administration of the Delhi Crown Lands*, p. 30.
[27] Ibid. [28] Ibid.
[29] *Report on the Administration of the Delhi Crown Lands*, p. 34.
[30] By realization I mean the point at which the final product is sold and the profit (or loss) is finally realized. In the case of a brick-making, for example, realization would happen once the bricks were baked and sold.
[31] For a complex and compelling account of the circulation of such forms of 'fixed capital', see David Harvey (1999), *The Limits to Capital*, new edn. (London: Verso), ch. 8.

to ninety years, and (vi) leases in perpetuity.[32] Leases drawn up with respect to state lands were consciously sensitive to the ways in which the circulation of commodities—lime, crops, buildings—was linked with urban space.

This idea that the lease drew together urban space and time is even more evident on examination of leases between private parties.[33] Time appears in these leases in a variety of ways. To begin with, the period of validity for most of the leases that I have studied was just one year,[34] which seems to have been the most prevalent term for rental documents. The upshot of the yearly term was that rent could, potentially at least, be revised fairly often. Did this actually happen? The extant record suggests that, in the areas we are looking at, it did. Thus, between November 1916 and February 1920, no less than eight leases were signed (in all likelihood) for two houses in Ballimaran.[35] Each of them involved different lessees, and rents were revised upwards, to varying extents, on each occasion. Similarly, for the two shops in Bazar Sitaram there are as many as ten leases over eight years from 1915 to 1923. Most, though not all, of these record upward revisions. That lease renewals encapsulated different possibilities—increase of rent, decrease, or neither—can also be said about the property located on the major thoroughfare through the old city, Chandni Chowk. Here, for instance, the leases signed by Musaddi Lal (son of Bhagwan Das) in 1919 and 1921 record exactly the same rent.[36] In contrast, the three leases signed by Kishen Chand

[32] DDA, CC Records, LSG-LB, F no. 1(46), 1939: Land Disposal Rules.

[33] The following discussion of rental leases (*kirayanama*) between private parties is based on analysis of 122 documents largely from two sets of private collections held at the Delhi Archives: the Mahant Jugtanand Collection (sixty-seven leases for three localities, 1900–25), and the Minamal Somany collection (fifty-six leases from one *Katra*, 1900–36). Most of the leases relate to four distinct sets of property in different parts of the city and suburbs: the densely populated intramural areas of Ballimaran (shops and houses) and Bazar Sitaram (shops and houses), the suburban area of Pul Mithai (land and houses), and Chandni Chowk (shops), the central avenue of the city. They are all handwritten in Urdu on legal stamp paper. The documents used here from the Jugtanand collection comprise all the leases extant from the relevant period held in that collection. For the purposes of this book, however, a random selection was made from the leases of the Somany collection, ensuring only that more than ten were present for each decade.

[34] More than ninety of the 122 leases. There is no mention of a term of validity in all but six of the rest.

[35] DDA, Private Archives, Collection no. 22, Mahant Jugtanand Collection. As will be discussed subsequently, the leases do not specify a unique number or marker for separate structures. Consequently it is impossible to state the number of houses involved with complete certainty. However, based on the dates of issue (some leases are within one month of each other) and amounts of the rent, two houses seems the most plausible scenario. The same caveat with respect to their number applies to all structures of a given type—shop, *kotha*, *balakhana*, and so on—within a given locality. The leases differentiate between structures; it is, for instance, clearly mentioned if a structure was a house or a shop.

[36] DDA, Private Archives, Collection no. 86, Minamal Somany Collection.

and his brother between 1918 and 1921 record first an increase in rent and then a decrease. The potential that year-long leases created for the periodic revision of rent was actualized. Rents were revised based on the presence of multiple claimants and linked to overall trends in the locality or even the city-wide trends isolated in Chapter 2. Further evidence for connections between space and time in leases can be found in their stipulations.[37]

At least two different styles of lease can be distinguished: those in which the landlord could have the premises vacated during the term of the rental contract, and those in which he or she did not retain this right. In the Mahant Jugtanand Collection, nearly all the documents follow the former pattern. In more than fifty leases of the sixty-seven, the notice period was just two weeks. While some leases of this kind can also be found in the Minamal Somany Collection, a majority of leases there state that the lessor cannot have the premises vacated during the term of the contract unless the lessee defaulted on the payment of rent.[38] These two formats would have had different implications for the security with which premises could be held, the former being more flexible for the owner than the latter. It is intriguing, then, that in the period from 1900 to 1913 well over half the leases in the Somany collection carry the clause about the vacating on receiving notice from the landlord.[39] In the rest of the period until 1936, only a fifth of the leases contain this clause. This shift in the style of lease seems to indicate a move towards a more secure tenure for the tenant.

Other evidence of the relative strengthening of tenants vis-a-vis landlords comes in the form of another stipulation that appeared in leases from

[37] Rental documents, being both formal and formulaic, tend to have repetitive stipulations. In the *kirayanamas* studied here, phrases referring to key elements—rent (*zar-kiraya*), pay/payment (*adaa*/*adaayagi*), notice (*ittila*)—and formulas for addressing the parties, particularly at the start and finish of the documents, remain more or less the same throughout the period and across the various localities and owners. It is possible, then, to trace the appearance or absence of stipulations in leases of various periods. Some of the vocabulary can be seen even in the much older tradition of lease-writing identified by J. S. Grewal in leases from the sixteenth century to the nineteenth century in small-town Punjab. Most of the documents he examined are mortgage and sale deeds, though there are also a few rental documents. These documents are, however, written in Persian, and overall it seems fair to say that the leases under discussion depart significantly in form and content. J. S. Grewal (1975), *In the By-Lanes of History: Some Persian Documents from a Punjab Town*, 1st edn. (Simla: Indian Institute of Advanced Study). For an exposition of north Indian urban form using these documents, see William J. Glover (2008), *Making Lahore Modern: Constructing and Imagining a Colonial City* (Minneapolis, MN: University of Minnesota Press), pp. 15–18.

[38] There are more than twenty documents that follow the other formula.

[39] The period of notice, however, is usually one month rather than the two weeks seen in the other collection.

around 1924. From around this date we see that an increasing number of leases explicitly state that the landlord cannot increase the rent during the period of the lease. It is not surprising, in a city in which the seasonal relocation of the state apparatus was established fact, that landlords would attempt to revise rents frequently. That this power to revise rents could be relinquished is a marker that the retention of tenants was perhaps more important than the ability to raise rents.

The appearance of three other clauses between 1915 and 1930, however, suggest that the period was not one in which the relative strengthening of the tenant was unmitigated. First, from 1918, most leases begin to prohibit the lessee from making any alterations in the premises. Then, from 1920 onwards, a majority of leases explicitly state that any kind of sub-letting of the premises is barred. Both of these clauses restrict the kinds of use to which a tenant could put the property. They also suggest that making alterations and sub-letting for higher rents were practices that needed to be debarred. Taken together, they reflect an effort by landlords to control the activity of tenants and ensure that rent on their property was accruing solely to themselves. Then, from around 1926, a clause stating that the landlord has the right to evict the tenant if he violates any of the conditions of the lease becomes more common. Curiously, stipulations about eviction were not common in leases from 1913 to 1926 but are to be found in leases before 1913. The wording in the earlier period, however, emphasized non-payment of rent (rather than conformance with all the provisions of the lease) as the basis for eviction. The fact that some tenants accrued rights to occupancy over time has been mentioned in the discussion of *katras* in Chapter 3. A more explicit rendering of the right to evict, then, would appear to run counter to the strengthening of tenants' rights that we have seen in most of the other new lease stipulations discussed previously.

The standard stipulations in the *kirayanamas* indicate overall the relative strength of the landlord vis-à-vis the tenant. For instance, the landlord was empowered to claim his dues (via the courts) from the mortgaged and unmortgaged property of the tenant (*jaydad makful-o gair makful*). Similarly, for the most part there was no reciprocity in the stipulations with respect to vacating the premises. In leases that allowed for it, the landlord could, by giving notice, have the premises vacated, while most of these stated that were the tenant to leave, he or she would have to pay the rent for the entire period. It is, therefore, within this overall context of the asymmetrical power of the landlord over the tenant that the lease also documented the ebbs, flows, and reconfigurations of the dynamic between landlord and tenant.[40]

If changes to the various versions of the lease correspond loosely (and with some lag) to the ups and downs of the property market, this is at least partly a result of the formal constraints of the production of leases. Over this period, leases had an accretive character, acquiring additional specifications without necessarily getting rid of older ones (unless they were flatly contradicted). Nevertheless, the general point can still be made that flexibility in the lease was reflected in more ways than simply the revision of rent. The different stipulations also reflected different ideas about how to relate to space—what could and could not be altered—as well as conjunctures in the relative power of landlords and tenants.

Any discussion of power as reflected in the lease would be incomplete without consideration of the way in which the state is present in these documents. First, they were all enacted on government-issued stamp paper. Second, each of them was attested by a court official. Third, almost all of them gave the landlord the power to approach the courts for restitution of rental arrears (along with legal expenses). The state appears in this manner as the ultimate archivist, guarantor, and enforcer of contractual obligations relating to property. Neither as a mode of implicating the state in rental transactions, nor in the novelty of the specific elements, were any of these three aspects unprecedented. The mortgages and sale deeds collated by J. S. Grewal for a small town in early-nineteenth-century pre-colonial Punjab also use stamp paper and attestations.[41] While explicit references to courts are not common there, various judicial procedures and provisions for sanction are invoked in those older leases.

One other element of the leases we have been studying is, however, novel and of a qualitatively different nature. Documents in both the collections studied identify the structure being rented out through reference to a house tax number and area code. The emergence of this mode of identification reflects a qualitative shift in how the state related to urban space: an expansion of the power of the state, but one achieved through the use of abstract representational forms. Indeed, the implicit point of reference for such numbers was the map or the list. House tax numbering, in other words, was also an attempt to connect the lease to the map.

[40] The most drastic transformation was, of course, the introduction of rent control in 1942. This will be discussed further in Chapter 6.

[41] Grewal, *By-Lanes of History*.

If the significance of the appearance of the house tax number in state practice is appreciated, two peculiarities must be confronted. First, even though the house tax was introduced in Delhi in 1902, the oldest document to use this method of identifying the structure dates to 1913. This suggests that the ambition of the state to number and consistently differentiate the various structures in the city was not simply coincident with the introduction of the house tax. Second, and perhaps even more puzzling, the appearance of the actual house tax number in the leases was essentially random. In documents drafted after 1913 there is no greater likelihood of finding this element in any given year or decade. In the Mahant Jugtanand collection they are found in documents from most (but not all) years after 1913, but very often a majority of documents in the year have no mention of the house tax number. Similarly, the house tax number appears in leases from all the localities which have been studied here. However, in none of the localities does a majority of documents carry the house tax number for identification. With the *katra* on Chandni Chowk from the Minamal Somany collection, the house tax number does not appear at all until the mid-1930s. Nor, even once it does appear, are individual shops within the *katra* assigned separate numbers. This absence cannot be attributed simply to the irrelevance of the house tax itself. From around 1915 onward, a large majority of documents in the Somany collection refer to the house tax as a distinct component of the monthly dues owed to the landlord.[42] We also know, from other evidence that, for many of the poor in the city, the payment of house tax was perceived as a claim to the legality of the settlement.[43] Thus, while the house tax itself was regularly collected, the grid of numbering brought in alongside was only patchily adopted.

Identifying houses in *kirayanamas* at this point does not appear to have needed state-designated numbers. Simply the identification of the owner of the premises and the locality was enough to situate the property. Nor was house tax numbering more common in situations where more precise descriptions of property were necessary, such as sale and mortgage deeds. Here we find much more elaborate descriptions of the interiors of buildings, on the one hand, and, on the other, the external boundaries of the house

[42] This separate statement of house tax liability is less common in the leases from the Mahant Jugtanand Collection but present in leases whether or not the house tax number of the structure is mentioned.

[43] See Chapter 7 for a discussion of one such case where the settlement was demolished as illegal but house tax had been claimed. In the aftermath of the demolition, this fact was presented as proof of the legality of the settlement.

were specified by reference to neighbours' property, and public landmarks that surrounded the premises.[44] The house tax number, however, is a conspicuous absence.

The modern state asserts its control over territory at least partially by connecting up various kinds of representations of space from the micro- to the macro-level: a government list could refer to numbers of houses which could, in turn, be located on an officially commissioned map, and so on. The 'truth' of these various representations and the density of their interconnections forms the basis of the claims of the state to objectivity and neutrality. What we see here, however, is that efforts to create this kind of density of interconnecting references in Delhi met with only partial success. Even as lease documents called on the state to act as arbiter and enforcer in some ways, they continued to utilize another domain of interpersonal and relatively traditional modes of identifying property. The ultimate paradox of the lease documents studied here seems to be that despite this interrupted and partial relationship to the forms of representation of the state, leases continued to function as a means of connecting urban property to the temporalities of accumulation.

Auctions

Of the various instruments studied in this chapter, the least readily recognizable as a 'representation of space' is the auction. It is, after all, a transaction or a practice, and has often been studied as such. My justification for treating it here as a representation, however, rests on two bases. First, auctions were very much part of the increasing density of interconnecting references to other representations of space. Second, and more significantly, unlike most market transactions, where the price of the commodity is known in advance of the purchase, an auction is a form of transaction which culminates in the establishment of a price.[45] As such, it is a form of practice that essays in the production of the key way in which commodified space is represented: a money value. Close attention to the form of, and justifications for, auctions can therefore reveal much.

[44] Various mortgage and sale deeds in DDA, Private Collections, Lala Jhabban Lal Collection, Collection no. 30. Significantly, this method of identifying various premises is also found in the deeds for a much earlier period in smalltown Punjab. Grewal, *By-Lanes of History*.

[45] Charles W. Smith (1989), *Auctions: The Social Construction of Value* (London: Harvester Wheatsheaf), p. 16.

Maps, in contrast to their implicit connection to leases (through the house tax number), had explicit connections to the auction. The image from the *Hindustan Times* (Figure 4.3), announcing an auction of properties in Sabzimandi, is fairly representative of advertisements that appeared in newspapers in the late 1930s.

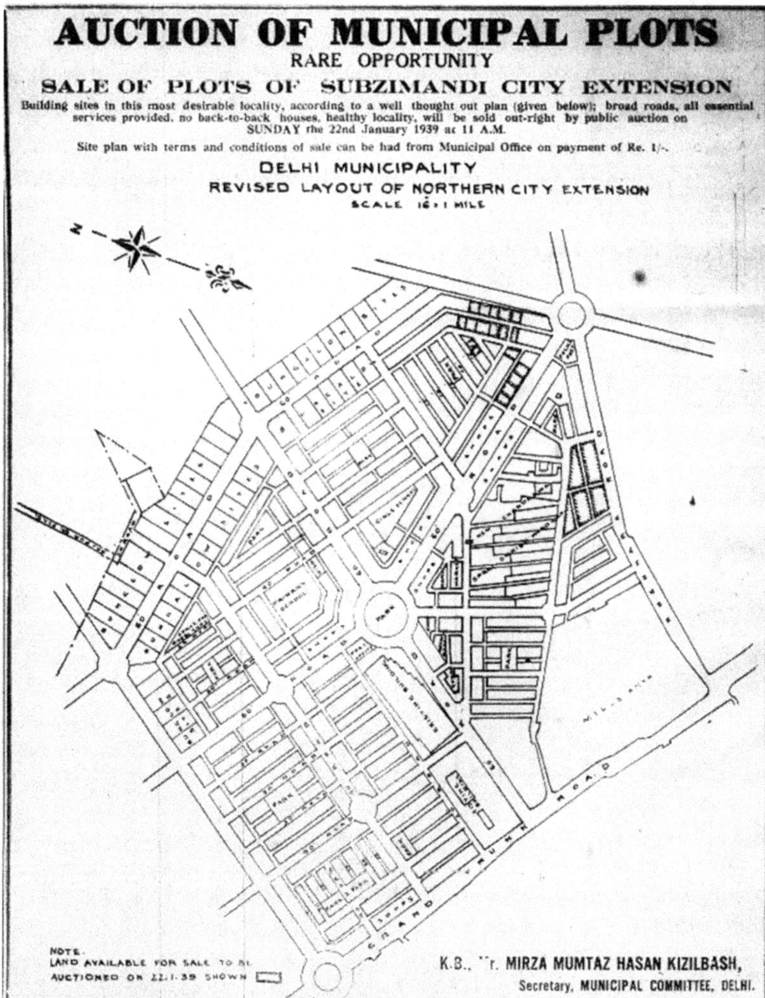

Figure 4.3. Advertisement for auction of plots in Sabzimandi. (*Hindustan Times*, 20 January 1939.)

The prominence given to the map in this advertisement is integrated into the enticement to participate in the auction of 'building sites in this most desirable locality, according to a well thought out plan'. Indeed, the very act of planning is part of what is being advertised by the image. This deployment of the map, however, was not exclusive to the external, public aspect of the auction; it can also be found in the conceptualization and analysis of auctions internal to official circles. Figure 4.4 is part of a report by A. P. Hume, Chairman of the DIT, concerning the results of an auction in Daryaganj. Here, the use of numbers in conjunction with the map was crucial to the discussion, which centred on the issue of frontage areas, corner plots, and sales of different kinds of structures.[46] Similar references to the numbering of houses and location through reference to maps can also be found in official reports about auctions in Daryaganj from two decades earlier.[47]

The crucial attribute of maps in auctions was not as accurate representations of size and distance. In fact, it was explicitly expected that those

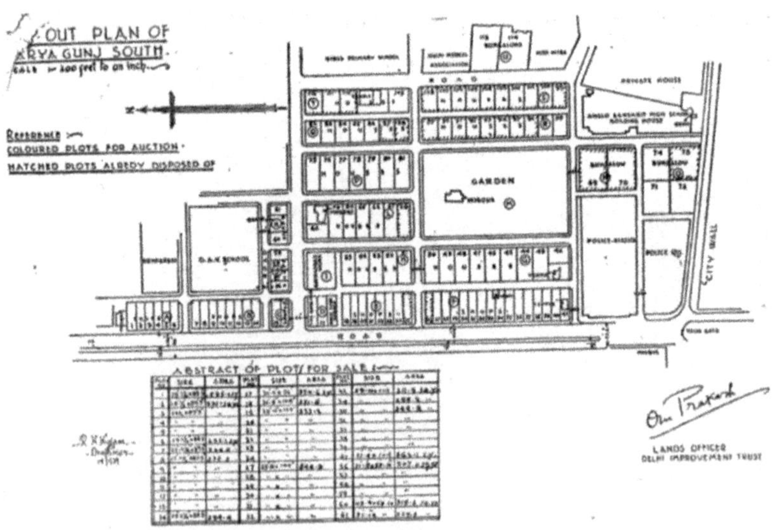

Figure 4.4. Layout of Daryaganj South. (DDA, CC Records, LSG-LB, F no. 1 (46), 1939.)

[46] CC Records, LSG-LB, F no. 1(46), 1939: From Chairman Delhi Improvement Trust to Chief Commissioner Delhi, 23 February 1939.

[47] CC Records, Education, F. no. 11, Part A, 1922: DC to CC, 21 April 1920.

bidding would have inspected the site themselves.[48] Maps served as reminders of location rather than reflecting any authoritative accuracy; what was most important was whether a shop was a corner plot or in the middle of a row. Nevertheless, advertisements used the visual conventions of authoritative mapping being diffused by the state. The idea was to convey uniform information that a potentially heterogeneous group of participants at an auction would consider accurate.

Of particular importance was an allied question: who was this community of potential auction participants? By the late 1930s the conclusion reached by DIT officials, at least explicitly, was that this community ought to be as wide as possible. Thus Hume, Chairman of DIT, could aver that one of the three crucial requirements for a successful auction was that there be 'extensive advertisement to the persons concerned of the fact that the commodity is available.'[49] Consistent with this understanding he had highlighted that in the case of the successful Daryaganj auctions of 1939, DIT officials and the auction agents had carried out considerable publicity.

> Judged by western, and particularly American, standards, the advertising would be described as negligible. Judged by Delhi standards, it was probably in excess of anything that has been attempted for land disposal sales.[50]

In the land disposal rules formulated by DIT, it was decided that notices of receipt of tenders or announcement of public auctions would be advertised in local papers, through fixing posters at suitable places, distributing handbills to the public, and 'if the Chairman so directs by beat of drum.'[51]

Where the auction was chosen as the mode for the disposal of government property[52] the ambition seems to have been to have as wide a dissemination of knowledge about the auction as possible. This is in marked contrast to the auctions of property held in Delhi after 1857, where participation was significantly more limited (partly by design).[53] By the late 1930s

[48] Ibid., Conditions of Tender appended to Chairman DIT to Chief Commissioner Delhi, 15 June 1939.

[49] Ibid., Chairman DIT to Chief Commissioner Delhi, 9 March 1939.

[50] Ibid., Chairman DIT to Chief Commissioner Delhi, 23 February 1939.

[51] Ibid., Chairman DIT to Chief Commissioner Delhi, 15 June 1939.

[52] There are certainly frequent advertisement of auctions, inserts about tenders received for sites, and other kinds of information disseminated in the local English-language daily *Hindustan Times* from the late 1930s onwards.

[53] See Chapter 1 and Vanaik, 'Changing the Plot: Property Relations in Delhi 1857–1920', ch. 1.

the ambition was to have every potential bidder participate in auctions. This marks an important and novel moment within state practice in Delhi—one where the image of the perfect market became an ideal complement to state actions.

It can be readily conceded, then, that auctions were a part of the interlinking chain of representations of property. There is a further reason, related more closely to the auction as a form itself, for why they might be treated as a representation of space. Economic sociologist Charles Smith points out that the invariable reason for the use of auctions to establish values stems from the prevalence of 'situations in which the conventional ways of establishing price and ownership are inadequate [...]'.[54] Smith argues that the reasons for uncertainty could be manifold, from uniqueness (as of a work of art) to the instability of market demand (as at auctions for fruit or fish); uncertainty, however, is the definitive cause for the deployment of auctions. The auction, he concludes, allows a community to resolve situations of uncertain valuations by arriving at a price for a commodity. That price, a money value, is perhaps the most important representation of commodified space.

It follows from this proposition that much can be gleaned through close attention to the nature and sources of uncertainty that prevailed where auctions were held. With respect to land and house property in twentieth century Delhi, at least three kinds of uncertainty were addressed by the auction. First, the question of the value and pricing of land. To a certain extent, and in contrast to many other commodities in everyday use, the value of land is fundamentally irresolvable. This is reflected in the debates around rent within classical political economy.[55] With respect to prices,

[54] Smith, *Auctions: The Social Construction of Value*, p. x.

[55] Debates about the status of rent within capitalism have continued since the canonical propositions of David Ricardo. The basic issue remains: is rent simply a payment to the residue of medieval political power—the control of land by a landowner—with no organic role within modern capitalism? Or can such a role be envisioned? Put another way, is the value of land simply an outcome of the use to which it is put? Or does the value of land play a role in determining the use to which land is put? For an account of theorizations of rent within classical political economy, particularly in non-Marxist theory, see Conway L. Lackman (1977), 'The Modern Development of Classical Rent Theory', *American Journal of Economics and Sociology*, 36 (1), 51–63. For a useful summary of the debates around these issues in the 1970s and 1980s (largely between Marxist and Marxist-inspired scholars), see A. Haila (1990), 'The Theory of Land Rent at the Crossroads', *Environment and Planning D: Society and Space*, 8, 275–96. An update of her survey and critique of some of her propositions is in Johannes Jager (2003), 'Urban Land Rent Theory: A Regulationist Perspective', *International Journal of Urban and Regional Research*, 27 (2), 233–49.

moreover, the situations in which past experience tend to break down as a guide to future pricing of land are manifold, and prominent among these are moments of land use change. Questions about the legitimate price of land are posed acutely at such moments, and auctions are one available mode of resolution.

After 1857, Daryaganj (a locality which had been the residence of the urban elite) was used to house troops stationed at Delhi. The effect had been to drastically devalue property holdings in the area.[56] Subsequent to the exodus of the army from the area in 1908, plots in the area were acquired, and it was proposed to redevelop the area as a whole. Acquisition of property began in 1914, and from the very beginning there were deep and irresolvable questions of how best to offer compensation. With very few sales occurring just prior to 1914, those that did happen were fairly volatile and a poor guide to pricing. Listing a series of these, the special acquisition officer pointed out:

> These instances are given in order to show the difficulty in arriving at the market value as defined in the Act. On one hand, there is a sale of vacant land at Rs. 3 a square yard [a relatively high amount at the time], and on the other there are sales of land with buildings at a price which would seem to give the land a *minus* value. These anomalies are difficult to explain.[57]

Acquisition pushed on regardless of these difficulties. A minimal redevelopment brought up the total expenditure on the area (including acquisition) to Rs. 161,270.[58] In June 1920, an auction of just twelve shops on the main road brought in Rs. 139,000 at a rate of Rs. 56 per sq. yd.[59] While officials had hitherto been confident of recouping the outlay on acquisition, these results were well beyond their expectations. With six acres more to be disposed of, the auctions of June 1920 had been the first concrete indicator of what to expect, and subsequent projections based themselves on the results of that auction.[60]

[56] Vanaik, 'Changing the Plot: Property Relations in Delhi 1857–1920', ch. 3.

[57] DDA, CC Records, Education, F no. 11, Part A, 1922: Special Land Acquisition officer to PA to CC Delhi, 2 July 1914.

[58] Ibid., CC Delhi to Secretary to Government of India, Dept. of Education and Health, 8 November 1921.

[59] Ibid., DC to CC, 7 July 1920.

[60] Ibid., CC to Secy, to GoI, Dept of Education and Health, 8 November 1921.

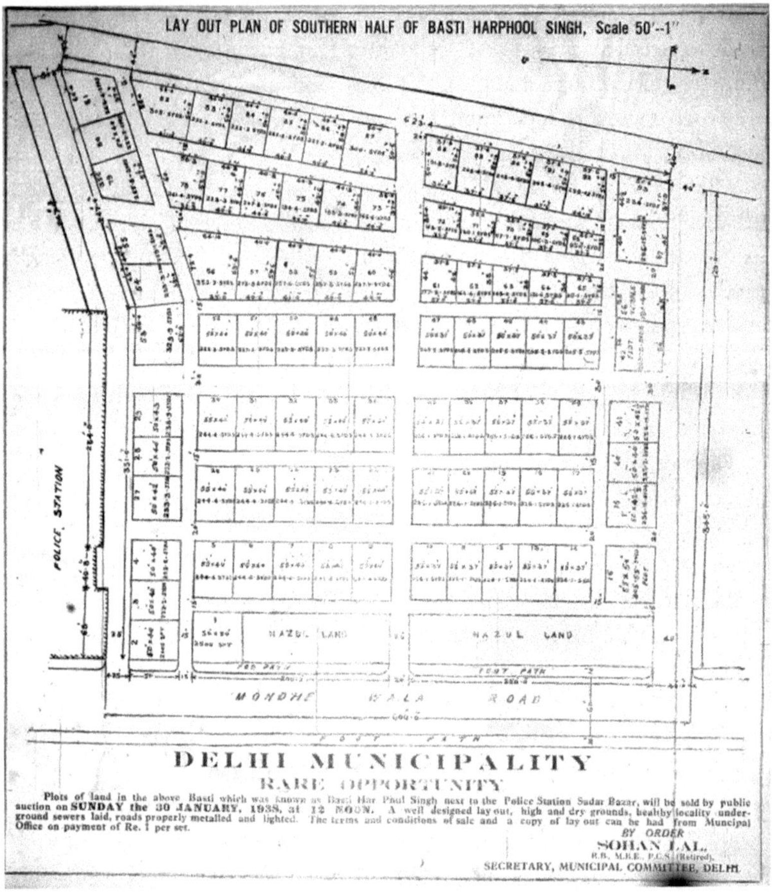

Figure 4.5. Layout of plots in Basti Harphool Singh. (*Hindustan Times*, 29 January 1938.)

On this occasion, and others—for instance, the Burn Bastion Road auctions in 1916—auctions were the only reliable guide to the value of a piece of land in a given area. The sheer alienness of planned enclaves in the old city also made pre-existing valuations moot. A particularly striking instance was the conversion of Basti Harphool Singh from a slum into a planned layout (Figure 4.5).

Other forms of uncertainty were more conjunctural. In 1919, forty of a total of 141 plots on Garstin Bastion Road, developed on lines similar to the very successful Burn Bastion Road layout, were sold through auction at

Rs. 61 per sq. yd.[61] However, with the slump in the 1920s, prices crashed. In 1930 the administration offered a plot to the Central Agency Ltd at Rs. 40 per sq. yd. The offer was rejected. In order to gauge what the price of land might be, exploratory auctions were held in September and November 1930. The best price that could be raised on those occasions were Rs. 28 per sq. yd. It was ultimately decided to offer it to Central Agency Ltd, on perpetual lease, at a reserve price of Rs. 35 per sq. yd. A fall and recovery of property values, then, could lead to uncertainties similar to changes in land use.

Auctions were used on these occasions to arrive at a price when the value of land was uncertain. Also characteristic on both these occasions, however, was that prices recorded at auctions could guide future pricing. This process of 'learning' could, sudden depressions apart, throw up more generally accepted prices, obviating the need for auctions. References to auctions dwindle in classified advertisements for property sales through the late 1930s. Simultaneously, the number of advertisements that mentioned prices and rents for properties increased steadily. Something like this is also evident in Hume's 1939 assertion that the DIT would be best off disposing of lands through private negotiations rather than via public auctions.[62] In his argument against the auction he posited that, even in theoretical terms, auctions worked best when three conditions were met: strong demand for land, a limited supply, and extensive advertisement of the availability of land.[63] As Hume pointed out:

> he auction system is admirable on a small scale for limited periods, but the successful disposal of a large amount of land over a long period requires a vast amount of personal interest and effort in the way of private negotiations.[64]

Throughout the correspondence on the subject, Hume takes for granted that 'market price' was something that could be, and was, known in advance of auctions, and any disposal of land should proceed on that basis.[65]

[61] DDA, CC Records, Education, F no. 4(128), 1930: DC to CC, 20 November 1930. The rest of the account of the Garstin Bastion Road properties in this paragraph is based on this file.

[62] DDA, CC Records, LSG-LB, F no. 1(46), 1939: Review of Sales in Daryaganj South, 15 February 1939.

[63] Ibid., Review of Sales in Daryaganj South, 9 March 1939.

[64] Ibid. The contention is particularly ironic in the context of Delhi, where in the aftermath of 1857, through a tremendously convoluted process, auctions were used to dispose of properties spanning almost a third of the city.

[65] Ibid., Review of Sales in Daryaganj South, 9 March 1939, and final Land Disposal Rules.

In response, the Chief Commissioner of Delhi argued for the continuing importance of the auction on the basis that private negotiations would inevitably lead to improper practices. The state was required to appear above suspicion, however groundless, and the public auction was the best way to assure this.[66] Here we come to a second form of uncertainty that auctions could address. For much of this period the legitimacy of the colonial state and its evaluations of property were under question. The state could not simply announce prices for land that it wished to lease or sell on the assumption that its procedure would appear impartial and free from manipulation. The auction offered a solution to public doubts about the state. Through the auction the colonial state could be represented as being both transparent in its actions and above particularistic interests.

Nevertheless, the final rules for land disposal formulated by the DIT in 1939 gave leeway to the chairman and board to decide on the apposite method of disposing of lands. Either receipt of private applications (a negotiated sale), a call for tenders (another form of auction), or conducting a public auction could be used to dispose of plots. In each sale, however, public notice of receipt and details of the offer were to be issued. Another important change was that the market rate for the plot in question was to be included in the terms of the advertisement for the plot, whether it was to be disposed of by auction, tender, or private negotiation.

In this reformulated auction, with its narrower brief and coexistence with the options of private negotiations, the uncertainty is not about price. Here the uncertainty stems from the state of the property market. Releasing too many properties at once could create a glut, while releasing too few might inflate prices. The auction with clearly marked parameters—prices, localities, and maps—emerges as a way of representing the efforts of the state to husband and carefully control the market in property. Here, rather than simply generating a price, the auction could emerge as a way of representing the state's knowledge of the situation of the property market—a signal, for instance, of a market in recovery.

It is indeed remarkable that throughout the period of this study, and especially towards its end, the auction was the preferred modality for the disposal of land by all the various state agencies active in Delhi: Daryaganj North, Burn Bastion Road, and others by the Delhi Municipal Committee,

[66] Ibid., CC to Chairman DIT, 7 March 1939. The Chief Commissioner also made the argument that the highest value could be achieved through auctions. This, however, is shown to be untrue by Hume in his response.

New Delhi by the Government of India and Daryaganj South, and many others by the DIT. In contrast, private individuals used auctions relatively infrequently. Revealingly, all the significant auctioneers in the city advertised their links to the state in their self description as 'government auctioneers' or 'railway auctioneers', even though they were also conducting private auctions.[67] Indeed, when government lands stopped being auctioned because of World War II, sales through other methods came to dominate the classified advertisements.[68]

At the beginning of the twentieth century and through the depression in the property market in the 1920s, auctions addressed uncertainties about the value of urban land. But they also were a means to suggest that transparency and an open market characterized Delhi real estate. The close proximity of the auction to the practices of the state, however, is usefully contrasted with the interesting role of advertisements vis-a-vis private actors in the property market.

Advertisements

As we have seen, the state was, through this entire period, a significant advertiser in the newspapers in all its various avatars—as DMC, DIT, and court-ordered partition or insolvency cases. The newspaper was also, however, a vehicle of choice for disseminating information about property for a section of the private property market.[69]

Hindustan Times was a newspaper in English, and therefore, circulated among the elite, professional classes (lawyers, clerks, and so on), and some sections of the business community.[70] This is indicated by the areas for

[67] Niadar Mall and Rangi Lall, and S. M. G. Beaty were the two largest auction firms active in Delhi.

[68] Significantly enough, the number of advertisements for sale of property were not reduced at this point.

[69] The following propositions are based on a comprehensive survey of classified advertisements in the extant issues of the Delhi-based, nationalist-inclined newspaper *Hindustan Times* between October 1924 and the end of 1944, held at the Cambridge Centre for South Asian Studies. This is a more or less complete run except for stray missing issues and periods when the newspaper was suppressed.

[70] Official circulation figures suggest that *Hindustan Times*, from its founding until 1947, was one of the highest-selling dailies in any language in Delhi. From a circulation of 3,500 from 1925 to 1932, its circulation jumped to 15,000 from 1933 to 1943, and remained above 18,000 from 1943 to 1947. All data are based on the quarterly statement of newspapers and periodicals published in Delhi Province from 1925 to 1947. The circulation of the English-language *Hindustan Times* remained higher than that of its Hindi-language counterpart *Hindustan*,

which property rentals were regularly advertised—New Delhi and the more elite or modernized portions of Old Delhi—which suggests that relatively high-ranking colonial officials and business elites were the targets. More interesting results emerge from the advertisements for sales of property. Advertisements for plots and structures in New Delhi and the Civil Lines (the parts of the city most associated with the colonial elite) dominated the pages until the early 1930s. In the period after this, plots in Old Delhi and, from around 1937, suburban developments (Karol Bagh, Paharganj, and DIT layouts) were the majority of properties advertised. These last were areas where a large number of the middle classes—sections of clerks, professionals, and small businessmen—were coming to reside. In short, the constituency of the newspaper advertisement spanned the colonial elite and the emerging middle classes. Omitted from the newspaper were the areas in which the more locally rooted segments of the trading community resided: the intramural wards to the south of Chandni Chowk.

If this was the audience, what of the advertisements themselves? The similarities in the form of the advertisement by the private property agency shown in Figure 4.6 and the Municipal Committee's advertisement for auction (Figure 4.3) are striking. They share the central placement of the map and the exhortation about the 'rare opportunity' involved, and underline the planned nature of the layout. There was, in fact, a symbiotic connection between the private property market and the state—one that centred on the presumed truth of government maps. This symbiosis was carried forward at an institutional level in the connections between the DIT and property agents. While the form of advertisement in Figure 4.5 was relatively rare for private bodies, layouts such as that in Figure 4.7, where DIT's notices for tender were associated with agents' advertisements for sale, were a common way of underlining these connections.

Thus, in a number of advertisements, the institutional authorizations by the state of private agents was carried over into a two-sided embrace of similar conventions of visual representation. While the examples cited so far were large-format advertisements, the more usual classifieds placed by private sellers also carried through some of the representations of space deployed by the state. In particular, the use of house numbers and standardized units of measurements became increasingly common from the

published by the same press from 1936 onwards and throughout this period. The *Statesman*, the loyalist English-language daily, had a higher circulation in Delhi than did the *Hindustan Times* for most of this period.

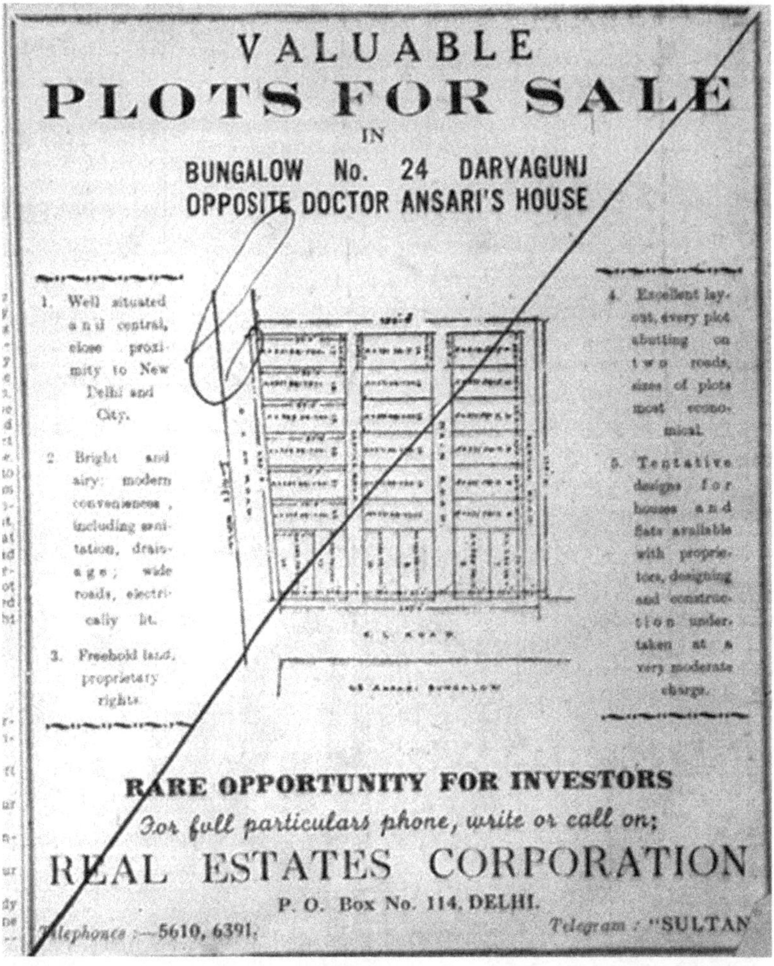

Figure 4.6. Advertisement by the Real Estates Corporation. (*Hindustan Times*, 27 June 1936.)[71]

1930s onwards. This is precisely the opposite of the more complicated picture we saw with respect to these elements in lease documents. The newspaper, then, could amplify conventions of representing space as property that the state was keen to promote.

There were, however, also significant differences between advertisements issued by the state and those issued by private parties. For instance, the

[71] *HT*, 27 June 1936.

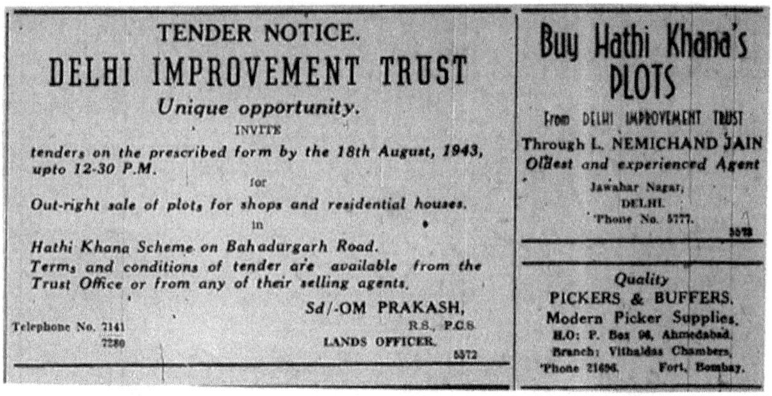

Figure 4.7. Advertisements of property, public and private. (*Hindustan Times*, 10 August 1943.)

Figure 4.8. The difficulties of tenancy. (*Hindustan Times*, 9 July 1932.)

signature of the state representative (even when there was no actual signature) came to signify a mark of authority in advertisements by state authorities, one that was not shared with the private sector. Nor were advertisements within the private sector as rigid in the imagery they were prepared to evoke. A more expansive set of references to the experience of renting and owning property than existed in DIT advertisements is in evidence in Figure 4.8.

Particularly from the mid-1930s, advertisements championed the idea of home ownership (Figure 4.9).

A number of interesting tropes were deployed here—the house as an expression of individuality and non-dependence. Thus, the Prudential Housing Corporation in its brochure (Figure 4.10) could aver that: 'Hired houses like hired clothes don't fit!' This is quite a departure from the

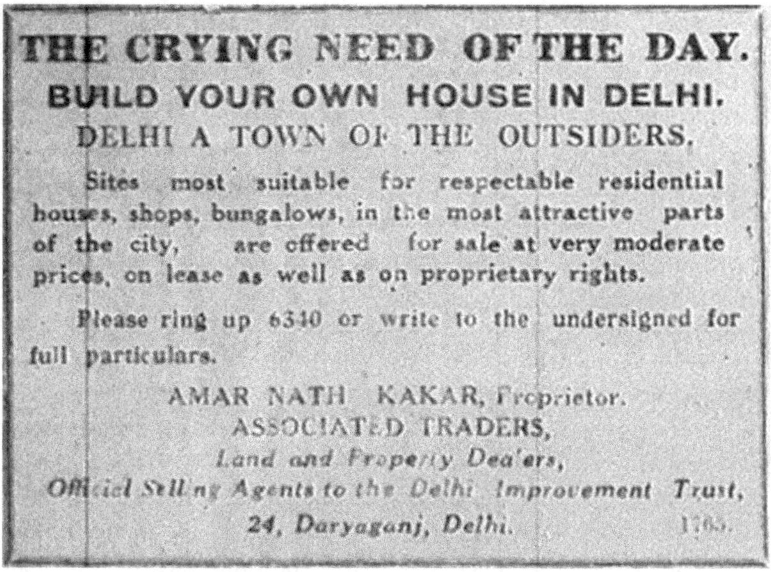

Figure 4.9. Promoting ownership. (*Hindustan Times*, 21 April 1940.)

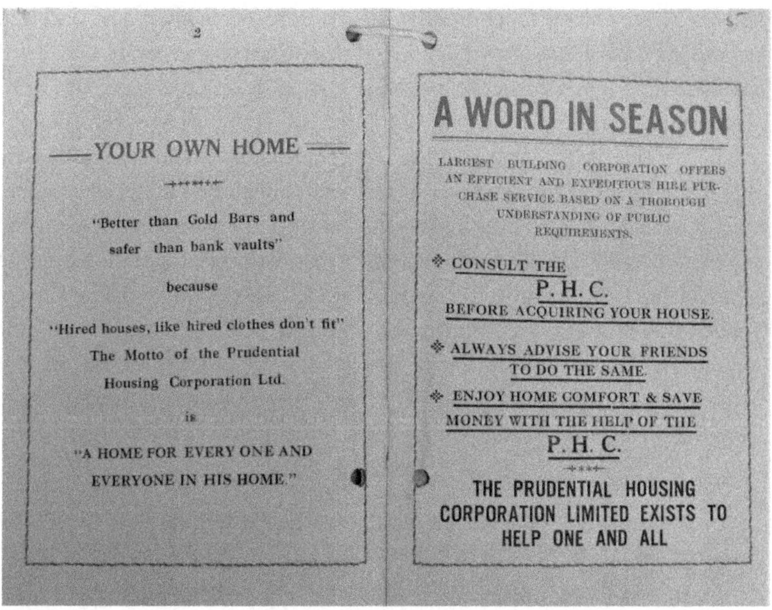

Figure 4.10. Homeliness. (DDA, CC Records, LSG-LB, F no. 1432, 1938.)

understanding of houses as structures which were expressions of rootedness and connection. Here, the constant construction that pockmarked large portions of the Delhi landscape, the sense of a landscape remade *de novo*—in New Delhi until the mid-1930s and in the DIT extensions soon after—was harnessed into a celebration of the individual and modern house owner. Delhi—the 'town of outsiders' (Figure 4.9)—could also be 'home' for a new and different kind of family than that found in the old city.

The image of the house used in Figure 4.11—another advertisement exhorting the construction of 'a home of your own'—would have been radically different from the layout of most houses in the old city. The text of the advertisement also evokes attributes of modern living: parks, roads, schools, electricity, and buses. This theme of a more modern house linked to the amenities provided by the state—sanitation, water, and electricity in particular, but secondarily roads and public transport—was in increasing evidence through the 1930s. Even the more quotidian classified advertisements, which were far less elaborately laid out, would highlight the presence of amenities: 'Flats in Ajmeri Gate Bazar consisting each of two rooms besides kitchen and bathrooms with electricity and water...'"[72]

The sense of a 'modern' fashion of living was seamlessly conjoined with the idea of the home as a sound investment. Whether as advice in the Prudential Housing Corporation brochure that houses were 'better than gold bars and safer than bank vaults', or as the more matter-of-fact suggestion in a classified advertisement that a particular structure was an 'ideal investment for capitalists, valued at around Rs. 60,000', it is within the realm of advertising that the most intensive image of the house as a commodity could emerge.[73] In a characteristic set of conjunctions, advertising could, often in the same document, reconcile images of the house as the acme of individual entitlement and expression, as felicitously dependent on the modern services of the state, and as an abstract commodity that could be traded for gain. The time cycles of financial investment and return were brought into consonance with the aspirational future-directedness of modern living. Indeed, the disjunction between the actual rhythms and patterns of life in Old and suburban Delhi from that promised in the advertisements is startling.[74]

[72] *HT*, 4 October 1932. There are numerous others along similar lines.

[73] *HT*, 2 April 1938. Classified advertisement for sale of buildings in Paharganj by Mohammed Umr, Dar-ul Umr.

[74] Sanjay Srivastava, analysing advertisements of DLF from the 1950s, locates this kind of 'utopian and commodified urbanism' of the 'consumer-citizen' in a very particular form of escape from post-Partition trauma. The 'fantabulous vision of post-partition utopia [was]

Figure 4.11. The modern family. (*Hindustan Times*, 17 November 1940.)

wrenched from the ascetic reaches of the Five-Year Plan state, and distant from the messianic—'slum-clearing'—gaze of the DIT.' My evidence would suggest that those post-1947 advertisements are better located as a continuation of a way of representing property ownership that began with the emergence of large real-estate firms in the mid-1930s. Sanjay Srivastava (2015), *Entangled Urbanism: Slum, Gated Community, and Shopping Mall in Delhi and Gurgaon*, 1st ed. (New Delhi: Oxford University Press), pp. xxvi–xxvii.

The newspaper—at least the English daily—saw a closer fit between state-authorized representations of space and those that emerged out of circulation outside the state. Within these advertisements, the state is presented as a unitary and reassuring source of guarantee: legitimate title, reliable amenities, and even secure loans. There is very little of the more chaotic aspect of the state seen in the other representations discussed so far: where maps might be out of date, house tax might be invoked and ignored, and auctions might be a search for legitimacy. That more fragmented terrain of the state was papered over in the newspaper advertisement. Indeed, private agencies built upon the reassuring cohesiveness of the state as it appeared in property advertisements, adding a further affective dimension: the promise of a modern home, freedom from the travails of the rental market, and the assurance of clear titles. In contrast to these ways of building up effective stories about new houses, a different narrative tradition took centre stage within the sphere of the state itself.

'Narrating' Property

The various representations of space studied in this chapter, with all their differences and specificities, have each highlighted two crucial attributes: a relationship to time, and a relationship to the state. We have seen that each of these representations of space was shaped and reshaped by the temporalities of the property market: maps came to be revised, the clauses and formats of leases underwent subtle alterations, the roles that auctions played changed, and the amount and patterns of advertising were transformed in response to various conjunctures. Alongside reflecting changes in the property market, for leases in particular and for maps to a lesser degree, the further issue of representing the changes that flowed from property circulation was a central concern, as the time period of the contract or the new morphology of the city that construction and demolition was constantly bringing into being.

As with the appearance of time, the different ways of representing space each had its own relationship to the state: differing degrees of dependence, and circulation within and outside it. We have seen, however, that in each of these representations, contingent, situated, and particularized forms of knowledge seeped into seemingly technical documents: maps would rely on local knowledge for update of surveys, lease documents would situate houses through locality and name of tenant rather than house tax numbers, colonial officials were concerned that their valuations of property appear to the public to be accurate and fair, regardless of their conviction that the best price had been achieved. In each instance, forms of knowledge outside the state and outside the technical apparatuses for objectivity were necessary supplements to official representations of space.

Recognizing this incompleteness of official documents allows us to situate more precisely the nature of state authority over representations of space. This was not an authority that derived simply from absolute control over space. The authority of the state in this sphere emerged, in part, from its physical role as archivist and controller of many of the representations discussed. The key instruments of the property market—maps, building plans, leases, and so on—were deposited with state authorities who would go on to aggregate, preserve, classify, and catalogue these documents.

The act of archiving was crucial labour, however, because of a second and even more significant activity: the ability to enunciate narratives about the property market. The very fact that the documents in the archives of the state were amenable to such narrativization was an outcome of the temporal reference preserved in each of these documents. Left as disparate pieces of paper in the archive, however, these individual references to time were only potential sources of authority. It was not until they were stitched together into narratives that their significance came to the fore. For the modern state, the ability to create these narratives about changes in urban space came to be crucial to urban governance.

The narrative impulse might be narrow and focused, or wide-ranging and expansive. Towards the beginning of the period of this study, R. B. Whitehead's report from 1910, and towards the end of the period, that of A. P. Hume from 1936, were exercises in the broad scale—efforts to 'narrate' the history of property in the city as a whole.[75] In the course of everyday activity, however, numerous reports on a microscale reproduced the basic pattern. An entirely unexceptional instance of this was the DMC's decision to construct shops on the site of an old police station in Kashmere Gate in December 1926.[76] The Deputy Commissioner of Delhi was reluctant to extend sanction for this, as the area was potentially to be declared a protected monument and the Municipal Committee's claim to the site was unclear. A municipal councillor, however, declared that the site was undoubtedly

[75] *Report on the Relief of Congestion in Delhi* (1937), vol. 1 (Simla: Government of India Press); *Report on the Administration of the Delhi Crown Lands*.

[76] TH, DMC Progs, July–September 1927, prog. No. 7, OM of 14 September 1927.

municipal, and he was asked to put up a note on the matter. The councillor, Lala Ram Pershad, reported that he had gone through the available records and found that the premises of the police station reverted to the police department when charge of the police force was shifted away from DMC. This meant that it was not *nazul* property—a fact further corroborated by *RADCL*. Pershad concluded that its non-use by the police established that the site belonged to the municipal committee and that

> Over and above all as it is a paying site, I will not recommend its transfer to *nazul* Department... if it is to be levelled and cleared then compensation should be paid to the Municipal Committee...[77]

While the proposal was ultimately dropped, consider the deployment of the archive and the relationship to the market in this instance. The process of consulting the records was initiated by the conviction of the municipal councillor. His subsequent narrative about the site was built up by consulting documents held in the archive, as well as large-scale reports. Its conclusions, however, seem to be rooted in at least two, more contemporary, concerns: the profitability of the site, and, without explicit mention, the tussle between DMC and the local administration over *nazul* lands which had just recently been transferred from the control of the DMC to the Imperial administration.

This combination of archival work and the building up of narratives was shared between the micro- and macro- level exercises. Thus, Hume's city-wide report contained an introductory chapter that outlined what he saw as the key moments of urban development in Delhi since the 1870s.[78] In that report, Hume cited Whitehead's conclusions from the 1910 report at some length.[79] Whitehead's report had a similar layout, containing reference to the prior report of Leslie Smith from 1873.[80] In their mutual reference these three reports—Hume's, Whitehead's, and Smith's—created an interlocking narrative that could stretch from the early nineteenth century to the mid-twentieth century.

The reports, as well as correspondence that grew around them, were combinations of contemporary surveys with corroboration from, and

[77] TH, DMC Progs., July–September 1927, prog. No. 7, OM of 14 September 1927.

[78] *Report on the Relief of Congestion in Delhi* (1937), vol. 1 (Simla: Government of India Press), pp. 3–13.

[79] Ibid., pp. 5–6.

[80] *Report on the Administration of the Delhi Crown Lands*, pp. 17–19.

presentations of, archival material. The process of narrativization, however, in these instances removed traces of the heterogeneous composition of the archive. Thus the variety of forms of knowledge that constituted individual documents, which, as we have seen, contained both technical as well as more experience-based forms of knowledge, would not be preserved within the narrative.[81] Through narrativization, a more secure form of knowledge could be generated for the purposes of state action. It was precisely through the narrative form that a more certain 'truth' about the state of urban development could emerge. This, however, is seen more readily in the reports at the macrolevel than those generated at a more everyday level where the inconsistencies were usually more evident.

Macrolevel reports were also composed as a form of intervention. While all efforts at narrating property were shaped by their contemporary milieu, the reports of Hume and Whitehead were also attempts to generate frames through which future action could be guided. Thus, Whitehead's conclusions advocated a more commercialized treatment of the urban holdings of the state.[82] Hume, in contrast, by recommending the establishment of an Improvement Trust, framed his report as an effort to solve a population-related problem by partially discarding the injunction to profit. In addition, these narratives also affected the particular technical instruments that the state was to use: leases, modes of survey, mapping, urban layouts, expansion, and so on.

A circuit of the narrative can therefore be described: beginning with the generation of individual representations of space, their collection and organization in the archive, drawing on the archive to construct narrative forms, the use of these forms of narrative to imbue directionality to future state action, which, in turn, dictated the forms of individual representations of space. This circuit of the narrative—drawing on and returning to the various individual representations of space—came to be crucial within the state.

On this view, one way of understanding the relationship of the state to the property market would be to gauge the degree to which the circuit of the narrative described dictated the form and content of representations of space in the city. If this circuit and the timing of the appearance of the various reports were to determine the basic form of the representations of

[81] In the case of the Whitehead report, part of the claim to greater accuracy was based on consulting an archive that Smith had not been able to consult in 1873. The question of the precarious and partial nature of the documents within these archives was inevitably ignored.

[82] Jyoti Hosagrahar (2005), *Indigenous Modernities: Negotiating Architecture and Urbanism* (London: Routledge), p. 137.

space in circulation in the city, the relationship of the state to space would be an especially privileged one. As we have seen, forms of knowledge beyond the state also imprinted themselves onto the representations of space. To various degrees—the personalized forms of property identification in leases, the inadequate revisions of maps, the partial circulation of advertisements—each of the representations of space were constituted in critical ways by processes that lay beyond the purview of the state.

Nevertheless this circuit served to place the state in an advantageous position with respect to knowledge of the property market compared to private actors. Other actors—from squatters to traders and industrialists—experienced the market as disjointed and individual events knitted together (to varying degrees) by business knowledge accumulated over a lifetime, private collections of records, and, of course, the narratives disseminated by the state. Through generating these narratives of property, the state could, potentially at least, make better sense of the market and leverage that position favourably in directions that it chose.

The state's use of the narrative was directed inwards towards itself rather than outwards towards the subjects of the state. This was in contrast to the visions of middle-class life being propagated by private actors in the property market. As we shall see in Chapter 5, coherence was a critical and difficult achievement for the colonial state. A semblance of coherence was achieved, however, through leveraging its role as promulgator of law and repository of representations of space. The circuit of the narrative explored here was a source of the relative strength of the state vis-a-vis the private property market. The narratives built up also served to smooth over the cracks and fissures in the accuracy of the documents, attempting to generate a seamless truth in large-scale narratives. This narrative capacity was one source of the power for the state. A fuller assessment of the power of the state within the property market, however, requires moving beyond the realm of representations.

5

Intimacy in Four Registers

State, Space, and Capital in Delhi

The preceding chapters have argued that while the state was an important actor in the property market, robust private property development remained the mainstay of housing provision in Delhi. The intention of these formulations has not been to marginalize the role of the state, but rather to argue for a more careful analysis of the relationship between the state and the property market on one hand and the state and urban space on the other. Chapter 4 began to do so somewhat obliquely, approaching the state via representations of space and concluding that the ability to generate narratives about property was an important source of its power. This chapter takes up the task of understanding the relationship between the state and the property market in more frontal fashion.

Over the twentieth century there was a heightened convergence of the state and the market in urban land and construction. In the nineteenth century the state had used the property market to cobble together a local support base. This had been accompanied by a concerted effort to clarify property rights in land. By about 1925, a further far-ranging and significant transformation in the relationship between the state and the property market was effected. This transformation can be understood in terms of four registers of intimacy between the state and the market. For one, the state internalized market valuations into its own everyday practice—a kind of ingestion of the property market. A second register might be thought of as affinity—an attraction towards the property market as an opportunity and means to make profits and boost income. A third register resembles something more like symbiosis—a coming together of state and urban property to the point where it becomes impossible to think about the latter except inasmuch as it was mediated by the state. The fourth register is that of the property market as nightmare, thwarting efforts of the state to serve the 'common good'. The gathering closeness of the state and property market over this period was no simple affair. A more complicated picture emerges, but one which reflects the maturing influence of each side of the relationship on the other. We might begin, however, with a more first-order question: what was the state in Delhi?

Possessing the City: Property and Politics in Delhi, 1911–1947. Anish Vanaik, Oxford University Press (2020).

DOI: 10.1093/oso/9780198848752.001.0001

The Fragmented State

The history of the agency (or agencies) that could be seen as the concrete manifestation of the state in Delhi can be divided neatly at 1911. Before that date, Delhi made an administrative outcrop of Punjab province in the aftermath of 1857, and had three centres of authority: the district administration, the Delhi Municipal Committee (DMC), and the army. The first two were connected through the office of the District Commissioner (DC), who was also the President of the DMC. The army controlled the area around the fort and old cantonment to the north. These were relatively clearly demarcated divisions, and it makes sense to speak of a separation between civil and military areas in Delhi. After 1911, however, the centres of state authority in Delhi steadily multiplied.

The immediate upshot of the announcement of the shift of the capital to Delhi was the creation of the Delhi Town Planning Committee, to work out a plan for the construction of New Delhi. Land acquisition and construction was carried out by its successor body, the Imperial Delhi Committee. Once the capital was built, the New Delhi Municipal Committee (NDMC) was established to take over administration of the New Delhi area. The status of Old Delhi, however, also underwent a change. It was now detached from Punjab province and accorded an independent status as a centrally administered region. The redrawn Delhi district, dominated by the city but including rural areas around it, was presided over by a Chief Commissioner (CC). The DC remained Chairman of the DMC, though he was no longer the highest civilian authority in the region. Both CC and DC were also concerned with the administration of New Delhi.

The Civil Lines, where most of the European residents of Delhi lived after 1857, had always had a somewhat anomalous status within Delhi. Although officially within the jurisdiction of the Municipal Committee, it received attention and resources disproportionate to its population and size. After 1911, the administration of the Civil Lines was hedged off from the rest of the city through the establishment of a Notified Area Committee (NAC) whose source of funds and control of expenditure was made partially independent of the DMC. Although the army moved out of Daryaganj into a new cantonment to the south of the New City, troops continued to be stationed in the fort. The latter was also formed into an NAC.

Two other bodies were to further complicate the picture. The Imperial administration spent six months of the year stationed in Delhi.[1] Apart from

[1] All reference to 'government' in what follows should be taken to be mean the central administration.

the host of clerks and junior administrators brought in its wake, the Viceroy and senior officials displayed an intermittent interest in the state of Delhi's built environment—its sanitation and housing in particular. The final piece of the puzzle was the establishment of the Delhi Improvement Trust (DIT) in 1937. It was constituted as a result of a report about the state of housing in Delhi commissioned by the Imperial government.[2] The author of the report, A. P. Hume, who had briefly served as acting DC of Delhi, was made chairman of the DIT. The latter came to control large amounts of land outside the New Capital into which Delhi was expected to expand.

By the end of the 1930s, the area of Delhi had no fewer than six separate bodies that represented the state: central government, local administration, the DIT, NDMC, DMC, and the Civil Lines NAC. Apart from these, other bodies—in particular, the railways, the Public Works Department, and the army—intervened in the city through channels that were at least partly autonomous. Even more than was the case in most urban centres, the state in Delhi was distributed across numerous agencies.

The jurisdictions of these various agencies, in terms of area and purview, were for the most part discrete (Figure 5.1). Nevertheless, the scope for confusion and mutual treading on toes remained considerable. Between 1927 and the early 1930s, for instance, the area outside the southern walls of Delhi (the northern boundary of New Delhi) became the site for what was to become a long-running dispute. The DMC saw this stretch as the best candidate for city extension, and was prepared to develop this land without any monetary assistance from the central administration. In May 1927 they approached the DC, hoping that the land could be transferred to them for this purpose.[3] In the course of investigations, it emerged that the jurisdiction of the DMC already extended over the land even though the Imperial Delhi Committee had acquired it.[4] This was not clarified for the members of the DMC until October 1929, when the CC stated to a deputation from the DMC that, with respect to the land in question, 'the New Capital Committee were [. . .] more or less in the same position [vis-à-vis the DMC] as a private landlord.'[5] The issue—of the demolition of the city wall along the southern edge of the city and the development of an extension towards New Delhi—dragged on for many years thereafter. Marking out jurisdiction was one part

[2] See Chapter 6 for an account of the different ways in which the DMC and the central government viewed the prospect of an Improvement Trust.

[3] DDA, CC Records, Education, F no. 4(100), 1928: Secy. DMC to DC, 10 May 1927, and DC to CC, 26 August 1927.

[4] Ibid., noting of 18 August 1927.

[5] DDA, CC Records, Education, Pt. B, F no. 4(105), 1929: noting of 24 October 1929.

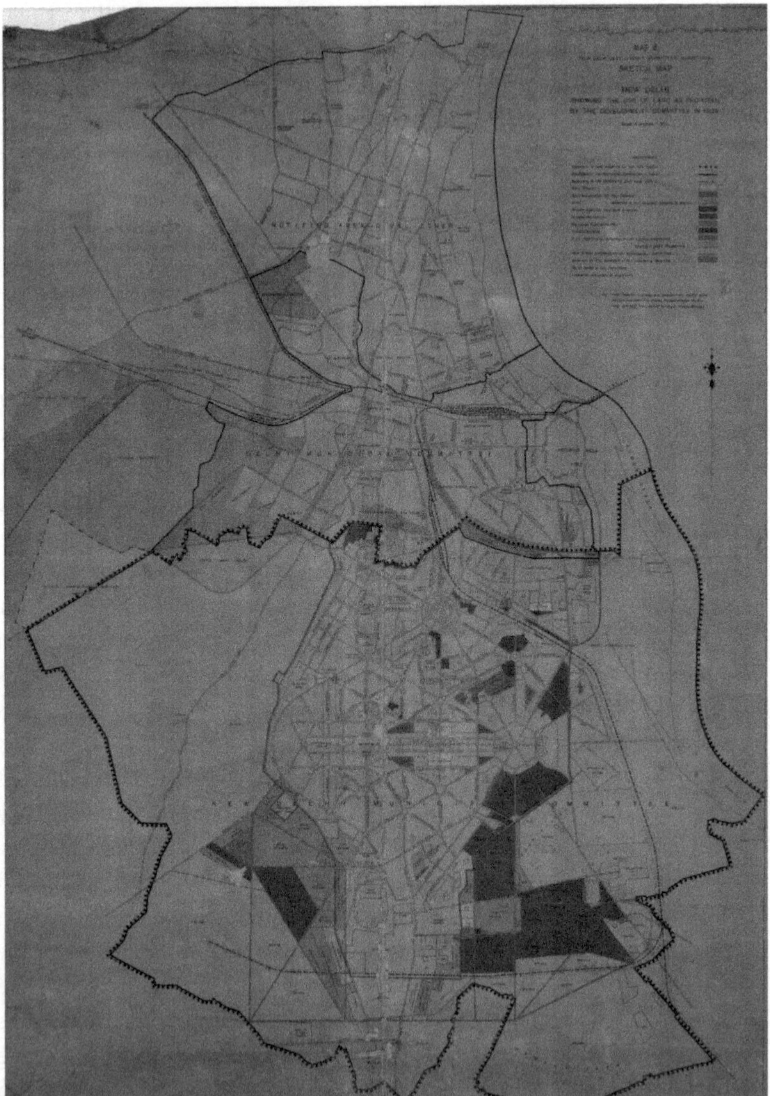

Figure 5.1. Sketch map of New Delhi showing jurisdictions

of the matter.[6] In the late 1930s and 1940s, the DIT planned to demolish the southern portion of the city wall and make space for the redevelopment of a slum located there. Officials rejected this plan too, partly on the grounds that bringing down the wall would make an unsightly old Delhi directly visible from the Imperial capital.[7]

Jurisdictional disputes could and did cut across this landscape in other complicated ways. In 1935, the DMC refused to provide drainage and essential services to government estates in Delhi. They argued that the government was, in effect, the biggest landlord in Delhi, and pointed out that they were refusing to sanction services 'to many important government estates in Delhi because they consider that Government should supply such services in the same manner as the private landlord is required to supply them.'[8]

The point that the state in Delhi over this period was fragmented might readily be conceded. Fragmentation itself had effects on how land and authority over it came to be utilized in the city. The incoherence of state efforts to build housing and infrastructure in Delhi can in part be traced to this. But we can make a further observation concerning the terms in which fragmentation came to be expressed with respect to land. It is striking, for instance, that in the disputes discussed previously, each public agency cast the other in the capacity of a private actor. The metaphor of the private actor, even when applied to state agencies, had great currency in the internal workings of the state.

Ingestion: Internalising the Market

The fiction that the different agencies of the state related to each other as would distinct private actors derived from an important shift in the administrative practice vis-a-vis public lands. Given what has been discussed about their overlapping jurisdictions, it is not surprising that there was a need for coordination between agencies from time to time. Logically, there were various ways in which coordination could be worked out. It is striking, then, that with respect to land exchanges, market values and prices emerged as the key mechanism for uncontentious transactions between state agencies.

[6] A stretch slightly to the west of that discussed previously (owned by the DMC in this case) was transferred to the jurisdiction of NDMC in 1934. CC Records, Education, Pt. B., F no. 4 (104), 1935.

[7] Stephen Legg (2007), *Spaces of Colonialism: Delhi's Urban Governmentalities* (Malden, MA; Oxford: Blackwell), pp. 190–209.

[8] DDA, CC Records, R&A, F no. 122, 1935: DC to CC, 26 March 1935.

This had not always been the case. In 1874, while *nazul* lands were assigned a monetary value, these were not handed over to the DMC by the district authorities in exchange for either rent or payment. Although the terms of the transfer to the DMC stipulated that *nazul* lands were only managed (not owned) by the DMC, the latter had the right to collect and utilize rents from the land as they pleased. Similarly, when the army moved out of the area around Daryaganj in 1914, the lands that they vacated were simply transferred to the DMC for redevelopment. Pipal Park, another plot in the vicinity of the fort, was handed over to the DMC by military authorities in 1918 without payment, with only the rider that it could not be alienated.[9] These were all instances of transfers between state agencies in which the monetary value of land played little part in coordinating the pattern of development and utilization.

In 1925, however, the government decided to resume the *nazul* lands that they had handed over to the DMC in 1874.[10] This decision was prompted partly by the fact that, due to the acquisitions for constructing the capital city, the government found itself in possession of new lands, apart from those it had historically inherited from Mughal holdings that constituted the *nazul* estates. Consolidating all these would make for more convenient administration. The Chief Commissioner also argued that that the DMC had not managed the *nazul* estates optimally. More crucially, it was argued that the municipality had received a grant (the income from *nazul* properties) whose value the Government had no means of adequately assessing. While resuming control of the *nazul* lands on these grounds, the loss to the Municipal Committee was acknowledged through a compensatory grant for 'loss of income' for twelve years until 1937.

The 1925 resumption of *nazul* estates heralded a change in the administrative attitudes towards land values; the state would now keep much closer track of the economic worth of its holdings. Thus, the Deputy Commissioner produced an annual report on the 'Financial Results of the Delhi Improvement Schemes' every year from 1928 until the establishment of the Delhi Improvement Trust. The report briefly summarized improvements being carried out in the *nazul* lands and any sales that had been completed.[11]

[9] DDA, CC Records, Education, F no. 39, 1918. Pipal Park, named for a common tree, was site for many nationalist demonstrations and meetings in Delhi from the 1920s onward. As a consequence, it increasingly came to be referred to by a homonym: 'People's Park'.

[10] An account of the various exchanges on the question is summarized in *Report on the Relief of Congestion in Delhi*, vol. 1, pp. 8–10.

[11] DDA, CC Records, Education, F no. 15, 1928: DC to CC, 17 May 1928. Reports with the same format are available for each subsequent year.

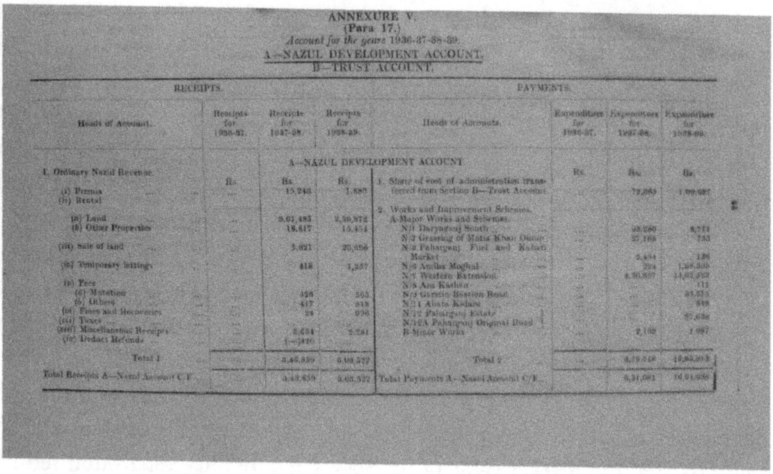

ANNEXURE V.
(Para 17.)
Account for the years 1936-37-38-39.
A—NAZUL DEVELOPMENT ACCOUNT.
B—TRUST ACCOUNT.

RECEIPTS.

Heads of Account.	Receipts for 1936-37.	Receipts for 1047-38.	Receipts for 1938-39.
A—NAZUL DEVELOPMENT ACCOUNT			
1. Ordinary Nazul Revenue	Rs.	Rs.	Rs.
(i) Premia	...	15,248	1,880
(ii) Rental			
(a) Land	...	3,01,485	2,30,872
(b) Other Properties	...	18,817	15,454
(iii) Sale of land	...	5,821	25,696
(iv) Temporary lettings	...	418	1,257
(v) Fees			
(a) Mutation	...	428	505
(b) Others	...	417	818
(vi) Fines and Recoveries	...	24	998
(vii) Taxes	...	...	...
(viii) Miscellaneous Receipts	...	8,634	2,281
(ix) Deduct Refunds	...	(—)420	...
Total 1	...	3,48,859	5,08,527
Total Receipts A—Nazul Account C/F	...	3,48,859	5,08,522

PAYMENTS.

Heads of Accounts.	Expenditure for 1936-37.	Expenditure for 1937-38.	Expenditure for 1938-39.
	Rs.	Rs.	Rs.
1. Share of cost of administration transferred from Section B—Trust Account	...	72,865	1,09,927
2. Works and Improvement Schemes.			
A-Major Works and Schemes.			
N/1 Daryaganj South	...	98,280	6,711
N/2 Grassing of Matia Khan Dump	...	27,168	753
N/3 Paharganj Fuel and Kabari Market	...	3,434	136
N/6 Andha Moghal	...	394	1,08,305
N/7 Western Extension	...	4,50,837	14,07,692
N/8 Ara Kashan	...	...	111
N/9 Garstin Bastion Road	...	...	33,513
N/11 Abata Kadara	...	...	518
N/12 Paharganj Estate / N/12A Paharganj Original Road	...	...	67,636
B-Minor Works	...	2,182	1,987
Total 2	...	[illegible]	[illegible]
Total Payments A—Nazul Account C/F	...	6,31,081	[illegible]

Figure 5.2. Nazul Development Account Statement, 1939.

The salient features of this were summarized in a table that compared expenditure and income on the seven schemes being carried out on *nazul* lands over the relevant period . Presentation in these terms—facilitating easy comparison of expenditure and income—came to be *de rigueur* for all improvement schemes, as was demonstrated by the even more elaborate accounts of the DIT for some of the same areas in the years following 1937 (Figure 5.2).[12] The mode of presentation of accounts prior to 1925 was quite different. In those accounts, there was no attempt to bring income and expenditure from a given improvement scheme onto the same page. Income from all *nazul* properties were clubbed together without highlighting the breakdown for individual schemes. Within expenditure, the utilization of special grants—for instance, the one grant-in-aid of the Garstin Bastion Road Scheme (on which more subsequently)—was separately enumerated without any mention of the income that had been derived from that scheme.[13] In short, the discussion around the transfer of *nazul* lands to the government redefined the improvement scheme as an enterprise whose profits had to be tangibly demonstrable.

12 *Administration Report of the Delhi Improvement Trust For Years 1937–1939* (1940) (New Delhi: Delhi Improvement Trust), pp. 44–55.

13 *Report on the Administration of the Delhi Municipality in the year 1920–21: General Administration* (1921) (Delhi: Municipal Press), pp. 10–25. The same format is followed in subsequent annual reports of the Delhi Muncipal Committee.

Ultimately, a newly created agency directly answerable to the central administration, the DIT, inherited the *nazul* lands in Delhi. The succeeding period was one of even more stringent accounting of transactions between different agencies. In 1938, when the NDMC wanted to construct residential quarters for the Lady Health Visitor they had appointed, the government informed the Chief Commissioner that while transfers to the NDMC had hitherto been conducted without charge, this was no longer to be the case.[14] Payment for such purposes would have to be made at the going market rate. In 1939 the NDMC asked for transfer of a plot at cost of acquisition—Rs. 200 per acre—in order to build a complex containing a Child Welfare Centre, a storekeeper's quarter, and a conservancy depot.[15] The response was that the portion of the plot required for the Child Welfare Centre would be transferred at Rs. 200 per acre, while the rest of the land would be transferred at the market value of Rs. 8000 per acre plus 5% ground rent.[16] The assumption seems to have been that if the NDMC was to receive rent from the storekeeper, the fact ought to be built into the transaction between the NDMC and the government, as it would between any buyer and seller.

Perhaps the clearest demonstration of the logic can be seen during the war. Land earmarked by the DIT to build housing for the poor was demanded by the Central Public Works Department (CPWD) to house the extra clerks required for wartime duties.[17] The need was understood to be temporary, and the land would revert to the DIT when the war ended. However, the CC advised the DIT to insert a stipulation that any buildings constructed by the CPWD would revert to the Trust after the war, without any charge.[18] The CPWD was adamant that such a free transfer was not a viable proposition. The DIT's subsequent negotiations with the CPWD concluded with the latter saying that on restoration of possession to the DIT, the CPWD could be paid at concessional pre-war rates.[19] The DIT remained concerned that this would not be a favourable transaction, and held that if they had to buy the buildings after the war, they must have some say about the specifications to which the buildings were built. This, the Trust explained, was necessary because CPWD was building to very low standards

14 DDA, CC Records, LSG/LB, F no. 1308, 1938, GoI Department of Education, Health and Lands to CC, 20 July 1938.

15 DDA, CC Records, LSG LB, F no. 3(37), 1939, CC to Secy to GoI EHL, 9 May 1939.

16 Ibid., Addnl Secy to GoI EHL to CC, 30 June 1939.

17 DDA, CC Records, LSG-DIT, F no. 1(58), 1944, Chairman DIT to CC, 26 January 1944.

18 Ibid., CC to Chairman DIT, 3 February 1944.

19 Ibid., Chairman DIT to CC, 28 August 1944.

and in some haste; retrofitting, and even demolition of these structures might be necessary. Consequently, the DIT must be compensated for any expenses incurred to convert the existing structures into poor class housing. Else 'the Trust may be saddled with an exceedingly bad bargain.'[20]

Two models of transfers between state agencies are in evidence here. By one model, the DIT and CPWD are both agencies of the state and are assumed to be coordinated by needs and principles that were not based on the value of property. This was the situation brought into being by the war. The irrelevance of monetary concerns was exactly what the DIT was pointing towards when they stated:

> The Trust has of course, done a service to the Government of India by readily supplying developed land at a time of emergency for Government purposes, without imposing the delay which would have ensued, if financial adjustments had been thrashed out in advance. But I doubt if the Government of India will agree that this consideration has any cash value [...][21]

It is revealing that such largesse in the matter of land transfers was thought of as a temporary consequence of heightened wartime needs, and that the suspension of economic valuation could hurt the DIT in the post-war period. This second model, where transfers of land within the state itself were made crucial markers of efficacy and efficiency, reflects the more intimate relationship between the state and the market.

Beginning in the mid-1920s, then, market transactions were steadily internalized within the operations of the state. This meant that changes in land prices, the buoyancy or depression of the property market, and other kinds of fluctuations were transmitted to the operations of the state as a matter of course. Even more significantly, they became a principle through which coordination of the efforts of various parts of the state could be effected. In many ways, this established limits to what the state could and couldn't achieve through agencies such as the DIT. Housing the poor, in particular, was an aim that could only sit uneasily with the growing need to manage property profitably. The ramified operation of the market within the state, then, served to generate certain kinds of state actions while delimiting others. Indeed, the determination and potential to generate profits out of urban development was an increasingly significant driver of state activity in Delhi.

[20] Ibid. [21] Ibid.

Attraction: Property Development by the State

I have previously alluded to the fact that the state was the largest landowner in the suburbs of Delhi. The lands seized after suppression of the rebellion of 1857 were augmented by the acquisitions carried out to build the new city after 1913. Despite sporadic efforts to develop *nazul* lands in a planned manner, most of the neighbourhoods that sprang up in the western suburbs (particularly those in Sadar Bazar and Paharganj) were developed by private owners. Beginning hesitantly in the mid-1920s and gathering pace from the mid-1930s, however, first the DMC and subsequently the DIT began to develop parts of these holdings in more systematic fashion.

Existing histories of the city have highlighted the ways in which the desire to turn a profit from these lands was an overriding consideration. Jyoti Hosagrahar, studying late nineteenth and early twentieth century extensions, concludes that 'improvement schemes that had initially been motivated by the abominable housing conditions, increasingly focused on facilitating commerce.'[22] Stephen Legg outlines the centrality of finance to the projects of the DIT in the 1930s. The DIT's pattern of urban development—the areas that were developed and the pace at which these were carried out—highlights the degree to which financial viability determined the efforts of the state. Therefore, even though housing for the poor, generalized insanitation, and congestion were the discursive tropes that led to the establishment of the DIT, an overwhelming number of the schemes that were actually realized were designed to generate a profit and, consequently, were directed towards the middle classes. Thus, the Daryaganj, Northern Extension, Roshanara Extension, and Karol Bagh schemes were carried out. while the Delhi–Ajmeri Gate Scheme and the schemes relating to the impoverished areas around Sadar Bazar and Paharganj remained a dead letter.[23]

The framing imperative to be financially profitable was supplemented by specific procedural aspects of the Trust's functioning. The use of auctions by the DIT has already been discussed, but from the 1940s, the DIT also came

[22] Jyoti Hosagrahar (2005), *Indigenous Modernities: Negotiating Architecture and Urbanism* (London: Routledge), p. 129.

[23] The report of the Delhi Improvement Trust Enquiry Committee, assessing the DIT's performance in 1951, stated that 'the policy of the Trust has not resulted even in a partial solution of the housing problem in Delhi' (p. 4), and elsewhere, that it had sold lands 'at huge profits after creating a monopoly, without any regard for the interest of the community or the object with which the Trust has been created' (p. 6): *Report of the Delhi Improvement Trust Enquiry Committee 1951*, vol. I (New Delhi: Government of India Press).

to rely on authorized sale agents to conduct its sales privately. An advertisement in *Hindustan Times* from 1942, for instance, announces that six firms had been appointed 'selling agents' for the year.[24] These firms, in turn, advertised the plots which they were authorised to sell in ways that were no different from any other private company.

The impulse to embrace the market to profit from state holdings was not restricted to the period of the DIT. Illustrative of the ways in which the diktats of the market could determine the nature and timing of state property development is the Garstin Bastion Road Scheme of the DMC. The GB Road scheme was modelled on the very successful development scheme along Burn Bastion Road (BB Road). The latter scheme, connecting Delhi railway station with the commercial suburbs just beyond the city walls, was one of the most spectacular successes of the DMC. The road, and plots laid out along it, had been constructed out of a special grant of Rs. 1.32 lakhs from the Government of India in 1913. The basic plan of the shops and godowns were specified by the President of the DMC.[25] By March 1935, the scheme as a whole had brought in a profit of Rs. 6.8 lakhs from initial sales and ongoing rent receipts.[26]

The GB Road scheme—running from Lahore Gate to Ajmere Gate—was sanctioned in 1916 with an even larger government grant of Rs. 2.5 lakhs. The unexpectedly large profit from the BB Road scheme was clearly the incentive to carry out this development, and GB Road was imagined as a similar commercial development. As has been discussed in Chapter 4, when the road was developed and plots finally laid out in 1919, the first lot of auctions fetched a promising amount. Subsequently, however, the general slump in the property market meant that no further sales were carried out until at least 1935.[27]

[24] The firms were Messrs Associated Traders, The Delhi Estate and Commercial Agencies, Messrs Shiv Charan Das and Sons, L. Nemi Chand Jain, Messrs Onkar Brothers, and Haji Mohammad Hasan. Two other firms—Messrs Madan and Co and Messrs Mohd. Ashfaq Mohd. Yaqub—are mentioned as having ceased to be agents of the Trust. *Hindustan Times*, 12 May 1942.

[25] For instance, TH, DMC Progs., BSC conf. at OM, 24 October 1916, progs. no. 18–22. A note informs that the Deputy Commissioner had personally approved the plans for building along Burn Bastion Road in ward 3. The personal intervention of the DC in sanctioning building applications was not common.

[26] *Report on the Relief of Congestion in Delhi*, p. 7.

[27] DDA, CC Records, Education, F no. 4(128), 1930, DC to CC, 20 November 1930. See the section entitled 'Auctions' in Chapter 4 for details about prices. Hume's report details a profit of Rs. 5,82,083 from the scheme, which corresponds almost exactly with the premia paid at the 1919 auction along with the ground rent at Rs. 2 per cent per annum. *Report on the Relief of Congestion in Delhi*, p. 8.

The next time that GB Road appears in the records is from an unexpected direction. From the 1920s, officials of the DMC had been determined to move women they termed 'prostitutes' away from the business areas around Hauz Qazi and Chawri Bazar, where they had resided for many decades. The earliest efforts to remove them can be dated to 1919, and it is only after considerable struggle and resistance in 1940 that DMC officials were able to report that 'Chawri Bazar, the stronghold of prostitutes for a considerable length of time, is after all free from them.'[28]

Various strategies of resistance were adopted by the women over the course of these two decades. Some defended themselves on the basis that they could not be moved out of houses that they owned—property ownership becoming a claim mobilized (unsuccessfully) against the DMC's assertion of public interest.[29] A more substantial obstacle to the removal efforts was a Lahore High Court judgement from the mid-1920s that forced the DMC to demonstrate in each case that the women they were evicting were 'public prostitutes' and not attached to a particular person.[30]

For their own part, the DMC opted to pursue the matter through aggressive prosecution of the women as well as their landlords.[31] In the proceedings on the matter, one of the key points of contention (for members of the Municipal Committee as well as the women themselves) was their proximity to the city. Most officials were inclined to move them out to the suburbs, and this was the ultimate destination for many of the women who took up premises in Tanda Natniyan in Sadar Bazar. However, a large number of sex workers also began to take up residence in the houses that had been built along GB road.[32] With its situation on the outskirts of the city and yet within the walls, not far from the New Delhi railway station or the Chawri Bazar-Hauz Qazi area, GB road emerged as a convenient via media—

[28] Particular note should be made of the military metaphor employed here. DDA, CC Records, Home, F no. 70, 1919, DMC resolution of 28 January 1919. The file reveals that the efforts of Christian organisations—the YMCA and SPG Mission—were particularly prominent in this regard. *Report on the Administration of the Delhi Municipality for the Year 1940–41, Vol. I: General Administration*, (Delhi: Municipal Press), p. 10.

[29] *Report on the Administration of the Delhi Municipality in the Year 1924–25, Vol. I: General Administration* (Delhi: Municipal Press), p. 9. These are among the few women who consistently appear in the records as property owners. It is also striking that in these instances they are identified as daughters of women, rather than men, indicating that they inherited their holdings from women.

[30] Moti Jan v. Municipal Committee Delhi *AIR* 1926 Lah. 461.

[31] TH, DMC Progs, OM, 20 July 1927, prog. 6, OM, 27 July 1927, progs. 4 and 5, OM, 14 September 1927, and many others. In a clear majority of cases the women were renting premises rather than owning them.

[32] *Report on the Administration of the Delhi Municipality for the Year 1940–41*, vol. I., p. 10.

neither too close to, nor too far from, the heart of the city.[33] The fact that GB Road could provide an affordable space near enough to the city, however, is at least in part traceable to the downturn in the property market which created devalued housing on a thoroughfare originally developed for a different purpose.

The various incarnations of GB road are indicative of the ways in which the property market could shape the manner and chronology of urban development by the state. The idea of developing GB road was an outcome of the DMC's search for a profitable avenue of urban development. Its failure—with only a third of plots being sold for almost two decades after it was created—was not an outcome of any inherent shortcomings in the layout. Rather, the generalized downturn in property values—related to other aspects of Delhi's economy—set sharp limits to the success of the scheme. In turn, the failure to generate profits on the scale expected opened up the possibility of the space being utilized in ways quite different from what was initially planned. The internalization of market-based valuations, then, also meant that state agencies viewed the property market as a way to generate revenues. This embrace of the market shaped the history of each housing or commercial layout of state agencies during this period.

Symbiosis: House, Neighbourhood, and the State

The separation of the public realm from the private is often seen as the *sine qua non* of modernity. In the colonial context, Partha Chatterjee's mapping of this distinction onto the inner and outer domains of the colonized subject has proved one of the most influential reformulations of the public/private divide during the colonial period.[34] For Chatterjee, the inner domain of spirituality, culture, and tradition was construed as one over which the colonized (male) subject could exercise control while the outer was the domain of materialism, technology, and subjugation. At a crucial point in his argument, Chatterjee suggests that the physical premises of the home was one of the points at which the separation of social space between the

[33] GB Road has continued to be the red-light district in Delhi—this despite periodic efforts disperse sex-workers. Perhaps the first attempt to clear GB Road was in 1944 when questions were raised in the Legislative Assembly about why 'the residences of immoral women' were not being removed from Garstin Bastion Road. DDA, DC Records, F. no. 15, 1944.

[34] Partha Chatterjee (1993), *The Nation and Its Fragments: Colonial and Postcolonial Histories* (Princeton, NJ: Princeton University Press).

colonizer and colonized was achieved.[35] There have since been a number of critiques of Chatterjee's idea that the separation of inner and outer domains was rigid. Swati Chattopadhyay, for instance, makes the case that inner and outer domains were subject to constant renegotiation. Rather than being stably defined, spaces understood as inner or outer, private or public, could change depending on the power dynamics between individuals moving through them.[36] In this section I take a cue from Chattopadhyay in approaching the relationship between the public and private in material terms. I argue that over the course of the twentieth century the intimate 'inner' domain of the house was made dependent on a relationship with the 'outer', technological, state-controlled domain, to the point even where this dependence itself could be taken for granted.

One index of the intertwining of the house and the state over the twentieth century is the trajectory of building bye-laws. The story of building bye-laws in Delhi is one of gradual imposition. A cursory requirement that the DMC would have to be intimated about intention to build had existed on the statute books throughout the late nineteenth century. It was, however, only in the early twentieth century, in the context of disputes with the army, that this intention to build needed to be accompanied by any set of plans.[37] Furthermore, only in 1914, with the pressure of living up to the designation of 'capital city', was a set of building bye-laws of any significance formulated. Only the symbolic burden of appearing as a capital city ought to, it would appear, coaxed Delhi's municipal commissioners into restricting building activity.[38]

Building bye-laws in Delhi were shaped by the confrontation between the sense that, on one hand, owners were likely to construct any kind of room to turn the smallest profit from rent, and on the other, that the state, by trying to regulate construction, was encroaching on the ability of landlords to build freely. One form that this confrontation took was the steady violation of bye-laws, mentioned in previously.[39] If permission were

[35] Partha Chatterjee (1993), *The Nation and Its Fragments: Colonial and Postcolonial Histories* (Princeton, NJ: Princeton University Press), p. 120.

[36] Swati Chattopadhyay (1993), *Representing Calcutta: Modernity, Nationalism and the Colonial Uncanny* (London: Routledge), p. 270.

[37] Anish Vanaik (2008), 'Changing the Plot: Property Relations in Delhi 1857–1920', (Jawaharlal Nehru University), p. 133–7.

[38] Colonel H. C. Beadon, then DC and Chairman of DMC, summarized the difficulties of getting this done in his address to the Executive and Finance Sub-Committee. TH, DMC Progs, E&FSC, 16 April 1913.

[39] See the section titled Coercion, Corruption and Power in Chapter 3.

not forthcoming, owners would nevertheless try to build, and hope that they would be subjected to only a mild fine. But within the DMC itself, municipal commissioners regularly tried to alter stipulations that they felt were restrictive. This was the case, for instance, with respect to courtyards within houses. The Junior Vice President contended in 1919 that Rule 27, which stipulated the acceptable size of courtyard in a given size of house, was only applicable to structures with rooms which were abutting the street, and should not apply otherwise.[40] Most buildings ought, therefore, to be exempt from the rule. The President of the DMC, however, argued that the rule applied to every courtyard:

> When courtyards were left inside houses they should be of a reasonable and healthy size. There is no obligation on anyone to leave a courtyard at all but the rule merely lays down that if people build houses with courtyards the minimum size of those courtyards is fixed. The rule is framed in the interest of the health of the *private residents* of the houses concerned.[41]

While considering building violations in 1929, however, the demand to clarify the definition of courtyard in Rule 27 was raised once again. The municipal secretary claimed that rules about sanitary courtyards were routinely violated with little consequence and should therefore be more clearly defined and stringently enforced.[42] These and other disputes over courtyards repeatedly arose in the face of landlords who were 'concerned with [their] rent only. It is immaterial to [them] if the house is a standing menace to the health of the inmates. One occupier will be replaced by another . . . '[43]

Challenges to the building bye-laws in the municipality were raised as a consequence of a robust notion of private property—a notion that jealously guarded the right of builders to construct as they felt fit, and, closely linked, determined that regulation be concerned with public spaces and not impinge on private space within the house. Counterposed to this idea of private property were two key discourses from within the state: public space and public purpose.

[40] Junior Vice Presidents of DMC were senior municipal commissioners and therefore members (either Hindu or Muslim) of the local elite. The President of the committee was an official: the DC.

[41] TH, DMC Progs, OM, 11 November 1919. Emphasis in original.

[42] 'At every meeting there are 2 or 3 cases in which the courtyard rule is set at naught . . . ' TH, DMC Progs, SM, prog. No. 2, 12 February 1929.

[43] TH, DMC Progs, SM, prog. No. 2, 12 February 1929.

The disputations over private projections on public streets (another repeatedly refined part of the bye-laws) generated the idea of of public space as analogous to ownership. The state owned the land of the street and, as in the case of any private owner, building upon it constituted an encroachment. The idea of public purpose was slightly different and can be traced in the rationale for sanitary houses with enough air circulating through them. Restriction on private construction here was construed as stemming from some general public good. Bye-laws regulating the height of buildings, for instance, spanned both ideas. These were justified on the grounds that light would be blocked from the public street. This would directly impact public property—the street—but also the health of those using the street. Skirmishes about building bye-laws cropped up regularly in the DMC, because it proved impossible to stably triangulate ideas of public space, public purpose, and private property.

The intertwining of public purpose, public ownership, and private ownership in the building bye-laws outlines the complicated ways in which the public did not begin at the door of the house. Internal elements of house construction, as well as its external impact, were brought within the purview of state intervention. Existing historiography has traced the intrusiveness of the state into the private domain (especially that of the poor) through deployment of the discourse of sanitation; for instance, as a result of plague measures.[44] Public purpose could also, on occasion, be mobilized to achieve private ends, as in the case of owners who tried to have indigent tenants evicted through sanitary statutes.[45]

Another way of linking public and private space over this period was, revealingly, far less contentious than building bye-laws. The first half of the twentieth century saw the creation of three kinds of flow which connected private and public space: drainage, water, and electricity. The history of the installation of these utilities is not my primary concern.[46] Instead I want to highlight the peculiar rapidity with which these came to be taken for granted as part of the structure of the private house.

[44] Rajnarayan Chandavarkar (1998), *Imperial Power and Popular Politics: Class, Resistance and the State in India, c.1850–1950* (Cambridge: Cambridge University Press).

[45] See Chapter 3 on housing the poor.

[46] Narayani Gupta discusses the troubled history of the intramural drainage scheme and also discusses the provision of water. Electricity was initially introduced in Delhi for the Durbar of 1902. Narayani Gupta (1981), *Delhi between Two Empires, 1803–1931: Society, Government and Urban Growth* (Delhi: Oxford University Press).

Advertisements in the *Hindustan Times*, from 1925 onwards, often allude to the presence of electric and sanitary fittings.[47] Electricity, sewage connections, and water supply were seen as important in advertisements for all parts of the city—New Delhi, Old Delhi (all parts), the suburbs, and the Civil Lines. The epithet 'modern' was often used in conjunction with these elements. The brochure of the Prudential Housing Corporation, under the section cheerily titled 'what the P. H. C. Can Do for You', outlined the following:

1. It can build you an ideal home [...]
2. It can build modern hygienic, sanitary, and up-to-date houses [...]
3. It can provide a building plot for you.
4. It will provide and fit modern furniture, sanitary and electrical fittings [...][48]

The 1940 advertisement for the Housing and General Finance Company also mentioned that its 'modern bungalow homes' had electricity, metalled roads, and a regular bus service. Brij Kishen Chandiwala's recollections from the early twentieth century suggest that even in more traditional houses in the old city these amenities were steadily becoming part of the structure of the house. He recounts, about the family house in Katra Khushhal Rai, that when the family first moved into the house in 1902 there were no taps, 'but taps were installed in the house at a time before my memory stretches.'[49]

The most striking evidence for the sense that the private house and public utilities were coming to be seen as the norm for a certain kind of existence, however, comes from the locality of Karol Bagh. Karol Bagh was initially earmarked for leatherworkers, but through the mid-1920s was redeveloped for clerks and government functionaries. Bishambar Prasad Gaur, the Honorary Secretary of the Karol Bagh Improvement Association, wrote to the Chief Commissioner of Delhi in 1935 outlining a history of the neighbourhood and the ad hoc nature of the installed utilities: 'On representations being made by the residents of this locality from time to time the Municipal

[47] For a representative sample, see advertisements of houses to let on the following dates: 18 September 1925, 5 May 1926, 1 January 1930, 4 October 1932, 27 March 1935, 3 July 1936, 30 April 1941, 5 February 1942, and others.

[48] DDA, CC Records, LSG-LB, F. no. 1432, 1938: Brochure of the Prudential Housing Corporation New Delhi.

[49] NMML, Manuscript Section, Individual collections, B. K. Chandiwala, Instalment II–III Subject Files, F no. 6, p. 24. Chandiwala was born in 1900.

Committee provided roads water supply and electricity'.[50] They highlighted, however, that a drainage scheme had not been provided. Part of the reason for the delay in this regard was that the *nazul* department and the DMC were blaming each other for not carrying out the necessary works. A year and a half later, the Association sent another summary of the continuing inadequacies of the locality.

> This area is devoid of any drainage system. The lanes are all Kacha and unlevelled and there is no lighting arrangement in the street. 'Khatta' where all the refuse of the City is dumped is too near the residential houses.[51]

There is in this correspondence an implicit ideal of the interdependent relationship between house, neighbourhood, and state required to conduct a respectable urban existence. Along with the individual house, then, the neighbourhood was also reconfigured through these emergent complementarities between public and private. This was not, however, a symbiosis generated spontaneously on the basis of a steady notion of modern progress. Many aspects of this complementarity had to be painstakingly created.

Historian Vijay Prashad has described the DMC's efforts, from the 1870s, to snap the relationship between sweepers and *mohallas* (neighbourhoods). 'From being part of the mohalla's fabric (although living outside it), the sweepers slowly became municipal employees with little direct link to the families in the homes along their routes'.[52] Even in the early twentieth century, however, a number of neighbourhoods could assert the right to determine how drains were constructed. The residents of Kucha Ram Rau, for instance, had open drains laid before the municipality could do so, and accompanied the action with a claim to ownership of the *Kucha* (*lit.* street). The ward member disputed this claim to ownership:

> *Kucha* is not the property of the owners of the houses situated in that '*kucha*'. There are many houses in that *kucha* and they are owned by different persons; the *kucha* should therefore be considered the property of the committee. The inhabitants' action of building drains and

[50] DDA, CC Records, Education, F no. 4(95), 1935, 'Letter from Hony Secy Karol Bagh Improvement Association to CC', 28 March 1935.

[51] DDA, CC Records, CC Records, Education, F no. 4(55), 1936, 'Letter from Hony Secy Karol Bagh Improvement Association to CC', 28 September 1936.

[52] Vijay Prashad (2000), *Untouchable Freedom: A Social History of a Dalit Community* (Oxford: Oxford University Press), p. 8.

steps to their houses without obtaining the Committee's permission is not justifiable.[53]

In this instance, the Building Sub-Committee demanded a declaration by residents that 'they will not regard the drains as their property.' If such an agreement were not forthcoming, the drains were to be demolished.

Kuchabandi (*lit.* closed street) sparked another controversy which reflected the tussle between neighbourhoods and the state. It was a long-standing practice by which neighbourhoods would install doors and gates at their various entrances, thereby determining the flow of people through the area. The DMC had an enduring conflict with these efforts to restrict movement on the grounds that this represented a claim analogous to ownership which could not be maintained on public land. In the mid-1920s, when the issue of *kuchabandis* exercised the members of the DMC, two kinds of justification were offered by various members defending gates.[54] One line of justification relied on the antiquity of the practice and structures in question. A second, much more commonly deployed in the 1920s, cited concerns about safety during riots. Indeed, a number of votes on this issue in the Municipal Committee broke along communal lines; when gates of Hindu localities were in question they were defended by Hindu members of the Municipal Committee, and those in Muslim localities by Muslim municipal commissioners. For colonial officials—whose opinion was the driving force behind the removal of gates and who held the balance of votes in the municipality—*kuchabandi* represented 'a permanent menace'[55] or 'signs of mistrust [between communities]'.[56] In a broader view, however, the events of the 1920s represented a particular inflection of a longstanding set of confrontations between the state and neighbourhood-based control of space. All this goes to show that the ideal of complementarity between the state and the house and neighbourhood did not slide smoothly into place in Delhi. The new complementarities represented a real break with older modes of urban living. The disappearance of that older conception of the neighbourhood and common space was effected through

[53] TH, DMC Progs, OM, 23 December 1907.

[54] See the following articles in *Hindustan Times*: 'Kucha-Bandis in Delhi', 24 December 1924; 'Kuchabandi in Delhi', 11 September 1925; 'Kucha Bandi Again', 29 January 1926; 'Juma Masjid: Removal of Street Gates', 30 June 1927; 'Delhi Kucha Bandis', 2 October 1927; 'Kucha Bandi Affair', 11 November 1927.

[55] *HT*,'Kucha Bandi Again', 29 January 1926.

[56] *HT*,'Kucha-Bandis in Delhi', 24 Deember 1924.

determined action of a variety of state agencies, often in the face of opposition by many communities.

In light of what we have seen of the relationship between state and *mohalla* it is possible to appreciate the novelty of a set of petitions from the mid-1920s onwards. These were collective appeals by owners of houses in various neighbourhoods that their lanes be taken over by the DMC to ensure sanitation. While the earliest of these appeals dates to the mid-1920s, they seem to have become more common in the mid-1930s.[57] In each instance the rationale was that the DMC could provide superior drainage and sanitation. The appeals of the middle-class residents of Karol Bagh that they be provided with 'modern' amenities represents a broader shift in conceptions of the relationship between the state and private property.

Within the state, at around the same time, there arose a question about whether the benefits of the increase in value of property that occurred as a result of provision of public amenities ought to be reaped entirely by the owners. The Taxation Enquiry Committee of 1924–25, keen to explore ways of enhancing revenues from cities, explicitly touched on this issue under the title 'unearned increment'. The idea referred to the fact that property values could rise even without any actual efforts by owners at improving land.[58] An allied term, concentrating on increases in value due to public amenities, was 'special assessments'.[59] The suggestion of the Enquiry Committee that levies be imposed on both these counts was taken up for debate and rejected by the DMC.[60] Particularly for the second of these forms of taxation, the (somewhat convoluted) argument raised by municipal commissioners was that improvements for poorer quarters would not be possible if they were made contingent on special payments, and 'special assessment made even in rich quarters to improve their surroundings would be considered a real hardship and would [...] be opposed by a majority.'[61] This reluctance of municipal commissioners to claim a share of the value accruing to private lands through public improvements is of a piece with their reluctance to enact

[57] For examples, see the following municipal proceedings: E&F SC, 13 June 1925, prog. No. 6; E&F SC, 3 August 1925, prog. no. 8; SSC conf. at OM, 10 July 1929, prog. No. 2; Sany SC conf. at OM, 24 July 1929, prog. No. 3; SSC conf. at OM, 3 August 1933, prog no. 12; E&FSC conf. at OM, 27 June 1935, prog. no. 20.

[58] *Report of the Indian Taxation Enquiry Committee, 1924–25*, vol. 1 (1926) (Madras: Government of India, Central Publication Branch), pp. 96–7.

[59] 'Special assessments... are essentially taxes on unearned increment, although the term 'unearned' is applied in a more restricted sense [...]'; *Report of the Indian Taxation Enquiry Committee*, p. 315.

[60] TH, DMC Progs., OM of 23 February 1927, prog. no. 3.

[61] Ibid.

restrictive building bye-laws and represents the difficulty of triangulating public purpose, public ownership, and private ownership.

In Delhi, neither the traditional house nor the *mohalla* within which it was situated, had been criss-crossed by public property on any substantial scale prior to the twentieth century. When an effort to do so was initiated in the twentieth century, despite a number of conflicts, a complementarity between the two was assembled. The modern city, then, cannot be seen as one in which the public and the private were severed. In fact, more characteristic was the manner in which the public within the intimate sphere—the presence of water, drains, and electricity—could enter the unthought-of 'modern' urban resident. As we have seen in the classifieds from this period, these were also quickly incorporated within the property market. The monetization of these utilities—initially as characteristics of a few houses and, over time, as elements that were expected in all 'modern' houses—moulded the qualitative aspect of the relationship between the state and the private citizen as well as between the state and the private property market. The inner and outer, the state and the private, were not simply opposites of each other in the modern city. They were, already in the colonial period, in a symbiotic relationship.

It is, however, crucial to take note of an asymmetry here. The houses and neighbourhoods described in this trajectory of interdependence of the private realm and the state were those of the middle classes and elites. The *chappars* and *katras* of the poor were increasingly defined precisely by the lack of this complementarity. For them, the state most commonly presented itself—as during sanitary inspections—in the form of a coercive force. It was precisely the notions of public purpose and public ownership, discussed previously as setting up the intimacy of the state with the houses of the middle classes, that could be (and were) turned against the poor.

Nightmare: Property Development Beyond the State

The fourth kind of relationship between state and market was far less harmonious. Discordant notes in the relationship between the state and market appeared most consistently in situations of land acquisition. There was, however, a lot of acquisition going around, but the prices of land meant that any process of acquiring land which at the same time sought to be fastidious about adequately recompensing landowners would be mired in disputes and alternative valuations. At times, the property market could effectively nullify aims that the state was keen to pursue. Blocked developments and transformed goals meant that the property market could take on the character of a nightmare for the colonial state.

With the announcement of the shift of capital to Delhi, land acquisition was conducted on a vast scale. For the most part, however, it was village lands—cultivated and uncultivated—that were earmarked for acquisition. With the exception of Paharganj, a minor portion of acquisition for New Delhi consisted of residential land and buildings. The DC of Delhi, while conducting the acquisitions, elaborated the need to make careful distinctions between lands which fronted on markets and those in more secluded bye-ways.[62] There seems, however, to have been little concern during these acquisitions about speculation pushing up the prices of land. In contrast, in the next period of large-scale acquisition (associated with the establishment of the DIT in 1937), fear of speculation driving up the cost of acquisition was pervasive.

As Hume put the matter in his confidential note: 'It is now clear that the work of the Delhi Improvement Trust will be largely vitiated unless control is secured over areas in which sporadic development has begun or is known to be contemplated.'[63] Hume often spoke in terms that viewed the DIT as mired in a swamp of speculative property trading.[64] This sense was probably not unwarranted. We have seen that Delhi in the mid-1930s saw a boom in the property market and that property was viewed as one of the few profitable arenas in which to invest. Commercial speculation was precisely what was on the CC's mind when he urged that swift sanction be accorded to the early acquisitions for the Roshanara Extension Scheme in 1939. These would, he hoped, be 'part of a protective "ring" of Trust operations'. The completion of this 'ring' was urgent, as 'private development has already begun [. . .] and unless strict control is established the outskirts of Delhi will be irretrievably ruined.'[65]

The metaphor of protection that can be found in so many discussions of acquisition, however, spawned a decidedly ambivalent vocabulary—one that pitted competing visions of the relationship between the state and the market against each other. Thus, on one hand, protection against 'unfair speculation' was crucial, particularly if the state was to provide subsidized

[62] DDA, DC Records, F no. 30, 1912. The difference between the valuations offered is very high: Rs. 40 per acre for grazing lands near the city, compared to an estimated Rs. 10,000 per acre for lands in Paharganj.

[63] DDA, CC Confidential Records, Education, F no. 4, 1937, Chairman DIT to Financial Adviser to CC, 8 April 1937.

[64] See, for instance, DDA, CC Records, LSG-LB, F no. 1289, 1938, note from A. P. Hume to CC, 8 February 1939.

[65] DDA, CC Records, LSG-LB, F no. 1(44), 1939, CC to Secy. to GoI, Dept of EHL, 30 March 1939.

housing for the poor.[66] On the other hand, the state itself was a protector of private property, committed to being bound by the real market value of property and to ensure that owners of lands were not undercompensated.

An revealing instantiation of the confusions generated by this structural issue can be found in one of the earliest instances of acquisition proceedings by the DIT. A scheme for the Andha Mughal area had been considered even before the DIT had been formally established, and notification of intention to acquire lands under the Land Acquisition Act of 1894 had been issued in April 1936. The DIT, which took over the scheme and acquired land under an Act with different provisions, issued a new notification in June 1937. Munshi Ram, the owner of 1.55 acres of garden land in the area, had, even before the April 1936 notification, cleared the trees and sold three plots of his erstwhile garden land as building sites. He went on to sell another twenty-eight plots before the June 1937 notification under Trust Law. By the time the award was actually granted, two houses had appeared on the land, and foundations had been laid for six other buildings—a fairly typical instance of private property development in the city's suburbs.

Om Prakash, the officer in charge of the land acquisition awards, announced, however, that compensation for Munshi Ram's lands would be based on the 'market value' of the plot in April 1936. Furthermore, since acquisition was proceeding on the basis of the DIT Act, 'market value' was to be calculated based on the use to which the property was being put at the time of notification. Since no construction had taken place on the land by April 1936, Munshi Ram and those to whom he had sold the plots would be compensated at the rate for garden land. Elaborating on the principles he had followed, Prakash stated that 'It is [. . .] not possible for the purposes of this Act to take into account any potential value of the land.'[67] He cited, at length, a judgement of the Allahabad High Court in support of this contention.

The CC, stating that these were the first examples of acquisition under Trust Law, took note of its variance from the Land Acquisition Act. Uniquely, under Trust Law, 'market value' had been expressly defined as 'the market value according to the use to which the land was put at the date with reference

[66] DDA, CC records, LSG-LB, F no. 1289, 1938, noting of Mohammed Sulaiman, 4 Octeober 1938.

[67] This understanding of 'market value' was based on a full bench ruling of the Allahabad High Court. It should be noted that the DIT used the stipulations of the UP Town Improvement Act. The acquisition stipulations of this Act were different from those of others, including the Land Acquisition Act of 1894. Hence also the salience of the Allahabad High Court judgement. DDA, CC records, LSG-LB, F no. 1289, 1938, Acquisition of land for the execution of the Andha Mughal Town Expansion Scheme.

to which the market value is to be determined.'[68] The CC went on to state that Munshi Ram's case demonstrated the absurdity of a 'rigid interpretation' of market value. Whether built up or not, the plot was no longer garden land in April 1936: Munshi Ram had provided clear indications that he was about to develop it as a built-up plot, and this was the basis on which people had bought the plots. In this case, awarding compensation at rates for garden lands was bound to result in unfair awards. This distinguished the CC from Hume, who took the view that it was imperative that the DIT acquire land on the most favourable terms possible. The CC averred:

> It is absurd that Government or any other authority should have the power to acquire a man's land without paying him the approximate price which he could obtain for it at a fair sale.[69]

The financial adviser to the CC concurred with the CC's assessment that recent sales were the best possible guide.[70] He pointed out that most Town Improvement Acts had 'deliberately omitted' a definition of the market value, leaving it to the collector and court to decide on a fair value. The DIT definition was a device for 'Trusts to acquire land at the outskirts of the towns at less than its true market value.' He pointed to the ambiguous nature of suburban land: 'Garden, agricultural, and even building land values on the outskirts of a rapidly developing town are constantly in a state of flux with a steady tendency towards increase.' As a result, income from land (as rent or marketing of produce) often lagged behind its capital value, which had a component that was sensitive to 'probable appreciation in future'. Compensation that was based on the net income from land—for example, aggregation of rent for a certain number of years—or its use at the time of notification, was bound to be unfair. He argued that only recent values of sales price ought to be taken into consideration for acquisition awards. Prices offered in 1925 and 1927, for instance, were no guide to prices in 1937. Realistically, he went on to suggest, a certain degree of unfairness was inevitable in any acquisition proceeding. The outcome in the case of Munshi Ram and the people who had bought land from him, however, had to be avoided.

On the question of what might be the best way to avoid such a course in the future, once again the administration was split. Another official, Khan

[68] DDA, CC records, LSG-LB, F no. 1289, 1938, confidential noting of CC, 25 July 1938.
[69] Ibid.
[70] Ibid., unofficial note of Financial Adviser to CC, 1 August 1938.

Bahadur Mohammed Sulaiman, strongly argued that acquisition law must be altered by suitably changing the definition of market value. Specifying a definition of market value removed the discretion of local officials who were best placed to judge such matters. The CC, declaring that 'I will be no party to expropriation', was prepared to countenance such an amendement to the law itself.[71] Opposed to them were the financial adviser and Chairman of the DIT, A. P. Hume.[72] They all argued that Trust Law must not be changed, and that fair practice and interpretation was all that was really needed. Awards should be based on recent transactions, acquisition as rapidly as possible after notification (so that property values do not change in the interim), and wide publicity of notification to prevent unwary purchases. On Hume's account, the actions in the case of Munshi Ram were simply an outcome of an overzealous interpretation.[73] A more correct interpretation would have arrived at a more liberal view of these cases. Hume, however, ended on a note which suggested that his inclination was just the opposite, stating that 'in the state of speculation which is rife in areas not yet fully protected by the Trust that the ruling [by the Allahabad Court] will yet be very useful.'

The serial vacillations in this case are in themselves revealing. More or less everyone seemed to agree that mistakes had been committed by the acquisition officer. Considerable nervousness about what was the best way of assessing land on the outskirts of the city ensued. At stake were two conflicting requirements: the need to appear fair in property acquisition had to be balanced against the need of the Improvement Trust to acquire land as cheaply as possible. This same basic conflict prompted a range of institutional arrangements over the rest of the DIT's period of functioning.[74]

The core of the issue, however, was the interface between the state and the market: ought the state be seen as protecting private property ownership and supporting 'market value' (recall the CC's reproach about expropriation)

[71] Ibid., unofficial note of CC, 8 August 1938, and Mohd. Sulaiman 4 October 1938.

[72] Ibid., unofficial note of Financial Adviser to CC, 1 August 1938; A. P. Hume, 8 February 1939.

[73] Whether the zealotry stemmed from Hume or Om Prakash is an open question, as Hume points out that he had 'brought the [Allahabad High Court] ruling to Om Prakash's notice fairly forcibly from time to time'. Ibid. A. P. Hume, 8 February 1939.

[74] Rather than acquiring outright, it soon became routine for the DIT to offer owners the choice of paying the costs of redevelopment and acquiring an adjusted plot of land in the new layout. An early instance of this practice was pioneered by the Municipal Committee in 1934. DDA, CC Records, Education, F no. 4(168), 1934, Resolution 24 of OM of DMC on 23 May 1934. For DIT, see for instance DDA, CC Records, LSG-DIT, F no. 1(46), 1942, Chairman DIT to CC, 17 March 1943.

or, alternatively, did the state need 'protection' against speculation? The incoherence on display in this set of proceedings is illustrative of why that interface could be seen as a kind of nightmare of antagonism. At one level this was an antagonism because of market values making state projects unviable. In a deeper sense, however, this was merely a manifestation of mutually irreconcilable impulses within the state: simultaneously, support for the property market, acting within it to turn a profit on its own holdings, and acting against it in the name of public purpose.

Conclusion

An assessment of the relationship between the state and the property market must begin from the acknowledgement that over the twentieth century the relationship between the state and the market was deepened. State lands were often treated in much the same way as a private owner might: different branches of the state exchanged property with each other on the basis of property value, and lands were developed with an eye on profit and loss. Even the more antagonistic expression of the relationship between the state and the property market derived ultimately from the state's pursuit of two conflicting ways of supporting the market. Whether in the register of ingestion, attraction, symbiosis, or nightmare, the dinner date of the colonial state and the property market was well and truly on, over the twentieth century.

An expanded class basis for the actions of the state in the city was also established in this period. Compared to the relatively narrow set of elites courted in the nineteenth century, the state was supportive of a larger swathe of the city's property-owning population. Public flows—water, drainage, and electricity—were quickly incorporated into the middle-class private sphere. Indeed, in Delhi, the increase in property values that derived from the addition of these amenities was smoothly assigned to landlords, without 'unearned increments' or 'special assessments' really being considered. The DMC commissioners were particularly receptive to the freedom of local landlords to build for profit, tempered only by the occasional efforts of colonial officials to rein in the worst excesses. By the late 1920s and early 1930s it also became common to find demands being made upon the DMC (and usually being favourably received) to provide amenities to houses and *mohallas* around the city. In contrast, the *bastis* and *katras* of the poor were defined by the lack of these kinds of complementarities with the state.

Indeed, notions of public ownership and public purpose could each be mobilized by the state (and at times local elites) against the poor.[75]

What can be said about what we have been tracking concerning the relative power of the state and property market in creating the built environment? Here, stock needs to be taken of tendencies that cut in either direction. On the one hand the state was, undeniably the largest property holder in the city. In addition, both at the beginning and the end of the period, large amounts of property were actively acquired and made urban by the state. With such a preponderant position within the market it is possible to envisage a role whereby the state's action came to determine the contours of the property market.

On the other hand, the fact that the state in Delhi was fragmented must also be considered, as must the curtailed budgets of the DMC and the imperative to meticulously tally profit and loss. A spectrum can be imagined, at one end of which would be the ways in which New Delhi was administered, with the DMC at the other. While private property and the market operated in both parts of the city, the differing pressures on, and capacities of, the various state agencies shaped very different cityscapes. The planned centralized vision and symbolic importance of New Delhi was enforced through strict building codes and tightly controlled rents. In most other parts of Delhi—intramural, extramural, and the newly developed DIT areas—the necessity to turn a profit, the influence of the propertied on the structures of governance, and the restrictions on administrative expenditure—all shaped a greater orientation towards profit and the market. Particularly illustrative of this is the fact that the slump of the 1920s and rise in the 1930s had such determinate effects on the properties of the state in suburban and Old Delhi. Both the depression and the recovery were outcomes of changes in the local economy, and not a result of the fiat of the state. It is, of course, well known that there was less planned development in Old Delhi than in New Delhi. What is being suggested here, however, is that the lack of planning was an outcome not of mere neglect on the part of the colonial state. The prominence of private development in the older parts of Delhi, rather, was the product of the complex relationship between the economy, local elites, and the colonial state that emerged over the twentieth century.

[75] This, I would suggest, is also the reason why a Foucauldian account of the governmentalization of the state and the steady extension of power over the body remains a partial one. The gainers and promoters of these changes are far more identifiable and active than a strictly non-agential Foucauldian account would allow.

6
Lineages of the Housing Question

> ... when money is available for parks, gardens, roads, and a hundred other things, it is incomprehensible that it should not be available for so urgent a purpose as providing habitable surroundings and houses for Harijans ...
>
> *Hindustan Times*, editorial, 29 April 1937

> The slums are appalling, conditions of life under crowding of 265 persons per acre (and in some parts at 18 sq yds per person) are not ideal and my mission at the next Simla visit will be to explain that fiddling about with a few open plots of land in Delhi will not solve the problem.
>
> -A. P. Hume, 6 September 1935[1]

The demographic transformations of the Industrial Revolution spawned both slums and urban reform in the large cities of Western Europe. Reformers decried the pitiful state of slum housing, condemned rack-renting landlords, and devised schemes to temper the effects of an individualized and unregulated housing market. Over the course of the nineteenth century, cities across Europe saw the emergence of the so-called housing question—an effort by industrialists and reformers to grapple with (what they identified as) the worst excesses of an industrializing modernity.

Friedrich Engels, Karl Marx's intellectual collaborator, was among the people whose response to the great concentrations of labour in European cities was to analyse working-class housing.[2] His take on the housing question, however, was far less complimentary.[3] His polemic against the bourgeoning urban reform movements made three points. First, that the bourgeoisie and reformist socialists loved talking about the housing question, and they

[1] BL, A. P. Hume, Letter to Parents, MSS Eur D724/7.

[2] Friedrich Engels (1972), *The Condition of the Working Class in England: From Personal Observation and Authentic Sources* (London: Panther).

[3] Friedrich Engels (1988), 'The Housing Question', in Karl Marx and Friedrich Engels (eds.), *Collected Works* (New York, NY: International Publishers).

Possessing the City: Property and Politics in Delhi, 1911–1947. Anish Vanaik, Oxford University Press (2020).

DOI: 10.1093/oso/9780198848752.001.0001

endlessly described and decried the physical and moral degeneration that plagued industrializing cities. Second, he pointed out that despite posing the question compulsively, bourgeois reformers were utterly unable to answer it. The best of their schemes did no more than displace the problem of insanitary and decrepit housing; slums banished from one location simply reappeared elsewhere in the city. Third, Engels argued that the question remained unanswered because it was the wrong question. In terms of the very problem it set out, the housing question was fundamentally a diversion—a merely minor manifestation of a deeper problem that must be solved in the realm of production. If the elimination of an economy based on profit was not envisaged, housing for the poor would never be decisively and finally improved. What Engels suggested, in short, is that the reformist energies invested in the housing question were a vast repository of bad faith—a form of political activity too timid to confront the real roots of the problem but inordinately vocal in proclaiming solutions. It is in this way that the appearance of the housing question is a diagnostic of the emergence in the political sphere of a charcteristically bourgeois set of evasions, and a terrain of struggle that might or might not expose this fundamental fact.

Was there, then, a housing question in Delhi? The epigraphs at the beginning of this chapter suggest that (certainly by the mid-1930s) a politics around housing provision had emerged which linked the issues of commodification, urban housing, and demographics—all the forces outlined in the previous chapters. Politics about housing emerged as a direct consequence of the property market and the ways in which the poor and lower middle classes were housed in Delhi. That there was a housing question in Delhi, however, is a general point. There are numerous particularities to be noted. Most significant of these is that Delhi was not an industrial city. This meant that neither from below—as a consolidated political constituency that struggled for rights—nor from above, as an administrative problem that industrialists wanted to solve was the issue of housing the working class, the typical form taken by the housing question in Delhi.[4] The politics of housing

[4] From the beginning of the twentieth century, a number of industrial enterprises did emerge in Delhi. These had a workforce that was largely immigrant. One of the largest such concerns—the Delhi Cloth Mills—also introduced a workers' housing scheme. Nita Kumar points out that this was a crucial way to stabilise its workforce which had no independent roots in Delhi. The housing scheme was also not a subsidised one—it generated a profit for the company. Nevertheless, it did not become a model for emulation among other industrial concerns. Nita Kumar (1989), 'Labour, Capital and the Congress: Delhi Cloth Mills, 1928–38' *Indian Economic and Social History Review* 26 (1) 29–59.

in Delhi had a more variegated lineage. The range of formulations of the problem, in turn, moulded state responses to it. This chapter tracks these 'lineages' of the housing question, from above and from below.

I begin by looking at two loci within the state which generated opposition to an untrammelled market. The first of these is Delhi's symbolic centrality and enhanced visibility—a result of being made the capital of British India. This gave a particular character to the issue of housing, generating doubts about the appropriate scale at which to view the issue of housing in the city: was it a local question or a much wider one? The second locus of opposition to the market from within the state came on the terrain of sanitation. Here, concern for the material fabric of the city, an organic consequence of sanitary discourse, prompted interest in housing arrangements and their improvement. Both these approaches to housing, however, posed solutions that were rooted in the authoritarian impulses of the colonial state.

More broad-based articulations of the housing question traced their roots to the steady rise of mass politics in the city from the 1920s to the 1940s. The Indian National Congress over this period used the Municipal Committee as an arena of politics in which to demand housing. There were, however, decided limits to the solutions that the Congress was prepared to envisage—limits that at times exposed fissures between leadership and rank-and-file members. Caste-uplift organizations were a second kind of organized formation that pushed for subsidized housing. The Arya Samajist and Gandhian inflexions of the caste question—the two most significant organizationally rooted initiatives in Delhi at that time—yielded forms of activity and thinking about housing very different from those seen in the municipal arena. Finally, the moment in which the politics around housing reached its most antagonistic pitch was the introduction of rent control during World War II. On this occasion, large portions of the middle classes, mercantile and salaried, in individual and collective forms, raised demands for moderating the property market. In a reversal of longstanding reluctance, the colonial state was forced to enact rent control legislation for Delhi in 1942 and then again in 1944.

These were five points from which a politics of housing issued. Two within the state, and three outside, they form a formidably diverse set of forces and point to the fractured nature of politics about housing in Delhi. The fractures were a key reason why the provision of housing for the poor was so inadequate: the political pressure for anything more than a superficial approach to (even the bad-faith politics of) the housing question quite simply did not exist.

The Imperial City

Expectations

In November 1912, G. de Montmorency, Secretary to the Chief Commissioner of Delhi, drafted a response to the report of the Delhi Town Planning Committee on the issue of expanding the existing city to the west.[5] The committee, established primarily to consider the site for the new capital, had advocated in favour of such an expansion and outlined the major categories of construction that would be necessary. In identifying a western expansion, the report of the Town Planning Committee was following a well-established course within arguments about Delhi's future.[6] Nevertheless, the report itself chose not to pronounce on the particular mechanisms through which development should take place—whether it was to be public or private investment that would be responsible for the development, how much area it would involve, and so on. It was left to Montmorency to supply details.

Montmorency's note recommended that 50 acres a year ought to be developed until a maximum of 2,500–3,000 acres was reached. This pace would accommodate a rise in population of 25,000–30,000 people per decade, and was deemed suitable for Delhi's anticipated expansion. Montmorency believed that the state should develop this land because, for one, left to themselves, owners of lands in the suburbs were reluctant urbanists.

> The hereditary cultivator has no use for capital as capital: his aspirations find their [fullest expression] ... in a good market garden plot where his customary trade can be pursued to monetary advantage ... [the buyer] in making his deal has not only to pay the market price for the land but also to purchase the unwillingness of the seller to sell.[7]

[5] DDA, CC Records, Home, Pt. B. F no. 379, 1915. 'Note by G.F de Montmorency', 14 November 1912.

[6] Apart from earlier reports, see *Report on the Administration of the Delhi Crown Lands* (1910) (Lahore: Civil and Military Gazetteer Press), p. 42; DDA, Commissioner's Office, F. no. 13, Vol. no. 1, Box No. 64, 1908; R. Humphreys, Deputy Commissioner to A. Meredith, Commissioner, 14 August 1908.

[7] DDA, CC Records, Home, Pt. B. F no. 379, 1915. Note by G. F de Montmorency, 14 November 1912. The contrast with what we have seen, in Chapter 5, of DIT's concerns about speculators rapidly converting garden lands into built neighbourhoods could not be more stark.

Apart from this unsatisfactory state of affairs, however, he also noted that the state was guaranteed to reap a handsome profit from any acquisitions it undertook. Summarizing various estimates regarding the economics of such a venture, Montmorency surmised, 'no apprehension exists as to the possibility of the venture being unprofitable to government.'[8] Finally, it was also important that the suburbs constructed were sanitary and capable of an aesthetic harmonization of the old and the new city, things that were best ensured by a unified vision that only the state could provide.

Subsequent events demonstrated that Montmorency's projection was an immense underestimation. Nor were developments taken in hand in quite the way he outlined. Nevertheless, his note highlights the degree to which the existence of New Delhi gave shape to the housing question as articulated from within the state. Parts of what Montmorency had suggested were well established in earlier reports; for example, the idea that the city would expand and the state could make profits from it. However, novel elements had also been introduced. Most prominent among these new aspects was the specification of an aesthetic standard to be achieved—a direct consequence of the new visibility that Delhi was assumed to have acquired.

The housing question in Delhi was rooted in a logic of expectation inaugurated by the shift of the capital. On the one hand, these expectations drew upon seemingly objective factors: population dynamics, prices of land, rents, and so on. The Delhi landscape was imagined as an expansionary entity, and administering the city involved anticipation of its future growth. But there was also a subjective dimension to the logic of expectation: an aesthetic ideal to which a capital should conform. While not the capital, sheer proximity ensured that Old Delhi would, to an attenuated degree, be measured against this ideal. In the actual course of events, Old Delhi constantly fell short of these expectations: it was never clean enough, movement through it was never as easy as desired, and the people that lived within it were deemed in need of reform. It is useful, nevertheless, to determine the relative weight of the elements within this logic of expectation—aesthetic, demographic, political, and economic.

The most direct outcome of Montmorency's report related to the labouring poor displaced as a result of the extension of Delhi. In the late nineteenth century, leatherworkers from within the city had been shifted to Karol Bagh, in the south-west of the extramural area. This was understood as an

[8] Ibid.

adequate distance away from the city for the continuance of their 'noxious trade'. Now that Karol Bagh adjoined the site for Imperial Delhi, these workers would have to be moved once again.

Rehgar Basti—the site selected to relocate (the already relocated) leatherworkers—was to consist of 972 compounds of 30 × 30 feet with annual rents (at rates considered nominal) on 90-year leases subject to regular revision.[9] The Imperial Delhi Committee, however, refused to pay for any engineering or earthwork in the locality, as the assumption was that the occupants would put in the manual labour required for establishing the settlement themselves.[10] Nor was it considered necessary to provide sewage or water supply, on the grounds that this was a rural settlement. About a year after the establishment of the area, discussions about providing drainage were begun, though nothing came of these. This was an early recognition of the state's responsibility to provide some form of housing, in this case through subsidized ground rent. Also in evidence at Rehgar Basti was a particular modality of providing housing. Particularly (though not exclusively) for the lower castes and urban poor, housing meant as little as the allotment of space.[11]

Most of the houses that came up in Rehgar Basti were built of mud, and this was more or less anticipated.[12] While contemporary sanitary expertise did not endorse this architecture, those objections were considered secondary. Much more significant was the financial viability of the scheme and the need to shift the industrial activity—leatherwork—away from the city. In the first instance of a pattern that would recur, fiscal stringency was deemed more significant than care for aesthetics or planning when it came to dwellings for the poor. We have seen how this concatenation of impulses within the state left an open field for 'private' construction to become the mainstay for the provision of housing in Delhi. The logic of expectation, established by the shift of the capital, had determinate limits. Aesthetic considerations were important, but, particularly with respect to the urban poor, this would usually mean banishment from visibility rather than the creation of better housing.

[9] DDA, CC records, Revenue And Agriculture, Pt. B, F no. 129, 1914.

[10] Ibid.

[11] In Karol Bagh, which was simultaneously being laid out for the middle classes, the plots were laid out and landscaped, although sewerage and water supply were still not provided.

[12] DDA, CC Records, Revenue and Agriculture, Pt. B, F no. 45, 1916; Chief Commissioner's note, 27 January 1916.

Scales

Another readily identifiable upshot of the visibility conferred on Old Delhi was a muddying of the issue of scale. Ought questions about Delhi's housing to be understood as delimited local problems? Or were they symptomatic of a much broader Imperial malaise? Should the Municipal Committee be the agency to address the question? Or did the responsibility lie at the doorstep of the Imperial administration? In 1934 *The Times of India* published an article entitled 'Delhi a Death Trap', based substantially on the annual report of the Health Officer of the Delhi Municipal Committee.[13] The sense of crisis this generated within Imperial circles was palpable[14]—so much so that the Viceroy felt compelled to address the question by commissioning a report on the measures needed to improve the slums of Delhi. Tasked with carrying out the study, A. P. Hume investigated the experiences of the Improvement Trusts of Calcutta and the United Provinces and Burma, as well as in a number of English towns.

This entire course of events is illustrative of the uncertainty of the scale at which the problem ought to be deliberated upon. Here we find that the report of a Delhi official was picked up by a newspaper based in Bombay. The prestige of that newspaper in Imperial circles, however, meant that the Viceroy felt the need to appear to address the issues raised in the article. The report that the Viceroy commissioned understood Delhi as sharing elements with a national and international network of cities that were deemed to have had similar problems. India-wide and even global scales of experience and practice offered ideas that might be valuable in solving Delhi's problems. Scales from the local to the global were all entwined.

The move away from the local also reconstituted the power dynamics within the bodies that would administer housing. The suggestion of an Improvement Trust for Delhi had been raised by the Delhi Municipal Committee since at least the mid-1920s. At that point, local representatives conceived the Improvement Trust as a means for obtaining more assured

[13] The 1933 health report had largely followed the text and findings of a number of earlier reports made by the same officer in previous years. These reports of the Health Officer had also been regularly reported in the nationalist-leaning Delhi-based English-language daily *Hindustan Times* since the late 1920s. The *Times of India* report was not, to the reader following Delhi's development, a startling or novel discovery.

[14] DDA, CC Records, Education, F no. 4(72), 1934: demi-official from Viceroy's private secretary to CC, 23 January 1934.

financial assistance towards development schemes.[15] In its final formulation by Hume in 1937, however, the DIT emerged as a way to restrict the influence of municipal commissioners—seen as obstructive, either for political reasons or else in thrall to local landed interests.[16] In this form, Imperial fiat could add an unpredictable element to the connections between political power and economic relations in the city. A. P. Hume, as the chairman of the DIT, and his successor, J. S. Hardman, carved out a sphere of power substantively independent of the Municipal Committee. While two elected members of the DMC were on the Board of the DIT, they were outnumbered by unelected official members.[17] The significance of this is underscored by the fact that the Municipal Committee, at this point in the late 1930s, was being elected on a wider franchise than ever before. A key demand of the increasingly vocal Congress was that the DMC presidents should be elected rather than nominated. The DIT was introduced as a body that could address the housing question (and much wider aspects of urban development) insulated from local political wrangling. At the same time, the influence of a certain category of local capitalists and developers could be incorporated through the nominations of the Chief Commissioner. Even at this early moment in the history of Delhi as capital, a sense emerged that the local urban fabric could not be shaped solely by local interests.

Political Struggles within the State

The spotlight on Delhi could at times also assist the DIT in its most formidable battle: that of extracting adequate loans and grants from the government. Thus, while commenting on an impending tour of the slums of the city by the Viceroy, Hume would point out that

[15] DDA, CC Records, Education, F no. 4(17), 1926.

[16] Prashant Kidambi argues that this was the case with the Bombay Improvement Trust as early as 1898. P. Kidambi (2001), 'Housing the Poor in a Colonial City: The Bombay Improvement Trust, 1898–1918', *Studies in History*, 17 (1), 57–79, at 58.

[17] In the first three-year period, the Board of Trustees consisted of the Chairman, an officer of the CPWD, the Chief Health Officer, a Financial Adviser, a nominee of the Chief Commissioner, and two members of the Municipal Committee (a Muslim and a Hindu). The Chief Commissioner's nominee was Lala Shri Ram (owner of one of the largest local industrial houses Delhi Cloth and General Mills), replaced for a year by Sir Sobha Singh (the leading contractor in the building of New Delhi), and subsequently Lala Shri Ram once again. *Administration Report of the Delhi Improvement Trust for Years 1937–39* (1940) (New Delhi: Delhi Improvement Trust), p. iv.

> these visits do some good by focusing attention on the work in hand and the finance department *babus* quail a bit when they refuse the necessary money if they know the 'Fountain Head' is personally interested.[18]

The element of visibility—the fact that the Viceroy or other senior officials could be taken to see the state of squalor in Delhi first hand—was an intermittent rather than continuous source of pressure. It meant that the Imperial impact was concentrated around periods of scandalous press coverage or the personal interest of a Viceroy.

A more consistent source of upheaval in the Delhi property market was supplied by the task of housing the Imperial establishment that resided in Delhi for six months. The houses provided for clerks in New Delhi were offered on subsidized rents, and clerks pleaded and agitated incessantly to access these houses.[19] Indeed, their agitations represent one of the very few routes through which housing was demanded as a right in Delhi.

Equally significant were the forms that these agitations took—usually routed through petitions and the newspapers. In 1929, for instance, a number of letters to the *Hindustan Times* highlighted the difficulties that house allotments were posing for clerks.[20] As Stephen Legg has argued, government officials, at all levels in the administration, were most comfortable operating through the points where the maturing public sphere and governmental procedure overlapped. Thus, on the one hand, clerks preferred to route their agitations through written representations. On the other hand, governmental reports would prove particularly sensitive to claims made in these ways. Hume's report on congestion in Delhi, for instance, projected that this segment of occupation—the lower grades of the service class—would provide the mainstay of population increase.[21] In the Legislative Assembly too, a very large number of questions posed about Delhi's housing landscape concerned areas in which administrative personnel had a stake.

[18] BL, India Office Collection, MSS Eur D724/11, letter from A. P. Hume to his parents, 6 February 1938.

[19] This meant that subsidized housing, shielded from the operations of the market, could be found in Delhi from the mid-1920s. For a fuller appreciation of clerks' agitations in New Delhi see Stephen Legg (2007), *Spaces of Colonialism: Delhi's Urban Governmentalities* (Malden, MA; Oxford: Blackwell), pp. 59–75. Much of this section derives from Legg's work and conclusions.

[20] A Sufferer, 'Wail of Houseless Clerks', *Hindustan Times*, 24 July 1929, 'The Houseless Clerks', *Hindustan Times*, 1 August 1929. Some Clerks, 'Clerks' Grievances', *Hindustan Times*, 11 August 1929. A Winter Destitute and Non Migratory Exiles, 'Quarters for Clerks in New Delhi', *Hindustan Times*, 22 August 1929.

[21] A. P. Hume, *Report on the Relief of Congestion in Delhi*, vol. I, pp. 27–8.

Most spectacularly, this is evident in the development of Karol Bagh. As mentioned in Chapter 5, it became a favoured location for Indian administrative officials to build their houses. Between the early 1920s and the 1940s almost every year saw some form of petition or question raised in the Legislative Assembly about conditions of housing or provision of amenities in the neighbourhood.[22] The subjects of these missives ranged from the sanitation of the area to the provision of piped water to houses, and from opposition to the construction of a TB hospital in the vicinity to demands for the construction of a temple and a mosque. The struggle to create a complementarity between the state and the private middle-class house in this neighbourhood was not simply granted automatically, but was achieved through dogged mobilization. No other single locality was the focus of comparable legislative attention or more determined writing of letters to the editor! Legg has argued that the deployment of the petition by government clerks was indicative of their ability to manipulate the internal gaps and contradictions in the liberal edifice of the colonial state.[23] This orientation, towards the internal operations of the state, was conjoined with an address outwards towards public visibilization through newspapers and other forums.

The manner in which the issue of housing was posed by employees of the Imperial establishment was a formative influence on how other groups in the city would come to think about the issue. The demonstration effect of the clerks' agitation in the late 1920s can be traced in the actions of the clerks of the DMC in demanding allotment of house sites at cost price in the Northern Extension Scheme in 1935.[24] Permission for this was granted and provided the impetus towards the creation of a cooperative society of clerks through which the transaction could be effected.[25] In the public visibilizing of Karol Bagh we also see a template for raising the issue in a manner that was to be taken up by the middle classes at large. The influx of the various levels of government servants was not a mere addition to the

[22] Newspapers: see *HT*, 26 November 1927, 14 September 1928, 24 September 1932, 25 June 1933, 8 February 1934, 13 February 1935, 27 March 1936, 17 December 1937, 6 March 1941. Questions in the legislative assembly: *HT*, 14 September 1928; DDA, CC Records, LSG, 565, 1938; DDA, CC Records, LSG/LB, 1(104), 1939; DDA, CC Records, LSG/LB, 1(42), 1940; CC Records, LSG (Medical), 7(197), 1945. Other petitions: DDA, CC Records, Education, 33, 1923; DDA, CC Records, Education, 4(35), 1924; DDA, CC Records, Education, 4(53), 1930.

[23] Stephen Legg (2007), *Spaces of Colonialism: Delhi's Urban Governmentalities* (Malden, MA; Oxford: Blackwell), pp. 66–70.

[24] 'Hauz Qazi Market to be Demolished', *HT*, 7 March 1935.

[25] 'Sabzimandi Extension: How Scheme is Being Held Up', *HT*, 10 March 1936.

population of Delhi. More than a simple increase in demand, their combative presence actively gave shape to the politics of housing in Delhi.

This can be held true more broadly of the Imperial impact on the housing question in Delhi. At one level, conceptions of the Old city were reconfigured when it was held up to the 'higher' expectation of being the capital. This also involved destabilizing the apposite scale at which housing in the city was to be addressed: local, all-India, or Empire-wide. The structure of expectation also carried with it the implication of a new temporal rhythm for the city, both in the form of statistical projections of future growth as well as the physical movement of the administration into the city in winter and away again in the summer. Finally, the Imperial aspect also brought with it practical modulations of power dynamics in the city: the elite and intermittent interventions of the Viceroy, as well as the subaltern and quotidian struggles of the clerks.

Health and Sanitation

Sanitary discourse is one of the few topics in South Asian historiography where the city has been seen as representative of the colonial experience.[26] Interventions in the cityscape carried out in the name of sanitation have typically been portrayed as a violent aspect of colonial rule, both physical and discursive. In the aftermath of 1857 the extensive rebuilding of a number of north Indian cities (including Delhi) involved the inextricable intertwining of military and sanitary considerations.[27] The outbreak of the plague at the turn of the nineteenth century became another moment where discourses of health, sanitation, and physical violence were linked to each other through measures such as forcible confinement of patients and aggressive fumigation of houses.[28] At a more discursive level, in Jyoti Hosagrahar's

[26] Here I refer to Janaki Nair's evocative assessment that the city has 'had a fugitive existence in the political, cultural, and sociological imaginations of Modern India.' In contrast to the countryside which is seen as the default spatial formation, the city has always been seen an unrepresentative space in the South Asian historical scholarship. With respect to the politics of sanitation, in contrast, the city does appear representative. Janaki Nair (2005), *The Promise of the Metropolis: Bangalore's Twentieth Century* (Delhi: Oxford University Press), p. 1.

[27] Veena Talwar Oldenburg (1984), *The Making of Colonial Lucknow, 1856–1877* (Princeton, NJ: Princeton University Press).

[28] Rajnarayan Chandavarkar (1998), *Imperial Power and Popular Politics: Class, Resistance and the State in India, c.1850–1950* (Cambridge: Cambridge University Press).

study of Delhi, colonial officials viewed opposition to large-scale reconstruction of the city as a manifestation of native ignorance about scientific norms of hygiene and health.[29] Nandini Gooptu, in her study of the labouring poor in the United Provinces, points out that concerns centring on sanitation were not restricted to colonial officials. Indeed, the middle classes shared in the identification of the urban poor as constitutionally predisposed to insanitation.[30]

Dipesh Chakrabarty and Sudipta Kaviraj, in their respective accounts of the relationship between urban refuse and modernity, explore the ways in which the binaries of private/public and inside/outside (of the house) relate to each other, in turn, inflecting conceptions of the personal and the civic.[31] Gyan Prakash argues that western discourses of public health pathologized the native body, despite the potential for a less invasive approach rooted in the panoply of statistical and medical knowledge collected by the state.[32] All three of these scholars identify the lability of sanitary discourse from colonial officials to native elites who would refract colonial ideas about cleanliness in their own interactions with poor and working people in the city.

Histories of Delhi have outlined developments analogous to each of these aspects.[33] Medical expertise and statistics were generated by colonial officials, official accounts often took the form of a disquisition about the lack of hygiene among natives, and Delhi's middle classes were eager to embrace some of these assertions.[34] Stephen Legg contends, however, that public-health expertise was a relatively weak influence on the physical environment. He documents a litany of dogged reports about deteriorating public health and the dangers of overcrowding in Delhi that were, just as doggedly, ignored by local officials. Legg concludes that 'in Delhi the domain

[29] Jyoti Hosagrahar (2005), *Indigenous Modernities: Negotiating Architecture and Urbanism* (London: Routledge), ch. 4.

[30] Nandini Gooptu (2001), *The Politics of the Urban Poor in Early Twentieth-Century India* (Cambridge: Cambridge University Press), p. 69.

[31] Dipesh Chakrabarty (2002), *Habitations of Modernity: Essays in the Wake of Subaltern Studies* (Chicago, IL: University of Chicago Press), pp. 65–79. S. Kaviraj (1997), 'Filth and the Public Sphere: Concepts and Practices About Space in Calcutta', *Public Culture*, 10 (1), 83–113.

[32] Gyan Prakash (1999), *Another Reason: Science and the Imagination of Modern India* (Princeton, NJ: Princeton University Press), pp. 123–58.

[33] Narayani Gupta (1981), *Delhi between Two Empires, 1803–1931: Society, Government and Urban Growth* (Delhi: Oxford University Press).

[34] For instance, reports and statistics about the state of public health in Delhi were regularly reproduced in the *Hindustan Times*. Many of the formulations there also found echo in letters to the editor.

of the economic . . . in most instances, [was] prioritized over the domain of the biopolitical.'[35]

More evidence of this diminutive status of sanitation is available in municipal building bye-laws. In the Health Officer's report of 1915, it was noted that the new building bye-laws which came into force were the minimum required for sanitary houses.[36] Already by the 1920 report, however, the officer was dissatisfied with the newly enacted bye-laws and hoped that 'these building bye-laws may soon be revised with the idea of inserting in them conditions essential to meet with the elementary principles of sanitation.'[37] In 1931, a note of resentment crept into the Health Officer's report:

> The fact that the Committee had overlooked cases of infrigements [*sic*] of building bye-laws even after the cases had been taken in the Courts and decided in Municipal Committee's favour, has created an impression in the minds of the public that a resolution of rejection of a building application is not a serious decision of the Committee . . . building bye-laws are now deliberately defied. High, ill-lighted, and ill-ventilated buildings have been erected and are being erected . . . [38]

That note of resentment is present even more clearly as the volume of building applications began to rise from the 1930s onwards. In his report of 1933, the Health Officer wrote: 'I have often wondered at the utility (rather the futility) of getting my opinions on the building applications when they are never placed on the agenda of the Building Sub-Committee, much less are they followed.'[39] By this point in the 1930s, the Health Officer would argue that the pressure of seeking votes explained the negligence in enforcing building bye-laws.[40] A more balanced assessment would take note

[35] Legg, *Spaces of Colonialism*, p. 163. Samiksha Sehrawat's empirically rich and compelling account of medical care in Delhi's hospitals also points to the disjunction between the colonial state's discursive commitment to public health and an unwillingness to stray far from the diktats of fiscal conservatism. Samiksha Sehrawat (2013), *Colonial Medical Care in North India: Gender, State, and Society, c.1840–1920* (New Delhi: Oxford University Press).

[36] *Annual Report of the Health Officer for 1915* (1916) (Delhi: Municipal Press).

[37] *Report on the Administration of the Delhi Municipality for the Year 1919–20, Annual report of the Health Officer* (1920) (Delhi: Municipal Press).

[38] *Report on the Administration of the Delhi Municipality for the Year 1930–31, Vol. II. Annual Report of the Health Officer* (1931) (Delhi: Municipal Press), p. 25.

[39] *Report on the Administration of the Delhi Municipality for the Year 1932–33, Vol. II. Annual Report of the Health Officer* (1933) (Delhi: Municipal Press), p. 60.

[40] *Report on the Administration of the Delhi Municipality for the Year 1934–35, Vol. II. Annual Report of the Health Officer* (1935) (Delhi: Municipal Press), p. 67.

of the fact that neglect of, and opposition to, building bye-laws was characteristic of the DMC from a period well before the extended franchises of the 1930s. What sense, then, can be made of the relative weight of sanitary and other considerations in the generation of the cityscape?

A large body of historiographical work has converged on the fact that sanitary discourse was coercive and directed against the poor, but only in exceptional circumstances (the Mutiny, plague, epidemics, and so on) were sufficient resources put behind them to make their proclamations reality.[41] Sanitary discourse provided colonial authorities with a useful discursive melange: science, an apolitical technical vocabulary, and the ability to direct action against the poor. For all the usefulness of sanitary discourse to the colonial agenda, actual translation of it into brick and mortar was complicated because of a less remarked upon aspect of sanitary discourse: its irreducible materialism. Where this materialism has been recognized it has usually related to the pathologizing of the native body, and more specifically the body of the poor.[42] Less often theorized for South Asian cities is that this concern about the body was conjoined with an intense focus upon the material fabric of the city. Officials concerned with sanitation, in fact, were unavoidably led to think about the physical landscape of the city and the conditions under which it was being produced.

The demonstrable dissatisfaction with building bye-laws was one manifestation of a preoccupation with the material which went further.[43] The various reports of the Health Officer feature a number of descriptions of individual houses and architectural formations in the city. At the level of the house, the circulation of air and light as well as materials of construction were investigated. Within the house, there is reference to the *pardah* system of confinement of women (in conjoined physical and exoticizing terms) and discussions of the ideal situation of latrines. Above the scale of the house, Health Officers discussed the physical configuration of houses as they came together to form neighbourhoods—where the sun was coming into the street, what kinds of drain best allowed for regular cleaning. Also highlighted were the non-built spaces within these configurations—parks

[41] Gooptu, *Politics of the Urban Poor*; Oldenburg, *Making of Colonial Lucknow*.

[42] Gooptu, *Politics of the Urban Poor*, p. 69.

[43] William Glover makes a similar point about sanitary discourse and the physical fabric of indigenous houses. William J. Glover (2008), *Making Lahore Modern: Constructing and Imagining a Colonial City* (Minneapolis, MN: University of Minnesota Press), pp. 129–38.

and *khandars* (*lit.* ruins)—and the practices that emerged around them. Sanitary discourse necessarily imparted materiality to the discussion of housing in the city. It is no surprise that the work of the Health Officer loomed so large in the reports that led to the establishment of the DIT. As Legg notes, Hume's report drew heavily on the metaphor of congestion which first emerged from the work of the Health Officer.[44] The house-to-house survey of two wards—another centrepiece of Hume's report—was carried out in conjunction with the public health establishment of the city.[45] Contiguous with its obsession about the body, then, public health discourses also transmitted a concern for the material fabric of housing in the city. This also generated a subsidiary outcome—one which stood in a somewhat contradictory relationship to the undoubted pathologizing of the poor within sanitary discourse.

More consistently than in discourses that emerged out of 'Imperial visibility' (discussed previously), and earlier than the nationalist configuration of the housing question (to be discussed), public health officials recognized the impossibility of reconciling complete freedom to build with the provision of equitable and decent dwellings for all the inhabitants of the city. Even more significant, Medical and Health Officers were likely to identify builders and property owners as part of the problem. As early as the 1920s, for example, the Health Officer criticized the financially successful Burn Bastion Road development and stated that in the Garstin Bastion Road development: 'For erection of rat-proof godowns we cannot depend on private enterprise as there are sure to be several defects in their proper construction.'[46] Undeniably authoritarian and depoliticizing, ways of thinking about the city that emerged from sanitary discourse nevertheless pointed towards the need for the state to intervene against the market.

The literature on sanitation in the colonial city, in fact, presents a paradox that is well borne out for Delhi: the near inevitability of a sanitary frame for thinking about the urban fabric (on the part of colonial officials and the urban middle classes) was matched by the near inevitably that most sanitation schemes would simply not have the resources

[44] The term was used in the Health Officer's description of the city as early as 1914.

[45] Hume, *Report on the Relief of Congestion in Delhi*, pp. 17–18. The results of this survey or a similar one also inform the Health Officer's report of 1936–37. *Report on the Administration of the Delhi Municipality for the Year 1936–37, Vol. II. Annual Report of the Health Officer* (1937) (Delhi: Municipal Press), pp. 45–7.

[46] *Report on the Administration of the Delhi Municipality for the Year 1923–24, Vol. II. Annual Report of the Health Officer* (1924) (Delhi: Municipal Press).

required to execute them. This latter outcome related back to another impulse within the state which derived from the fact that sanitary discourse was inevitably a materialist one. The concern with physical particularities shown by sanitary officials made them consistent and early opponents of rapid construction for pure profit. Despite its weak implementation and authoritarianism, sanitary discourse did grapple with the housing question in Delhi.

The Congress and the Housing Question

There were articulations of the housing question that derived directly from the arena of popular politics. Indeed, increasingly strident agitations are one of the defining characteristics of the period. For a Congress seeking to construct a mass-based anti-colonial politics, developing an urban base required practical engagement with the trio of commodification, the state, and urban demographics. Over the twentieth century this was an engagement that yielded ambivalent results.

Municipal administration was one of the key arenas through which the Congress sought to create its urban base. Until at least the mid-1920s the issue of mass housing had never been raised within the DMC. The committee was content to take note of the squalid conditions in which the poor were housed and occasionally order action to mitigate this or that aspect of dwellings deemed inadequate. In part this was an outcome of the close ties between urban landlords and municipal commissioners.[47] With the increasing prominence of more radical nationalists in the DMC, the studied silence of the committee about housing began to be challenged.

In February 1924 the municipal engineer suggested that unused plots and *khandars* in localities around the city be acquired. His argument was posed in terms of facilities for children.

> I find that the facilities for open air life and play enjoyed by the children of wards 1 and 2, parts of wards 3, 4, and 11, 12 owing to the close proximity

[47] Deputy Commissioner of Delhi, Lieutenant-Colonel Beadon (in his capacity as President of the Delhi Municipal Committee) pointed to the nexus between landlords and Municipal Commissioners in stating that building bye-laws were delayed because 'the subject is one which so closely affects the people, especially landlords, that all new proposals have met with great opposition.' Rai Sahib Madho Pershad (1921), *The History of the Delhi Municipality, 1863–1921* (Allahabad: The Pioneer Press) p. 230.

> of these wards to the various gardens, parks. and open spaces are altogether missing in wards 6, 7, 8, 1, 10, 13, and 14…The children in these wards specially those of middle and poor classes are generally found congregating and playing in narrow streets and galis which besides the consequent inconvenience and risk to traffic therein and themselves is not much conducive to health.[48]

He urged that, given the crash in property prices in the early 1920s, the moment was opportune for such acquisition. Delay now would mean that 'the municipality shall have to pay lacs where only thousands are required now.' In August 1925 a sub-committee was appointed to investigate the matter, and the main body of its report was penned by Asaf Ali, a rising nationalist leader with the Congress.[49] Ali's report of 22 October 1925 broadened the proposal about parks to discuss the question of housing in the city. Empty and disused plots had been identified by the committee, and he suggested that they

> should be the first to be acquired; for although the cost may amount to perhaps two or three lakhs…after an expenditure of a little more money they are bound to yield us perhaps double their value, besides providing decent tenements for those who are looking for but cannot find them today. But it is an undertaking that only a City Improvement Trust, and not the Municipality, can venture to tackle.[50]

This was an audacious manoeuvre, turning an inquiry relating to the health of children into an opportunity to lobby for the provision of housing more generally. In one sense, Ali was merely resuscitating what had been taken for granted by colonial officials in the immediate aftermath of the shift of the capital to Delhi: that more housing would be needed and that the state had some responsibility to ensure this construction.[51] At the same time, this was a shift in the substantive basis upon which the claim was being made. Asaf Ali argued that the state had a responsibility to provide housing based on need. This was not part of early formulations of the idea of the Improvement

[48] TH, DMC Proceedings, Executive and Finance Sub-Committee meeting, 23 January 1925.
[49] Asaf Ali, after his return from England where he studied law, rose to prominence in Delhi during the non-cooperation and Khilafat movement of the early 1920s.
[50] TH, DMC Proceedings, E&F SC, 22 October 1925.
[51] Pershad, *History of the Delhi Municipality*, pp. 200–1.

Trust. Beadon's proposal for a Trust in 1913 was, apart from 'relieving congestion', based on the observation that builders needed help, since 'land has become so valuable that capitalists cannot build, and improvements, however pressing, cannot be effected.'[52] These deliberations had been undergirded by a perceived need to bring in improvements and support landlords rather than affirmation of a responsibility to provide housing.

In effect, Ali was inaugurating a more radical set of proposals that could place the agencies of the state in the service of popular causes. Something along these lines can be traced over the 1930s and 1940s. Bishambar Dayal, an important local Congress leader, in his 1931 letter to the *Hindustan Times* said that the 'solution [to the housing problem] lies in constructing thousands of houses provided with sanitary and other arrangements... These should be leased at cheap rents to the poor and middle classes for their residential purposes.'[53]

From the point of view of colonial officials, the growing power of the Congress (and other elected representatives) was a cause of much hand-wringing. It was noted previously that by the mid-1930s the Health Officer, somewhat speciously, was portraying the neglect of building bye-laws as an outcome of democracy. In this case he was echoing a sentiment that was gaining currency in official pronouncements. Thus, the annual report of the Delhi Municipal Committee of 1927–28 contained a similar formulation accompanied by the plea that oversight of building cases should be handed to executive officers disconnected from the hurly-burly of politics.[54] Even more explicitly directed at the Congress nationalists was the barb in the report for 1930–31. Against the backdrop of mass mobilizations for independence, the report noted:

> The Committee was given *Purna Swaraj* [*lit.* complete self-rule] so far as it related to the disposal of building plans, as the permanent Official Chairman seldom stayed back when the proceedings of the Building Sub-Committee were laid for confirmation before the weekly general meetings.[55]

[52] Ibid.

[53] Bishambar Dayal, 'Housing Problem in Delhi: Danger to Health from Overcrowding', *Hindustan Times*, 1 January 1931.

[54] *Report on the Administration of the Delhi Municipality in the Year 1927–28, Vol. I. General Administration* (1928) (Delhi: Municipal Press), p. 13.

[55] *Report on the Administration of the Delhi Municipality in the Year 1930–31, Vol. I. General Administration* (1931) (Delhi: Municipal Press), p. 57.

It went on to suggest that 'The year may well be called as a year of "general massacre of all building bye-laws"... It has to be noted with regret that... the authority of the Municipal Committee [has been] distinctly weakened thereby.'[56]

As has been suggested previously, the eventual constitution of the Improvement Trust, although it had been demanded repeatedly by the DMC since the mid-1920s, was designed to reduce the latter's influence on the city. Commissioners drove at this in their remarks that officials ought to have recognized the importance of DMC 'by allotting a majority of seats on the Trust to the Committee'.[57] This plea was, of course, studiously ignored by the DIT. The DMC and the DIT were institutions marked by the tussle between colonial officials and the Congress. Officials hurled accusations of corruption, nepotism, and incompetence at the DMC, while the Congress made increasingly robust claims to representing popular opinion and interests.

Nevertheless, a certain ambivalence remained within the nationalists' formulation of the housing question. Ali, it should be remembered, argued both for the provision of housing by the state based on need, and that this could be made to turn a profit for the body that carried out such a plan. Even in 1938, his thinking about the finances of the Delhi Improvement Trust, while more liberal than what colonial officials envisaged, remained restricted to a balance-the-books premise: '... if the city improvement is conducted along sound lines... the Trust is bound to lose heavily, in the first instance... [which will] be more or less balanced by profits on schemes of extension.'[58] Here the relative fiscal conservatism of Ali can be attributed in part to the limitations of operating within the state. For pronouncements in this sphere, deference to the balanced budget is not surprising. The impulse, however, also points towards a deeper dilemma at the heart of how the nationalists were prepared to think and mobilize around the housing question. Here, the attitude of the Congress to rental disputes in the city sheds interesting light.

In September 1931, around the time that Gandhi was attending the Round Table Conference, a campaign against high rents sprang up in Delhi in the form of *kiraya* (rent) committees in the city. The forms of agitation that it deployed drew very clearly upon the models of the Civil

[56] Ibid p. 58.
[57] TH, DMC Proceedings, Ordinary Meeting, 28 July 1938, prog. No. 31.
[58] Ibid.

Disobedience Movement: picketing landlords who did not reduce rents, and organizing various sub-committees for 'defence' and 'finance' in case police or legal action were taken against protesters.[59] It also seems clear that workers of the Congress party were involved in these agitations. The Delhi District Congress Committee, however, was eager to dissociate itself from the movement, stating:

> National workers and the members of the Congress in their individual capacity are free to take part in any committee or activity they like... The Congress should not be considered responsible for any activities for which it has not notified the public.[60]

On the issue of rental rates themselves, the statement went on to say, in a typically Gandhian formulation, that 'the Congress Committee shall be glad if the landlords and tenants would settle the question of the reduction of rent amicably.'[61]

The incident around the *kiraya* committees highlights a number of interesting facets of the ways in which the nationalists confronted urban housing. To begin with, nationalist mobilizations injected a populist dimension into politics, putting forward new principles of national autonomy and self-determination. An unavoidable side effect of this mobilization was that questions of urban living, including housing, were also opened up. Even more significantly, within the Congress rank and file, there were those who were prepared to push the implications of this critique into mobilizations against landlords. For the main body of the organization, however, a more circumspect attitude was typical. While in general terms they were prepared to criticise landlords, they were more reluctant to carve out a sphere—either conceptually or in practical terms—for action entirely independent of the market.

For nationalist agitators, cities were important because they were points where a variety of different scales coexisted: the international, national, regional, and local could all be found in the circuits of movement of people and goods through the city. Equally significant, these various transactions, with their multiple spatial implications, were not harmonized into a unitary dynamic. The symbolic and practical connections between the various scales

[59] 'Agitation Against High Rents', *HT*, 11 September 1931.
[60] 'Kiraya Committee: Congress Secretary's Statement', *HT*, 25 September 1931.
[61] Ibid., *HT*, 25 September 1931.

that intersected in the city remained fluid. Manu Goswami has persuasively argued that the creation of the nation involved acts of scaling and rescaling – reimagination and specification of the linkages between the local and units larger than it.[62] For the nationalists, the city—with the multiple possibilities of scalar action that it opened up at symbolic and physical levels—was a crucial arena of intervention. Here, two modes of generating scale were particularly important. On the one hand, urban spaces could be ones from which images of oppression and of a new nation-in-waiting could be effectively projected. On the other hand, this was also a space within which a relationship between their own political activity and the circuits of capital and commerce could be established. Often these two could go together; for instance, when the indigenous bourgeoisie would throw its weight behind popular Congress agitations for *Swadeshi*.

With the question of housing, however, the mutual coherence of these ways of scaling threatened to come apart. The symbolism of the inadequate provision of urban housing was a powerful stick with which to beat the colonial state: such a state of affairs would not be allowed to prevail in a state with more care for its citizens. At the same time, particularly when turned towards the question of who made profits, a critique carried too far could disrupt connections with urban traders and landlords. The housing question thus posed a dilemma for the nationalist leadership. Ultimately, the predilection of Congress workers notwithstanding, the organization favoured a course that did not oppose profiteering in urban property.[63]

In this, Congress leaders converged with the path treaded by the officials of the DMC. The Secretary, for instance, repeatedly condemned landlords who were making profits from the new schemes of the mid-1930s, but admitted that 'at the same time I am anxious to... not incur the hostility of the capitalist class if it can be helped.'[64] The denigration of democracy by officials in local administration was a hostile reaction to new styles of politics. At the same time, officials shared with the Congress a schizoid relationship to the wider questions of urban housing—acknowledging the problems of profiteering while being wary of addressing them head on.

[62] Manu Goswami (2004), *Producing India: From Colonial Economy to National Space* (Delhi: Permanent Black).

[63] We have seen in the Introduction that the dilemma as well as its mode of resolution cast a long shadow. In the post-Independence enquiry into the operations of the DIT, denouncement of speculation in property went hand in hand with a recommendation that private builders be encouraged to play a greater role in housing. *Report of the Delhi Improvement Trust Enquiry Committee 1951 Vol. 1* (1951) (New Delhi: Government of India Press), pp. 2–18.

[64] 'Solving Delhi's Housing Problem: Expanding City towards North', *HT*, 21 May 1934.

There remains, however, yet another political avenue through which the Congress came to raise the issue of housing. The next section considers how caste more generally and, more specifically, how nationalist mobilization around it, shaped the housing question.

Caste and the Housing Question

We saw earlier in this chapter that residents of Rehgar Basti, who carried on so-called polluting or 'offensive' trades, were forced to move when the new capital was announced. This was a second displacement of people who had previously been moved out from intramural areas to the suburbs. Rehgar Basti, in fact, instantiates the ways in which pressures originating in the coming of the Imperial capital and discourses of sanitation were refracted through a symbolic order based on the institution of caste. At the same time, it is in the context of caste that the Congress, and reforming forces outside it, were prepared to go furthest in their advocacy of state-subsidized housing.

It must be stated at the outset, however, that the fact that caste structured the housing question in Delhi should not be taken to mean that caste operated in a singular spatial pattern. The leatherworkers of Rehgar Basti had been assigned an area where ground rent was to be paid to the state and no facilities of sewage or water were provided (until much later). Predictably, within a few years of its establishment the *basti* was deemed insanitary and the blame laid at the door of its inhabitants' supposed predilections. In this instance, rather than addressing sanitation, housing, or the deprivations of caste effectively, the intervention reproduced (and even heightened) in the urban setting the logic of spatial segregation embedded in the caste system.

A different spatial pattern was exhibited in the contestations between the Municipal Committee and sweepers. Vijay Prashad's compelling long-run history of DMC's efforts to control the militancy of Delhi's 'mehtars'[65] suggests that a crucial turning point was the displacement of low-caste agricultural labourers from the Punjab countryside and their subsequent migration to the city. The rural 'chuhras'—who were now to be irreversibly

[65] Prashad points out that 'mehtar', in its origins, was an omnibus term created around the profession of sweeping rather than strictly speaking a caste designation, since it spanned a variety of caste groups who shared relatively little apart from being considered to occupy the lowest rungs of the caste hierarchy. Vijay Prashad (2000), *Untouchable Freedom: A Social History of a Dalit Community* (Oxford: Oxford University Press).

characterized as sweepers—did not share the mehtars' history of assertive collective action. As a result, they were considered more pliable by the authorities. One of the key means by which rural sweepers were drafted into the workforce was through the construction of houses for them. The Health Officer noted in 1915:

> The construction of sweepers' huts is solving a housing problem for the outside sweepers, the bringing in of which class is an essential requirement... as it has been found out by experience that they work much better than the city sweepers.[66]

The terrain of struggle, however, continued to be fraught. Even in 1920 the Health Officer felt it important to point out the centrality of house construction.

> The outside sweepers who have proved more useful than the city sweepers find great difficulty in obtaining lodging accommodation, hence they leave the city to work in the fields. The Municipal Committee should adopt a definite policy in providing these sweepers with some lodging accommodation, and a large number of sweepers huts should be constructed at an early date.[67]

In this avatar, then, housing could emerge as a strategic asset. The creation of small numbers of sweepers' huts in localities around the city, while seemingly running counter to the principle of spatial segregation, would reproduce caste hierarchies in two ways. First, it undercut the hard-won organizational strength of the urban sweepers. Second, and equally important, it served to disperse the labour force being used to replace them.

Both these instances—where divergent spatial patterns of segregation from and integration into the city reproduced a similar social outcome—point to the intimate relationship of caste, labour, and urban space. The labour of the castes seen as ritually impure was essential to the functioning of a city. This was true of sanitation, in common with other urban centres in India, but also in industry (leatherwork, for instance, was a mainstay of the Delhi industrial landscape). The question of how people ought to be

[66] *Annual Report of the Health Officer for 1915* (1916) (Delhi: Municipal Press), p. 21.

[67] *Report on the Administration of the Delhi Municipality for the Year 1919–20, Annual report of the Health Officer* (1920) (Delhi: Municipal Press), p. 23.

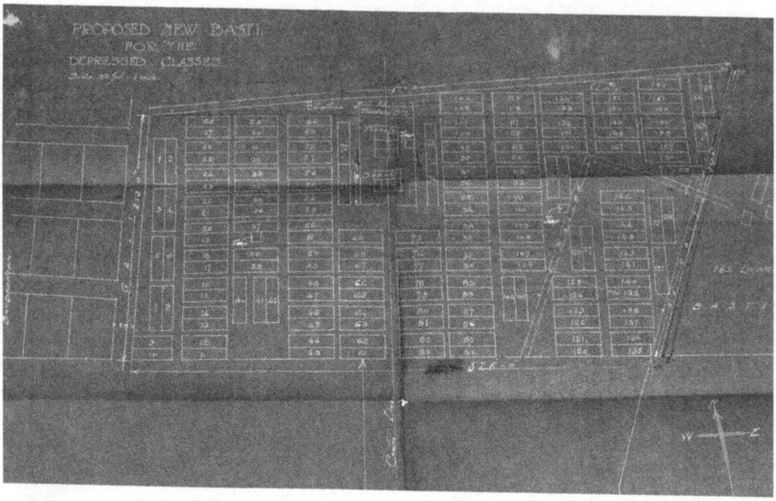

Figure 6.1. Layout of Shraddhanand Basti, Paharganj. (DDA, CC Records, Education, F no. 24, 1926: DC to CC, 23 July 1925.)

distributed in space was inevitable given the stipulated spatial separations of the caste system. This, in turn, meant that dealing with caste inevitably posed questions about housing. Conversely, any resolution of the question of housing in Delhi required engagement with the question of caste.

There is ample evidence of the significance of both aspects of this formulation. From the mid-1920s, militant Hindu outfits, looking to mobilize among the the people they considered untouchables, saw housing as central to their project.[68] In August 1925 the Dalituddhar Sabha, established in Delhi during the 1920s, applied to the District Commissioner with plans for a layout of a 'model village' to be established in the Paharganj area. Their layout included space for 213 cottages surrounding a school and a temple (Figure 6.1).[69] The rate of the ground rent was supposed to be the minimum possible—a figure which the administration ultimately fixed at 12 annas per 100 sq. yards. The lease also included conditions discouraging transfers of

[68] The term 'militant hindu' is used by Vijay Prashad, who sheds light on the many aspects of this phenomenon as they related to the labour of sweepers and displacement of many of their alternative belief structures. His work does not emphasize the importance of housing in this convergence. Prashad, *Untouchable Freedom*; see especially ch. 4.

[69] DDA, CC Records, Education, F no. 24, 1926. Ramanand Sanyasi, Dalitudhar Sabha, Delhi to Deputy Commissioner, 17 August 1925.

plots, and stated that any transfers must be to another member of the 'Depressed Classes'.

In many ways this was fundamentally continuous with the form of intervention already seen in the case of Basti Rehgar. It involved the allotment of plots at a subsidized ground rent (based on earning capacity of the allottees rather than market rates for land) and assent to the segregation of the 'Depressed Classes'. In this case, however, the process was to be carried out through the intermediation of the Dalituddhar Sabha, an Arya Samajist caste outreach organization. What did the intermediary role entail? Most immediately, this meant that a temple and school in the locality were to be leased directly to the organization.[70] The allotment of individual plots was also to be on the basis of the recommendations of the Sabha. The usefulness of this kind of approach for organizations like the Dalitudhar Sabha, effectively positioned as sub-contractors for housing allotments, can be readily appreciated.

Indeed, recognition of the significance of this position is evidenced by the fact that in 1931 the rival Depressed Classes Association chose to attack the Dalituddhar Sabha on the allotment of sites in this layout.[71]

> All India Dalitudhar Sabha is a caste Hindu Arya Samajist organization... [the Chief Commissioner should] make enquiries personally whether it is a case of wrong distribution of Government favours. If it be found so, the lands so granted should be confiscated to the State or should be given to the All India Depressed Classes Association for making distribution in a proper manner.[72]

Subsequent enquiries revealed that, out of the 106 plots ultimately released, only forty-five had been built upon. Of these, a majority had been allotted to Malis—technically not counted among the 'depressed classes', but, according to the Secretary of the Dalituddhar Sabha, deserving of sites since they

[70] DDA, CC Records, Education, F no. 28, 1928. CC to GoI, 23 April 1928, and GoI to CC, 17 May 1928. DDA, CC Records, Education, F no. 24, 1926. Ramanand Sanyasi, Dalitudhar Sabha, Delhi to DC, 17 August 1925.

[71] The Depressed Classes Association seems to have had members from a relatively wide spectrum ranging from the Congress to those who supported Ambedkar's political perspectives. According to Saurabh Dube, in the 1930s the organization was increasingly influenced by the latter. S. Dube (1998), *Untouchable Pasts: Religion, Identity, and Power among a Central Indian Community, 1780–1950* (Albany, NY: SUNY Press), p. 149.

[72] DDA, CC Records, Education, F no. 36, 1932. Ram Pershad, Honarary Provincial Secretary, All-India Depressed Classes Association, Delhi, to CC, 2 April 1931.

had 'in no way been admitted to privileges of "twiceborn"'.[73] A majority of them were masons or shopkeepers, in slightly better circumstances and consequently able to build much sooner than most of the other allotees. In a few cases they were even able to rent out the houses.[74] Based on these irregularities, the administration decided to resume direct control and allot the sites themselves. In a move that demonstrated the tenuousness of housing grants by the colonial state to dalits, the administration now agreed that space for dalits should be made in other, less valuable areas and that these plots be auctioned to recover amounts closer to the (far more lucrative) market rates.[75]

The proceedings around the Shraddhanand Basti span the period over which the caste question went from being relatively marginal to the Congress, to when it became both central and contentious. Whereas initially Gandhi was associated with the Shraddhanand Basti through the Arya Samaj,[76] over the 1930s the Congress began to establish its own organizations of outreach and mobilization among the Dalits.[77] At the same time, the period saw the rising significance of Ambedkar as a national figure who opposed both the Arya Samajist and Gandhian visions of politics. Through all this, housing remained relevant to the variety of political strategies being pursued.

The impact of the Gandhian emphasis on caste, however, was significant. Much historiography has highlighted the ways in which Gandhi's approach drew on discourses of sanitation in ways that reinforced the pathologizing of dalits.[78] In Delhi, Gandhian initiatives on caste took the form of a variety of high-visibility low-impact activities: visits to bastis, efforts to reform supposed vices, and cleaning drives. Less ephemeral than these, however, was the emergence, from the mid-1930s, of a tradition of writing about the city. The form brought together caste, sanitation, and housing. These accounts shared both the intermittent periodicity and sense of self-satisfied civic

[73] DDA, CC Records, Education, F no. 36, 1932. Secretary, Hindu Depressed Classes Mission, Delhi, to DC, 7 July 1931.

[74] Ibid.; noting by Nazul Tahsildar, 18 September 1931.

[75] Ibid. See also the correspondence in DDA, CC Records, Education, F no. 64, 1936.

[76] 'Model "Basti" for Untouchables', *HT*, 25 September 1928; 'Shraddhanand Nagar: Mahatmaji to lay foundation', *HT*, 8 July 1929. In November 1931 the Shraddhanand Dalituddhar Sabha denounced Ambedkar and named Mahatma Gandhi 'the true representative and friend of the depressed classes.' 'Delhi Depressed Classes', *HT*, 8 November 1931.

[77] The nationalist party within the Delhi Municipal Committee also began to take up the question actively. 'Delhi Municipality's Move: Harijan Uplift', *HT*, 11 November 1933.

[78] A. Rao (2009), *The Caste Question: Dalits and the Politics of Modern India* (Berkeley, CA: University of California Press).

Figure 6.2. 'Giving positive proof of their willingness to treat the Harijan as one of themselves: a fair worker drinking water served by a Harijan.' (*Hindustan Times*, 2 May 1933.)[79]

virtue of the calls issued by the Congress to its volunteers to clean up slums (see Figures 6.2 and 6.3, especially the captions).

The earliest instance of this kind of writing can be identified in a 1933 article which was reprinted from *Harijan*, in the *Hindustan Times*, entitled 'How Delhi Neglects Those Who Keep the City Clean'. It describes a visit during which the author accompanied A. V. Thakkar of the Harijan Sewak Sangh (one of Gandhi's more prominent Delhi associates) to various *bastis* in the city. Set at the time of one of Gandhi's fasts, the author writes that he visited the *basti* because he 'decided to look for Hari [a name for Vishnu] among the Harijan and to pray to Him to save us all by saving Bapu.'[80] The peculiarity of this formulation is matched by a recurrent rhetorical trope in the article: the alternation of factual minutiae and heightened rhetorical expressions of divinity or horror– for instance, the description of sweepers' quarters as reminiscent of hell juxtaposed with factual details regarding distances of dwellings from public latrines.[81]

[79] *HT*, 2 May 1933.

[80] 'How Delhi Neglects Those Who Keept the City Clean', *HT*, 17 May 1933.

[81] They also occur in N. R. Malkani's report about sweepers' slums in Delhi. 'Dewan-i-Khas and Suiwala Basti: Heaven and Hell', *HT*, 10 September 1933.

Figure 6.3. 'A group of men volunteers who helped clean up a mohalla of the untouchables on Sunday. There was not a trace of superiority complex in the volunteers. The party willingly posed for our cameraman with the hitherto-looked-down-upon emblems of the sweepers' trade.' (*Hindustan Times*, 2 May 1933.)

Where the account about Thakkar's visit differs from others is in the fact that the author records the voices of resentment and anger expressed by the residents of these areas. In doing so, he presents a rich mix of moods – humour ('Bhangis [caste-term for sweeper] are blessed with a charm which . . . keeps them from falling ill')—scorn ('certain ladies . . . came with brooms in their hands and went away after they had done a little sweeping over this place')—and anger. In the article, these voices were emplotted to highlight the dangers of so-called lower castes converting away from Hinduism and to make the case for the importance of measures such as education to avoid such an outcome. Nevertheless, the voices continued to carry a militant charge that perhaps explains their absence from later accounts.

Two accounts from the mid-1930s seem to divide the emphasis on factual detail and rhetoric between them. S. R. Venkataraman's article of 1936 fell on the 'factual' side. He sought to create a 'typology' of slums in Delhi of which he found four: those where the industrial workers lived, where wage earners lived, where skilled and unskilled labourers lived, and where sweepers lived.[82] He decided to describe only those inhabited by sweepers,

[82] S. R. Venkataraman, 'Slums in Delhi', *HT*, 12 October 1936.

since these were, he claimed, in the worst state. His stated aim was to provide a factual overview of prevalent conditions. In each of the four slums around the city that he visited, his account provided a description of the neighbourhood, an individual dwelling, and ended with a list of the 'needs' that required to be fulfilled.

Six months later, Rameshwari Nehru's account of her 'Harijan Week' visit to the *bastis* in Delhi placed more emphasis on the shock of the conditions: 'I am fairly acquainted with their [the 'harijans'] living conditions in many parts of India . . . Never before [Delhi] had I seen even sweepers living in such filthy conditions.'[83] In this case, while not absent from her own account, she chose to bracket the empirical dimension by referring the reader to 'go and see these for themselves. As for description, a detailed and clear account of these bastis is given in the report written by Professor Malkani and issued by the Harijan Sevak Sangh.'

The charge placed on individuals to gather knowledge about the *bastis* is, in fact, a cornerstone of all these accounts. A second element is the kind of knowledge to be gathered. As Venkataraman expressed it:

> Attempt should be made to survey all the slums in the city to collect facts about housing, sanitation, water supply, latrines, schools for children, lights, toddy shops, indebtedness, etc.[84]

In fact, this is precisely the form taken by one of the most significant post-independence surveys of slums in Delhi in 1956. The Bharat Sevak Sangh's report, endorsed by Prime Minister Jawaharlal Nehru, was very much a continuation of the urban sociology generated out of the Gandhian approach to caste.[85] The tradition of writing about the city that the Gandhians initiated might be their most significant contribution to the housing question in Delhi.

That report, as well as the articles discussed here, all shared a common assessment of the solution to the prevalent squalor in dalit *bastis:* the Municipal Committee ought to be held responsible for housing sweepers, since they were the employers. Here we approach the crux of the potentialities and problems of this particular configuration of the housing question.

[83] 'Harijan Bastis in Delhi: "Abodes of Human Misery"', *HT*, 29 April 1937.

[84] S. R. Venkataraman, 'Slums in Delhi', *HT*, 12 October 1936.

[85] Bharat Sevak Samaj (1958), *Slums of Old Delhi: Report of the Socio-Economic Survey of the Slum Dwellers of Old Delhi City* (Delhi: Atma Ram and Sons).

From within this tradition, the recognition that the material surroundings of dalits needed amelioration was accompanied by the proposition that dalits were unable to pay for the necessary measures. Housing must be provided for them in non-economic forms. This was undoubtedly the clearest and most radical case that the Congress was prepared to put forward in Delhi—a straightforward political articulation of the right to decent housing.

There remained, however, something transactional about the political demand. Rather than a call that anyone ought to be able to make upon the state, it was, in this Gandhian fold, the forms of labour that sweepers did (and should continue to do) that legitimized the demand for housing. The Gandhian approach to the more general caste question thus created a dual constriction. On the one hand, it insisted on the continuance of traditional labour by those who had always carried it out. With respect to the housing question, however, the converse was also palpable—a lack of interest in the possibility of political struggle geared towards housing being viewed as a responsibility of the state to its citizens *tout court*.

Rent Control

In all the struggles surveyed so far, the issue of housing and commodification rarely crystallized as a straightforward battle between tenants and landlords, emerging instead, for example, from state discourses and caste struggles. Even when commodification was presented as the central cause of crisis, as during the *Kiraya* committee agitations of 1931, political expression in these terms was thwarted because the Congress leadership would not take up the issue on a wider scale. The significant exception to this was agitation over rent control over the 1940s, when struggles between landlords and tenants, as landlords and tenants, came to a head.

The idea of controlling rents and prices in Delhi had been floated from time to time over twenty years. Particularly during the Durbars, prices and rents would rise precipitously, though they would usually resume normal values after the conclusion of these Imperial galas. The first serious call for levels of rent to be controlled by the state arose in 1920. In that year, a deputation of citizens sent a memorial to the Chief Commissioner complaining about high rents and asking that a law similar to those operative in Calcutta and Simla be introduced in Delhi.[86] Deliberations about the issue

[86] The deputation was led by a barrister. DDA, CC Records, Home, F no. 238, 1921: memorial from citizens of Delhi to Chief Commissioner, 12 July 1920.

continued until the summer of 1922, but it was concluded that the high rents were correcting themselves, rendering legislation unnecessary.[87]

The issue did not arise again until the outbreak of World War II. Concerns about price rises affecting the conduct of the war effort prompted notification of the New Delhi House Rent Control Order in September 1939 under the Defence of India Rules. This was made applicable to New Delhi and the Civil Lines Notified Area but not the rest of the city and suburbs.[88] Pressed repeatedly to extend rent control to Delhi as a whole, the Punjab Urban Rent Restriction Act 1941 (PURRA) was made applicable to the city in December 1942. Formulated very differently from the New Delhi law, the latter continued to allow landlords considerable powers.[89] Inundated by complaints about continuing harassment of tenants by landlords, the authorities were forced to promulgate the Delhi Rent Control Ordinance (DRCO) in June 1944. At least for Old Delhi and its suburbs, then, rent control was a measure that that authorities were reluctant to enact.

The reasons presented for this reluctance were both practical and theoretical. When petitioned between 1939 and 1942 about why rent control had been selectively introduced in New Delhi and the Civil Lines, officials maintained that the administrative apparatus required for these smaller well-planned areas was more manageable. Appointing a Rent Controller for Delhi as whole, it was argued, involved a different order of complexity. Within the state, however, a more theoretically grounded set of reasons had also been consistently argued. In the twenty years between 1922 and the eve of introduction of rent control in Delhi in 1942, officials maintained that the market would correct rents automatically.[90] Interference in the market would create perverse price distortions. It was better to increase the supply of housing and rely on the market to correct rents and prices. Again this was

[87] DDA, CC Records, Home, F no. 65, 1922: Chief Commissioner to Government of India in Home Department, 2 June 1922.

[88] It was subsequently extended to Daryaganj and the Western Extension Area in August 1942.

[89] Neither the Delhi Rent Control Ordinance nor the Punjab Urban Rents Restriction Act (PURRA) were formulated under the Defence of India Rules. Its provisions were, consequently, somewhat more lax. The major criticism of the Rents Restriction Act was that it continued to allow landlords to evict tenants. This was possible under PURRA with six months notice or, if the building were required by the landlord for his own purposes, with no notice at all. DDA, DC Records, F no. 216, 1943. Noting of 4 September 1943: Summary of Provisions of Punjab Urban Rent Restriction Act 1941.

[90] DDA, CC Records, LSG-PWD, F no. 62, 1939: demi-official from CC to Deputy Secretary to GoI Department of Labour, 31 October 1939. For the 1920s, see DDA, CC Records, Home, F no. 65, 1922: CC to GoI Department of Home, 2 June 1922.

argued, both in the 1920s and during World War II. In the latter case the Chief Commissioner averred that 'considerable areas of land adjoining the city have been or are being developed by the Delhi Improvement Trust and the Delhi Municipal Committee and as building proceeds the city rents are bound to fall.'[91] The averseness of the state to intervention in the rental contract, then, was based on its understanding of the role of the property market in the city.

The long history of unwillingness to legislate rent control also throws into sharp relief the prevailing circumstances that prompted the state to finally introduce the measure. In fact, the situation in the city before and during the enactment of rent control reveal sharp antagonism between landlords and tenants. Among the early and militant proponents of rent control in Delhi were the members of the Merchants' Association. They claimed, over a series of resolutions and missives from July to November 1939, that merchants and shopkeepers in the city were being squeezed by landlords. In October 1939 they claimed to have inquired into 5,000 cases of rents over the previous decade. The results suggested an average increase of more than 50% and that 'return on the capital invested in building is 12% to 16% in Delhi City'.[92] Comparing the fate of business incomes and those from property, they concluded that circumstances had been moving sharply in favour of the latter. Another fissure in the social landscape was being brought into existence by the legislation of rent control in New Delhi rather than in the city as a whole. This 'create[s] envy and bitterness between the two sections of the population in the same town.'[93] The sharp lines drawn in the correspondence of the Merchant Association—between landlords and high officers on the one hand, and tenants, small business owners, and the salaried classes on the other—are a pointer to the more general hostilities that were gathering as rents skyrocketed. Once again, demographics and the reduction in the amount of construction because of wartime shortages (from the 1940s) did play a role. However, the terrain was defined by the relative power of landlords and tenants in Delhi which, historically, as we have seen in previous chapters, were freighted in favour of the former.

The extension of PURRA to Delhi in December 1942 intensified the tussle. Anticipation that some form of rent control would be introduced

[91] DDA, CC Records, LSG-PWD, F no. 62, 1939: demi-official from CC to Deputy Secretary to GoI Department of Labour, 31 October 1939.

[92] Ibid., Dr M. N. Kaul, Honorary Secretary, The Merchants Association, to Chief Commissioner Delhi, 12 October 1939.

[93] Ibid.

had already prompted eviction notices and demands for higher rent in the city.[94] Once PURRA was enacted (and with the subsequent application of DRCO), landlord–tenant relations took on a harsher aspect. The most common form of clash was verbal harassment by landlords, with repeated demands that tenants vacate premises.[95] This was often followed by the disconnection of electricity and water supplies to the tenants.[96] Finally, numerous reports suggest that threats of violence and instances of physical assault—by landlords or by people hired by landlords—were also common occurrences.

A number of landlords—perhaps those less willing to enhance rent through such means—appear to have sold their properties. In many cases, harassment of tenants commenced in the wake of such sales.[97] Other forms of illegality also appear to have been common. Thus, tenants were routinely asked to pay an undocumented advance in order to enter into a rental contract in the first place. Indeed, in a number of cases a portion (sometimes the larger part) of the rent was paid outside the sum noted in the *kiraya-nama*.[98] Particularly after the end of the war, when there was assurance that the state would not requisition property, landlords were prepared to leave houses vacant unless their conditions were met.[99] Thus, even after legislation by the state, they were able to use a variety of means—including illegal ones—to claim higher rents.

Resistance to the power of landlords called into being organized associations, especially among the salaried and commercial middle classes. We have already encountered the Merchants' Association. Over this period, a Tenants Union (based in New Delhi) and a Tenant's Association and Rent

[94] Ibid., Sham Lal to Chief Commissioner Delhi, 4 November 1939.

[95] A common trope in the complaints about this is that of wives and children being harassed by the landlord while the petitioner, usually a man, was away at work. DDA, DC Records, F no. 266, 1942: Mohd. Hussain Khan to CC Delhi, 18 November 1942, Manzur Ahmed to DC Delhi, 4 December 1942.

[96] See various petitions in DDA, DC Records, F no. 314, 1944; DDA, DC Records, F no. 216, 1943. Incidentally, the very fact that this was a weapon in the landlord's arsenal indicates the degree to which these flows from the public sphere to the private had become markers of middle-class life.

[97] DDA, DC Records, F no. 321, 1944: Mohammed Ishaq to DC Delhi, 10 April 1945, Debi Saran to DC Delhi, 15 May 1945, various tenants to Messrs Haji Mohd. Ibrahim Mohd. Amin, 5 April 1945, and others. DDA, DC Records, F no. 314, 1944: Fatma Begam and ors. To DC Delhi, 14 November 1944.

[98] Ibid., Sher Singh to DC Delhi, 11 December 1944; DDA, DC Records, F no. 314, 1944: Hira Lal to Additional Dist. Magistrate, Delhi, 19 October 1944. DDA, DC Records, F no. 325, 1944: DC Delhi to CC Delhi, 5 August 1946.

[99] DDA, DC Records, F no. 325, 1944: DC Delhi to CC Delhi, 5 August 1946.

Payers' Association (both based in Old Delhi and its suburbs) were also established. Much of their activity consisted of bringing violations of the rent control acts to the attention of the authorities.[100]

Antagonism between landlords and tenants, then, were sharpened over this period. They spanned the gamut of possibilities, from illegal extractions and physical violence to individual and collective resistance. Middle-class involvement, in this instance, was wide, and shaped the character of the overall struggle. The fact that the state was drawn into the conflict between landlords and tenants was an outcome of the impact of rising rents on clerks—an issue about which they had agitated for many years. Petitions, meetings, resolutions, and drafts of model provisions in legislation are littered throughout the proceedings about rent control.

The introduction of rent control in the 1940s was one of the few moments in which the housing question presented itself as divided straightforwardly between landlords and tenants. On this occasion, rather than conceptualizations of public good, the state's role was, perforce, understood as a balancing between the interests of different classes. Indeed, it was that class struggle that established the broad parameters, though not particular details, of the state's intervention.

The Housing Question Resolved?

By the mid-1930s the question of housing had emerged out of immensely complex and cross-cutting strands of politics. While the demographic issue was most starkly identified as the key problem in discourses that emerged out of sanitation and the 'imperial' aspect of Delhi, more sophisticated connections between social oppression, state authority, commodification, and the social structure are evident in a whole range of other struggles.

Between 1933 and 1937 the DMC announced a number of extension schemes to address the 'congestion' revealed by the census of 1931. In rapid succession, the relatively minor Shadipur Extension and Deputyganj Parao schemes and significantly larger Northern Extension scheme were announced. Also on the agenda was the clearance of Basti Harphool Singh—the largest and most notorious slum in the city until its removal in

[100] DDA, DC Records, F no. 216, 1943: Veerendra Swarup to DC, 29 August 1943; DDA DC Records, F no. 325, 1944: Genl. Secy. Tenants' Union to DC Delhi, 8 July 1946; DDA, DC Records, F no. 314, 1944: Nanak Chand to L. Dhanpal Singh, 7 October 1944.

1936. Whereas the scheme was announced in the wake of the Viceroy's visit to the area in 1928, acquisition and resettlement continued for almost a decade. The rehousing consisted of plot allotments in Rehgar Basti and other areas further out from the city. The slum was replaced through auctions with a modern well-built locality (Figure 6.4), but its impact on the provision of mass housing was marginal.

The Delhi Improvement Trust, with its wide-ranging powers and scale of operations, was established in 1937. Government-owned (*nazul*) lands, which had been recalled from municipal control in 1925, were handed over to the DIT. As Legg has pointed out, one of the impulses embedded

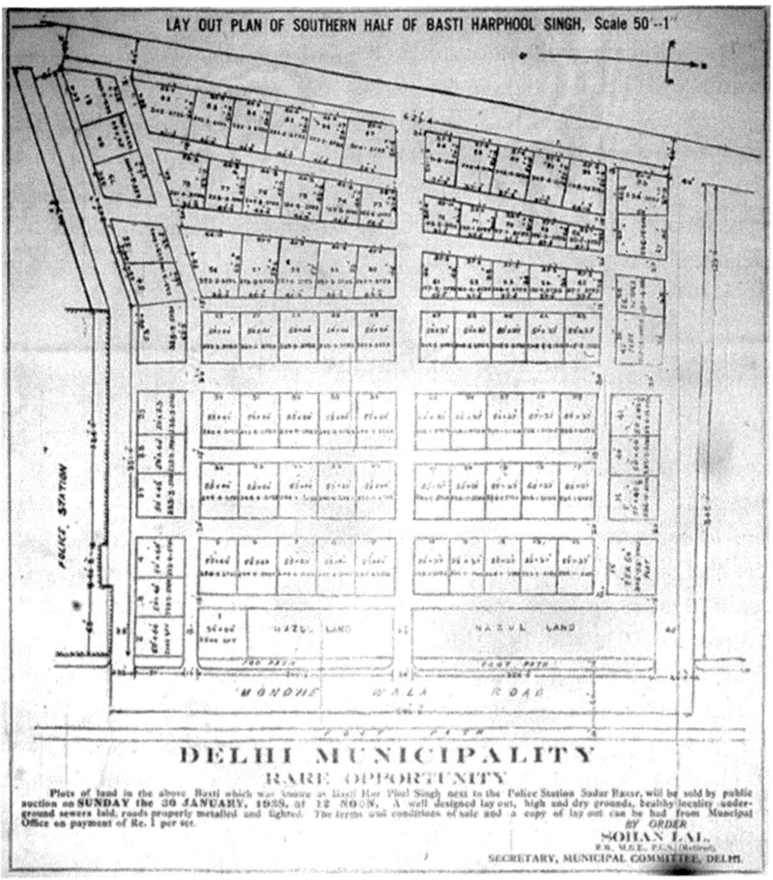

Figure 6.4. Auction of plots in Basti Harphool Singh. (*Hindustan Times*, 29 January 1938.)

within the DIT was the idea that housing the poor could not be carried out without some form of subsidy.[101]

In and of itself, this need not be seen as a radical departure. From a variety of perspectives—sanitary expertise, caste-based politics, nationalist conceptions, and even municipal executives—this was an idea that had a long history, if not deep roots, in 1930s Delhi. Each of these perspectives was, however, internally riven. If sanitary expertise carried a radical sense of materiality, it was also hostile to populist and democratic styles of politics. The Congress nationalists and various other actors in the municipality consciously felt the need to balance this impulse to subsidize housing against allowing landowners and capitalists a free hand in development. Caste-based agitations probably generated the most widely accepted claims to a far-reaching welfarism centred on housing. They carried their own ambiguities, however—most notably, the reproduction of spatial segregation and symbolically degraded forms of labour for dalits. Nor were they, in their Gandhian version, extendable to the unmarked urban citizen. Finally, the class-inflected struggles that arose around the question of rent control, though sharp and with far-reaching consequences, never moved beyond the model of private provision of housing.

In the end, it is not surprising that, as has been pointed out by Legg, the DIT's most successful schemes tended to relate to middle-class accommodation rather than accommodation for the lower middle classes and the poor.[102] Some of the most vibrant militant formulations of the housing question were articulated by clerks and traders. Weaker forms of struggle to contain the market in housing had little chance of shaping the DIT's projects, particularly given the DIT's constitution as a body intended to contain popular impulses in Delhi's urban politics. In this period, then, hesitant political battles to mitigate the market, predictably yielded little that resembled a right to housing for all urban dwellers.

101 Legg, *Spaces of Colonialism.*

102 Ibid. This was also the conclusion of the post-Independence survey of the working of the DIT. *Report of the Delhi Improvement Trust Enquiry Committee.*

7

Grave Investments

Property, Abstraction and Sacral Spaces

On the morning of Sunday 23 May 1937 the Deputy Superintendent of Police of Delhi, along with a small group of policemen, went to clear a settlement that had arisen on a Muslim graveyard in the suburb of Paharganj. He had been there before, just under a month earlier, trying to convince residents of some *chappars* (thatched temporary huts) in the area that they should move elsewhere. The issue was doubly complicated by the fact that the inhabitants of the graveyard were largely (though not exclusively) lower-caste Hindu migrants. On that day, just over a dozen huts were dismantled by the police. After they left, a large group of local Muslims, who had gathered for the festival of Barawafat, proceeded to demolish at least another dozen huts. The next morning, another group of 400 people proceeded to ransack 200 more huts and a temple that stood on the graveyard.

For almost two weeks this incident kicked up a furious political storm in Delhi. Happening against the backdrop of the formation of Congress ministries in the various provinces and a city that by the late 1930s had an established history of inter-religious clashes, the communal polarization that ensued was hardly surprising. S. Abdul Hamid, a local political leader, declaimed:

> The Mussalmans of Delhi are feeling greatly agitated over the encroachments on the land of the Nabi Karim graveyard, the more so as non-Muslims were allowed habitations, who defiled the Muslim graves most flagrantly ... the establishment of the temple in a Muslim graveyard is by itself a standing proof of encroachment upon the land of the graveyard as it is impossible to believe that a temple could have been built there in any other circumstances ...[1]

[1] DDA, CC Records, Home, Part B, File no. 124, 1937: 'S. Abdul Hamid to Chief Commissioner, Delhi, 28 May 1937'.

Possessing the City: Property and Politics in Delhi, 1911–1947. Anish Vanaik, Oxford University Press (2020).

DOI: 10.1093/oso/9780198848752.001.0001

At around the same time, Sadhu Shyampuri, an itinerant holy man from Sheikhupura in Punjab Province, had started squatting on municipal land and was beginning to build an improvised temple in the very heart of the city: the grounds of the Town Hall.[2] The municipal authorities, who considered the structure an 'encroachment', had had him evicted on and off since 1936, when he first started worship there. Shyampuri claimed that this had been the site of a temple until 1857 and had been demolished in the aftermath of the bloody events of that year. In pursuance of this claim he started slowly expanding the area over which he had built (so far) temporary structures. In early August 1938, however, matters reached a head as a group of Hindus tried to build a permanent structure on the site. The police prevented this, and cleared the platform at which *aarti* (worship) was being conducted.

This sparked escalating tension in the city and a steadily increasing Hindu mobilization. Muslim groups began to claim that the site in question had been the location of the mosque of Nawab Said-ud-Daula. In early September an agreement between Hindu and Muslim leaders was reached that, so long as the *Sankh* (conch shell) was not blown, *aarti* could resume at the site until the case was decided in the civil courts. The temporary calm was broken a week later when Munawar Khan, upset at the worship and sound of the *sankh*, entered the temple premises and stabbed the Sadhu. The wounds were relatively minor, but the attack became the occasion for full-scale mobilization by Hindu groups in Delhi. Spearheaded by the Hindu Mahasabha and Mahabir Dal, they launched successive waves of protests and processions through the main thoroughfares. Groups of young 'satyagrahis', usually under the auspices of the Mahabir Dal, flocked to the city from across north India. By January 1939, more than 879 of them had been arrested.

Perceived assaults on sacral sites became, in both these incidents, moments of community mobilization. This entire process was marked by an intriguing set of convergences. In both cases there was an extended period of 'encroachment' which went largely unnoticed. This was followed by a relatively sudden movement from its being a localized site of dispute to one over which people became incensed and were prepared to mobilize. Finally, in both cases these wider circles of mobilization were led by groups

[2] The following account is compiled from reports contained in DDA, DC Records, F. no. 34, 1938; DDA, CC Confidential Records, F. no. 47, 1938, and DDA, CC Confidential Records, F. no. 30-C, 1939.

with affiliations and arenas of activity that extended far beyond the local urban contexts of the property disputes.

This chapter suggests that there is a connection between the modes of community formation in evidence here: the more general commodification of urban space, and the specific effects of this on religious places from the start of the twentieth century. In a city where profit and loss from urban space was moulding the urban fabric, religious structures were no exception. Effective management of temples and mosques came to require that wealth be generated and accounts be maintained. At the same time, sacral sites were also seen in precisely the opposite manner, as outside of the process of commodification. Indeed, there were numerous efforts, especially at the local level, to prevent illegitimate commodification of religious structures. The contradictions between treating religious structures as any other urban space and as an exceptional space outside the process of accumulation characterized this period. Increasingly, through the 1930s, a resolution was offered by reconfigured collectives that defined themselves against local managers and claimed to operate in the interests of the community as a whole. Abstract space, then, called forth more abstract conceptions of community.

The Experience of Abstraction

Between 1900 and the late 1930s, Delhi had undergone periods of bust and boom in property values. Throughout, this period was also marked by an accelerating growth of population. We have seen earlier that suburban land, hitherto market gardens, peri-urban settlements, and artisanal neighbourhoods, were the first port of call for poorer migrants drawn to the city. The new *bastis* into which they moved were hubs for the commodification of suburban land in Delhi.

The graveyard in Nabi Karim (with which this chapter began) is an excellent instantiation of what was entailed. The *chappars* in the Nabi Karim graveyard were not of an especially long standing. According to a report by resident magistrate Narinder Singh, most of them had emerged in the mid-1920s, with others of yet more recent vintage.[3] Around that time,

[3] The graveyard itself had existed from before the 1880s and is supposed to have counted among its interrees the celebrated Delhi poet Zauq. DDA, CC Records, Home, Part B, File no. 124, 1937: Confidential report by Narinder Singh, Resident Magistrate, 25 May 1937.

gravediggers had begun to sell off plots of land. Initially they were sold to relatives, but very soon after, these plots were sold to people outside the community.[4] The new owners built *chappars* and some mud huts that were organized into eleven *katras* leased out to people coming into the city.[5] In the present case, these were members of artisanal castes (Kumhars, Kolis, and Bandhanis).[6]

What we see here is the prolonged process through which the land of the graveyard was brought into the realm of traded commodities. To begin with, a confluence of interrelated demographic, political, and industrial processes generated pressure upon marginal land in the outskirts of Delhi. These processes did not, in themselves, call into being a commodified landscape. Before selling the land, the gravediggers had to move the courts to establish their right to alienate the land. Although they won that legal battle, confusion persisted over what portions were state lands and which parts were 'legitimately' owned by the gravediggers.[7] Figure 7.1 indicates the interspersing of government land and private lands in the locality. The areas shaded dark grey were *nazul* or state-owned, and those coloured white were privately owned.[8]

Having won the case over ownership, the gravediggers sold off the land to another set of individuals. There are a number of telling differences between the gravediggers who brought the land into the commodity circuit and those who purchased it from them. To begin with, while the gravediggers were all Muslim, they sold land to Hindus as well.[9] Again, unlike the gravediggers—who actually worked in the area and whose claims to it were probably won on the basis of longstanding occupation, access, and use—those who purchased it were not doing so to work or live on it. Members of the Delhi Municipal Committee (DMC), while deliberating on the matter in 1937, referred to the people who owned the Nabi Karim land as a class of

[4] It would appear that while most of the land came to be owned by Muslims, there were some Hindus who had also bought these plots. Confidential report by Narinder Singh, Resident Magistrate 25 May 1937.

[5] DDA, CC Records, LSG, LB, Part B, File no. 5(37), 1939: Proceeding of an Ordinary Meeting of the Delhi Municipal Committee, 27 May 1937.

[6] DDA, CC Records, Home, Part B, File no. 124, 1937: Confidential report by Narinder Singh, Resident Magistrate, 25 May 1937.

[7] Ibid., Deputy Commissioner, Delhi to Chief Commissioner, Delhi, 4 June 1937.

[8] DDA, CC Records, Revenue and Agriculture, F no. 97, 1931: Nazul Officer's note, 23 July 1931.

[9] DDA, CC Records, Home, Part B, File no. 124, 1937: Confidential report by Narinder Singh, Resident Magistrate, 25 May 1937.

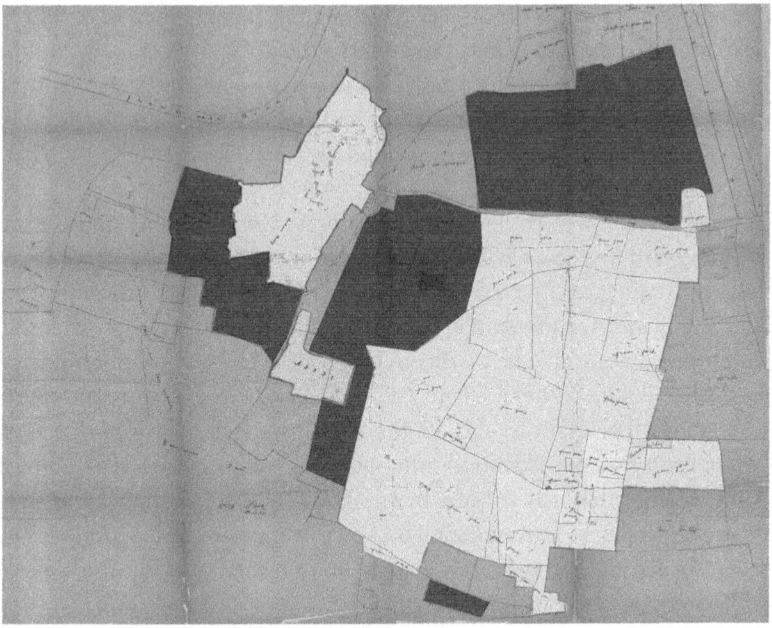

Figure 7.1. Map of Nabi Karim Graveyard and Qadam Sharif, *c.*1931. (*Nazul* officer's note, 23 July 1931.)

'Shylocks' who had little regard for the comfort or conditions in which their tenants lived.[10] This criticism notwithstanding, it appears that the municipality was quite prepared to confer a certain legitimacy on these structures, as house tax was collected regularly. Indeed, many took this payment as a sign of the legality of the settlement. Documents of ownership and possession also circulated for the *katras* and *chappars*.[11]

[10] DDA, CC Records, LSG, LB, Part B, File no. 5(37), 1939: Proceeding of an Ordinary Meeting of the Delhi Municipal Committee, 27 May 1937.

[11] In one instance, an occupant was even able to produce a sale deed (though it is equally clear from the context that he was unable to read it). In open court, Bawa Vichar Nath, the pujari of the Shiv temple erected on the graveyard, produced a deed of sale recording the transfer of the property to him from a Kanhya. However, it also appears to have stipulated that he could not erect a religious structure upon the land—a clause of which he is reported to have been entirely unaware until the deed was read back to him in court. 'Alleged Demolition of Mandir: Five Muslims on Trial: Recording of Prosecution Evidence', *HT*, 5 June 1937.

What is outlined above is (in a paradoxical formulation) the *experience* of spatial abstraction. In the broad sweep of the present account, a piece of land which began as a graveyard, relatively sparsely populated by people who labored on it, ended up as a densely populated suburb, largely occupied by people of a different religious faith. Little memory or sentiment tied those who were so brutally ejected from the spot on 23 May to the graves or the people buried in them. As such, between the start and end points of this narrative, we have seen it become less tied to particular uses and significations and more liable to be commodified, traded, and represented as a commodity.

This process of abstraction can also be illustrated through a number of intermediate points. Before the 1920s the gravediggers had worked on the land; by fighting the court case (and subsequently selling the plots) they decisively altered their own relationship to the graveyard. The differences between the gravediggers and those who bought the land was yet another alteration of relationship to the land. A third shift is evident in the relationship between the landlords, who acquired the land to turn it over for a profit, and those who rented the lands from them to live on. This rapid succession of different functionalities represents a process of abstraction as lived reality rather than idealized schema.

This exposition of the experience of abstraction lends support to two propositions. First, abstraction does not annihilate the capacity of space to be meaningful; rather, it attenuates the ability of space to sustain stable meanings. In the Nabi Karim graveyard, one set of concrete relationships to space was replaced by another, very different one. The temple which was built by Bawa Vichar Nath, for instance, represented an effort to make the space significant for the people living in it at the time. Rather than an absence of relationships to space, then, the experience of abstraction was that of shifting relationships to space. Indeed, its phenomenological manifestation was the presumption that change in the use of space is inevitable. Abstraction as experienced, in other words, was the interchangeability of concrete meanings rather than the absence, or hollowing out, of meaning altogether.

The second caveat follows from the first: precisely because meaning was never evacuated from the process, countervailing tendencies to increasing abstraction can be seen at every point of the process. For instance, the fact that most of the people who bought plots from the gravediggers were Muslim probably has everything to do with the networks of information and structures of community that lay outside the circuits of property circulation. Again, as mentioned previously, the sale deed of the plot upon which the temple came to stand stated that 'the site has been sold for residential purposes and not for erecting any religious building.'[12] Setting aside the legal tenability of such a clause, it preserves a conception of the particularity of the space in the instrument of sale. Finally, the relative social homogeneity of the actual residents of the area—largely workers from artisanal castes (reports seem to mention three castes specifically) and poor Muslims—points towards other ways in which cultural particularity and non-market relationships were preserved within a larger formal process of commodification.

Abstraction, then, proceeded in a contested and reversible fashion, constantly generating its opposite: particularities and non-market relationships. Through the rest of this chapter I argue that sacral spaces in cities ought to be understood in terms of this contested and paradoxical process of abstraction. There was a constant back and forth between seeing sacral spaces, on the one hand, as intertwined with the everyday life of people and thereby outside the process of commodification, and on the other hand, as spaces liable to be bought and sold for a profit just like any other. We can investigate this further by unpacking a crucial metaphor frequently arising in cases relating to religious sites: management.

Managing Sacral Spaces

In Delhi it had historically been common for mosques or temples to have shops, houses, or plots attached to them. The rent from these usually served to defray the ongoing expenses of the mosque or temple.[13] For some of the

[12] As reported in 'Alleged Demolition of Mandir', *HT*, 5 June 1937.

[13] Zafar Hasan's list of archaeologically significant monuments in Delhi includes a number of mosques where shops are attached. Some of these have inscriptions stating that the attached property belongs to the mosque/God. Among the more irreverant is an endowment created by Sadho Ghosan (a milkmaid): 'No one except God should be heir to the three houses and if there should be any, the skirt of his garment would be in my hand on the day of judgement'. Entry number 258 in Archaeological Survey of India, *List of Muhammadan and Hindu Monuments: Vol. 1: Shahjahanabad* (1916) (Delhi: Government of India Press).

larger institutions these could be fairly extensive holdings, while smaller ones might have a few shops in the neighbourhood or even attached to the temple in question.

The Thakurdwara of the Charandasi Gosain Sadhus of Delhi situated in Mohalla Dassan was a medium-sized temple in a neighbourhood which had a number of such structures. Between 1900 and 1925 the temple complex and associated order of *mahants* (priests) was headed by Mahant Basant Das and Mahant Gulab Das successively.[14] The Charandasis owned three pieces of property scattered around the city (Figure 7.2). One lay just outside the walls of the city to its north-west in an area called Pul Mithai, while the others lay in two of the most important commercial and residential neighbourhoods of the old city: Ballimaran and Bazar Sitaram.[15]

There are marked differences in the treatment of the urban and the suburban plots by the Sadhus. Between 1909 and 1918, all the suburban plots, with one exception, were rented out to Rajput families. They all consisted of land with a few *chappars* on them, probably being used for cultivation at this point. The thirty leases from these plots refer to seventeen different individuals from just ten families. There is, then, a pattern of repeatedly leasing out the same plot of land to the same individual, as happened with Jawahar (son of Bakhtawar), Tota Ram (son of Ram Prasad), and Devi Das (son of Sewa Ram) in 1909, 1913, and 1915.[16] There are also instances of brothers leasing out lands at the same time, and sons leasing out

[14] Bernard Cohn discusses the eighteenth-century involvement of Gosains in trading networks of northern and eastern India. He also points to the ways in which they became more purely religious figures dealing in landed property in the nineteenth century. Bernard S. Cohn (1964), 'The Role of the Gosains in the Economy of Eighteenth and Nineteenth Century Upper India', *Indian Economic and Social History Review*, 1 (4), 175–82. William Pinch suggests that by the late nineteenth century, along with this shift in their economic profile a much wider set of religious figures had begun to call themselves 'Gosain'. William R. Pinch (1996), *Peasants and Monks in British India* (Berkeley, CA: University of California Press), pp. 43–5. See C. A. Bayly (2012), *Rulers, Townsmen, and Bazaars: North Indian Society in the Age of British Expansion, 1770–1870*, 3rd edn. (New Delhi: Oxford University Press), pp. 241–42.

[15] The following discussion is based on information compiled from sixty-eight vernacular lease documents preserved in the collection relating to the Charandasi Sadhus in the Delhi Archives. DDA, Private Archives, Collection no. 22 Mahant Ram Rup Ji collection, and Collection no. 23 Mahant Ghanshyam Das ji collection.

[16] DDA, Private Archives, Collection no. 22 Mahant Ram Rup Ji collection, Documents number 122, 130, 139, 120, 129, 143, 119, 131, and 142.

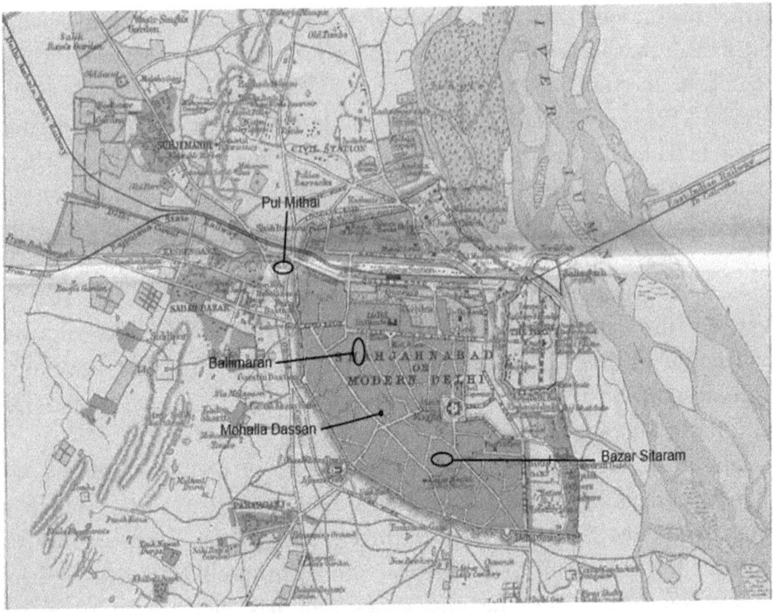

Figure 7.2. Properties owned by the Charandasi Sadhus in Delhi.

the land after fathers.[17] Finally, in a number of cases, new leases were issued for the same rent as during the previous period.[18] The overall impression is that of a group of families renting out the temple lands to carry on traditional occupations in the suburbs.

The structures in the urban area are a study in contrast. The thirty-seven lease documents pertaining to these houses and shops refer to thirty-four different individuals (Table 7.1 displays their castes). The diversity of castes and religions is in marked contrast to the suburban plots. In no instance is there clear evidence that the property was taken up by sons after fathers, or that siblings held the land at the same time. There are only two instances of the same individual renting shops in successive periods (in both instances the rents were increased). There is also a lease document relating to the Ballimaran property for almost every year from 1912 and 1922. These record

[17] Nandu and Ganesh, sons of Matadin, leased out land in 1913. Ibid., documents number 127 and 253. Hira Lal, son of Ghisa, and Panna Lal, son of Hira Lal, in 1913 and 1914 respectively. Ibid., documents number 128 and 16.

[18] Tota Ram, son of Ram Prasad, in 1913 and 1915: Ibid., documents number 129 and 143.

Table 7.1. Castes of individuals renting from Charandasi Sadhus.

Locality	Houses	Shops
Ballimaran	Mali (3)	
	Mahajan (2)	Vaish (1)
	Khatri (3)	Shaikh (1)
	Kayasth (2)	Pathan (1)
	Kahar (1)	Kahar (1)
	Jaini Aggarwal (2)	Brahmin (2)
	Brahmin (1)	
Bazar Sitaram		Shaikh (5)
	Pathan (1)	Pathan (1)
	Brahmin (1)	Khatri (1)
		Aggarwal (1)

a steady upward trend in the rents charged.[19] Unlike the suburban property, whose relative stability of both lessees and price has been noted previously, property in the city was traded relatively often to a much wider diversity of individuals, and with regular revision of prices. This is not especially surprising given what we have seen of property trends from this period.[20] However, it does suggest that properties connected to temples were dealt with in ways similar to any other in the city. Furthermore, it also indicates that personnel associated with temples behaved with orientations to space and time in much the same way that any urban property owner did: revising rents and searching for new tenants from time to time.

Property ownership, then, became a template for an orientation towards time and space in the management of temples and mosques in Delhi. At one level, this connected shrines to the ups and downs of the property market of the city. Thus, the rise and fall of the rental rates had a tangible impact on the life of the temple and those associated with it.[21] The documents of the Charandasi *mahants*, for instance, record the purchase of a Dodge car by

[19] Ibid., documents number 126, 13, 255, 137, 138, 260, 149, 265, 157, 161, 162, 163, 292, 301, 303, 172, 334, 339, and 178. Something similar could also be said about the Sitaram Bazar property, which has a lease document for almost every year between 1914 and 1922. The pattern of increasing rents is also attested to.

[20] Chapter 2 suggested that the sharp acceleration of suburban construction dated only to the mid-1920s.

[21] It is not being suggested that rents were the only source of this connection. Collections of cash from devotees are another obvious source—one that was probably even more significant for smaller shrines—which would have risen and fallen with a variety of other economic considerations. Nevertheless, these represented a particularly close-knit relationship between property markets and urban sacral spaces.

mahant Basant Das in 1920.[22] This new idea of management was a modification of historical connections between shrines and their supportive endowments. Most critically, the ideal of management was made measurable and liable to representation in specifiable units, comparable across many different places and times. Thus, a report on the Jama Masjid from 1941 could commend the managing committee for 'husbanding the resources of the Jama Masjid and for creating a large capital fund in the shape of house property.'[23]

The ideal of management of urban shrines, as it emerged in early twentieth-century Delhi, entailed a particular way of connecting space and time. For temples, mosques, and graveyards this engendered the peculiar dilemmas arising out of the vacillating course of abstraction referred to earlier. It is not surprising, then, that intersecting developments in colonial legal practice, communal mobilization, and wider social processes of commodification through the 1920s came to operate upon and mould precisely this question of management.

An Urban Commons?

In the case of the Mohalla Dassan Thakurdwara, there is one point of partial convergence in the make-up of the tenants of suburban properties and those in the city. The localities from which the tenants of the various properties of the Charandasis hailed were all very near the structures in question.[24] I suggested previously that the processes of abstraction was two-sided—always containing countervailing tendencies. This is well attested to in the relationship between sacral space and neighbourhoods.

The announcement of Delhi becoming the new capital saw a shift in the relationship between public space and private space. A series of building bye-laws looked to regulate private building, and the Municipal Committee tried, with limited success, to prevent projections over public land, and, with slightly more success, to regulate architectural elements such as overways,

[22] DDA, Private Archives, Collection no. 22 Mahant Ram Rup Ji, document number 211.

[23] KB Sheikh Khurshaid Mohammad (1942), *Report on the Delhi Masajid and Delhi Muslim Wakfs Bills* (New Delhi: Government of India Press).

[24] There are a few exceptions. At the Ballimaran property, two tenants—one from Lahore Gate and the other from Kinari Bazar—can reasonably be said to hail from a distance further away than the immediate neighbourhood.

chabutras (platforms in front of houses), and *kuchabandis* (gates of neighbourhoods).

Temples, mosques, and graveyards, simply by virtue of being urban spaces, were embedded within the broader shifts in municipal regulation. Glancing through the municipal records, for instance, it is clear that procedures for applying to build, extend, and repair sacral structures were subject to the same bye-laws as were other construction. Applications for temples and mosques came up regularly in the proceedings of the Bbuilding Sub-Committee of the DMC, and it was part of the routine duties of the Naib Tahsildars to inspect and report on building activity in such structures. Applications to extend or build new temples involved submitting plans and obtaining permission to build (*ittilanamas*), much as any house or shop would need. If a plot for a temple was being applied for in a neighbourhood, then a map of the sort shown in Figure 7.3 might be used to

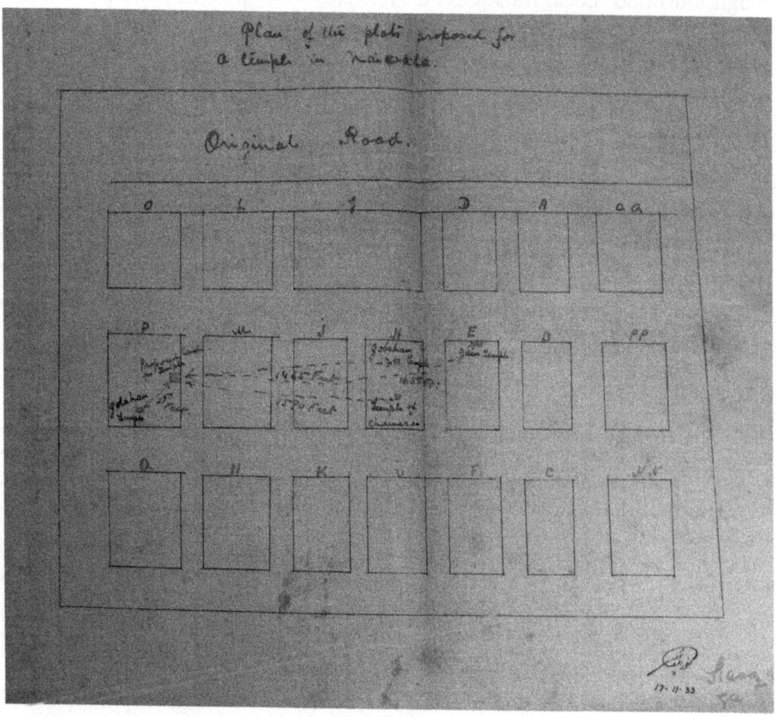

Figure 7.3. Plan for a temple off Original Road. (*Nazul* officer's note, 23 July 1931.)

represent it.[25] Apart from rents and values, then, urban shrines also shared a mode of representation with other structures in the city.

The statutory similarity of shrines and other construction notwithstanding, the treatment of these spaces by DMC was different from that of other structures around the city. First, religious structures were routinely pardoned for violating building bye-laws.[26] Indeed, often shops and houses attached to temples and mosques also had violations overlooked. Second, almost all kinds of projection onto public lands from sacral structures and shops and houses attached to them were usually pardoned, whereas they were more usually seen as encroachments when done by private parties.[27] Third, these buildings were also exempted from house tax. All these measures were conducted while explicitly taking note of the fact that sacral spaces were not expected to be commodified, and implying a contrast between these spaces and others which would be subject to more stringent regulation.

Sacral structures were also seen as having a strong relationship to the neighbourhood. Local mosques and temples were integral parts of communities and the lifeworld of the neighbourhood connected to these sacral structures.[28] The relationship was two-sided, local notions of identity being shaped through these institutions and vice versa. Disruption of this relationship could be seen as disrupting the life of the community. For instance, in 1915 the attendees of the Masjid Darzian Bara Hindu Rao were dissatisfied with the Imam of their mosque. Rather than concentrating on pastoral duties among their own children, they felt that he 'devotes too much time to the instruction of Pathan youth…'[29] In order to restore the customary relationship between the neighbourhood and the mosque, they agitated to get rid of him.

[25] DDA CC Records, Education, F no. 4(68), 1934: DC to CC, 4 Januaty 1934. Between 1916 and the 1920s, Qarol Bagh was a suburb from which the so-called 'offensive trades' were banished from the intra-mural parts of Delhi. From the late 1920s a series of planned layouts, initially by the Delhi Municipal Committee and subsequently by the Delhi Improvement Trust, replaced the earlier arrangements, pushing the groups carrying on these trades further away from the city. This is discussed in Chapter 6.

[26] Thus, in the course of considering what would ordinarily be considered an encroachment, members of a sub-committee consisting of two Muslims and one Hindu could recommend that 'Haji Sahib has done it as a *charitable* act. The Building Sub-Committee is rather indefinite and as a matter of policy we would recommend to overlook the affair. *It is a mosque case*.' TH, DMC Progs., SM, 10 April 1923, Prog no. 11 emphasis added.

[27] TH, DMC Progs., OM of 17 August 1927, confirming E and F SC, 8 August 1927, prog no. 27.

[28] For a discussion of *wakfs* and neighbourhoods, see Gregory C. Kozlowski (1985), *Muslim Endowments and Society in British* India (Cambridge: Cambridge University Press).

[29] DDA, CC Records, R&A, F no. 118, 1916: demi-official note to CC, 15 November 1915.

Structures like the Masjid Darzian, carrying the caste name of the community that frequented it, were common in Delhi and part of a longstanding tradition of sacral structures being established in conjunction with neighbourhoods. In 1923, Muslims from the emerging planned neighbourhood of Karol Bagh petitioned the Deputy Commissioner for land to build a mosque—a request which was granted.[30] A casteist segregation is evident in the 1933 request of the Sanatani Hindus of Karol Bagh for another temple in the neighbourhood, since they would not worship in the temples for Julahas and Chamars (whom the Sanatanis considered low-caste) that were already established in the area.[31] Religious structures were often erections based more on local sentiment than official permission. The temple of the Raidasis of Delhi, for instance, was adjudged an encroachment on *nazul* land and dismantled—an act that prompted a large mobilization of people in the locality.[32] Something similar happened while the Shiv Mandir agitation was raging. An unrelated order for demolition of a different temple happened to coincide with a *hartal* (protest) over the Shiv Mandir issue. The temple under demolition orders was described as being used by the 'Harijans' of Sabzimandi, and they went on to 'enlist the sympathy of the more fanatical Hindus' to amplify their protest.[33] The existence of the temple in this suburb—quite probably a recent one—points to the persistence of the practice of setting up sacral structures in conjunction with new neighbourhoods. While this was a longstanding tradition in urban centres, the nature of the relationship between neighbourhoods and religious structures shifted over time.[34]

I suggest that in Delhi of the mid-1920s these structures were acquiring a new valence. For one, the rapidity with which new neighbourhoods were springing up at this point was creating a new landscape of sacredness in the city. There were, quite simply, many more religious structures. More significant was the fact that the rapid and accelerating transformation of urban space cast sacred places in a new light. Against a more unstable and changing cityscape, sacral structures now began to appear as stable anchors.

[30] DDA, CC Records, Education, F no. 33, 1923: grant of land in Qaraul Bagh to the Muhammadan residents for the construction of a mosque.

[31] DDA CC Records, Education, F no. 4(68), 1934: DC to CC, 4 January 1934. See the map of the locality shown in Figure 7.2.

[32] 'Removal of a Temple' *HT*, 10 October 1929.

[33] DDA, CC Confidential, F no. 47 of 1938, CC to Secy. to GoI, Home Dept., 12 August 1938.

[34] For an exemplary demonstration of this for a number of shrines in Delhi from the fourteenth century onwards, see Sunil Kumar (2002), *The Present in Delhi's Pasts*, 1st edn. (New Delhi: Three Essays Press).

The causes for the sense of a shifting urban landscape (and the generation of concerns about it) were manifold. One obvious occasion for the expression of such fears was the building of the new capital. The newspaper *Comrade*, edited by Maulana Mohammed Ali, ran a series of articles in 1913 entitled 'City of Tombs'. This highlighted the ways in which the construction of Imperial Delhi was leading to the destruction of tombs and graveyards.[35]

> We all desire to see Delhi freed from the gloom of past years; but no one could have desired that those responsible for the creation of the new Delhi should act as if this could be done by removing the mementoes of 'the regal woe of many a vanquished race' and destroying every trace of her 'splendid tragedy of ancient things'.[36]

Accounts like these emplotted interventions in urban space within narratives of Mughal decline and opposition to the colonial present. On one hand, this imparted to the affective cityscape a sense of transience, 'every trace' slipping away. On the other hand, the narrative came to be crucial to the construction of political communities—a project in which both Ali and the *Comrade* (through the Khilafat movement) were deeply involved. Indeed, this initiated a theme that was revisited repeatedly throughout the 1920s. In 1924, a meeting organized at the Fatehpuri mosque (the second largest congregational mosque in Delhi) under the joint auspices of the Anjuman Muhafizul Muslimin, Paharganj, and the Provincial Khilafat Committee, identified a number of structures threatened by 'the building of the New Capital or the extension of Railway Lines.'[37] They declared that this had led Muslims to be in an 'extraordinarily agitated' state, and that any violence that occurred as a consequence should be understood to stem from this threat.

The sense of a mutable urban landscape was, however, far more widespread than the site for the new capital. Consider the following letter, signed simply 'an Ex-Citizen', referring to the area within the walls of the city:

> here are, I understand, scores of other cases of men of worth and fame who flourished in the last century, but who died in comparative poverty,

[35] *Comrade*, 24 May 1913, 21 June 1913, and others. [36] Ibid., 24 May 1913.

[37] DDA, CC Records, Education, F no. 57, 1926: letter of Secy. Anjuman Mahafizul Muslimin, Paharganj, Delhi, to CC, *c*.1924.

> or whose unthrifty children and heirs sold out the properties 'for a song' to the moneylenders, and the latter converted them to small houses, shops stables and katras. In such cases it should be possible to spot houses and courts of historic value, and it is these I am most anxious about, as after a few years it would be very difficult indeed, even perhaps impossible to trace them.[38]

Space commodified, then, was viewed as being unstable: physically in the first instance, but also in terms of what it could signify and symbolize. Against this generalized sense of an unstable urban fabric, sacral spaces came to be seen as points which could endow upon more stable identities upon neighbourhoods and communities. Particularly in Old Delhi, as the 'Ex-Citizen's' letter pointed out, the process of commodification lay at the heart of what made urban space mutable. Sacral spaces began to be seen as outside such a process.

From the early twentieth century in Delhi it is possible to trace tensions between, on the one hand, custodians of shrines, and, on the other, residents of various localities. These tensions hinged precisely on the unacceptable commodification of sacral space. A good case in point is the suit from 1934 brought by three residents of Paharganj against the trustees of the temple of Sada Shiv Bhola Nath with respect to property attached to the temple in their locality. The temple was created on the basis of a trust established in September 1899. In 1900 the creation of this trust was challenged by Mohammed Sultan on the grounds that the presentation of it as a temple was 'fictitiously entered in order to defeat his [Sultan's] right of preemption.'[39] On that occasion it was asserted that a foundation for a *Shivala* (temple) had been dug. Ram Chand, successor to the purchaser of the plot in question, even described himself as the manager of the temple.

The situation changed, however, when the new capital was built just a little south of Paharganj. Property values in the neighbourhood increased dramatically, and Ram Chand proceeded to build pukka buildings on the

[38] *Comrade*, 5 July 1913. The author of the letter goes on to suggest: 'With a view to preserving the memory of these great men and of their homes and habitations, I suggest that we should institute a scheme of memorial tablets – bearing names and dates. These marble tablets may be fixed up in the walls, or, when houses have or will disappear, on stone posts on a side of the road nearest to the actual spot.'

[39] Prem Nath and Others Vs. Har Ram and Others, *AIR* 1934 Lahore 771. The entire account of this property is based upon this source.

land and lease out another part of it to others, who built houses on it.[40] He built another Shiva temple in Mantola, a suburb further away. In his will of June 1918, Chand named his sons as inheritors of the property under ordinary family law (as opposed to managers of the temple). In the suit of 1934, Ram Chand's sons claimed that dedicating the land to a temple in 1899 had indeed been a ploy to prevent preemption and that the property had never been constituted as a trust at all. This claim was struck down in court, and the properties were declared a part of the temple trust. It is remarkable that residents of the neighbourhood had followed the tortuous trajectory of Ram Chand's transactions and intervened to prevent any possibility that the land be treated as private property.

While this case referred to property attached to a shrine, it was often the shrine itself which was at risk of being sold. Processionists planning to offer a *punkha* (*lit.* fan) at the temple in Gali Khajurwali Masjid found themselves rebuffed by a Muslim peon appointed by the Hindu owner, Benarsidas. It turned out that the property had been recently purchased by the latter and that he intended to turn it to another purpose.[41] Reconciliation between custodians and the neighbourhood often involved innovating new administrative arrangements. In 1934, residents of Baradari Nawab Wazir brought a case against the *mutawalli* (variously custodian, trustee or caretaker) of their local mosque, accusing him of mismanaging it. The judge tried to conciliate all parties by decreeing that a committee consisting of 'the representatives of the *Mohalladars* as well as the nominees of the *mutawalli*, would be in a better position to collect the necessary funds than the *mutawalli*, himself who has lost favour with some of the worshippers who visit the mosque.'[42]

Not all such disputes, however, were routed through the relatively sedate settings of the courts. In early 1927 the local chapter of the Mahabir Dal forcibly took over a temple at Pahari Imli, claiming that the *mahant* had removed the idols and was renting out portions of the temple.[43] These events at the Pahari Imli temple precipitated the creation of a Mandir Raksha Committee in Delhi, which was closely associated with other Sanatani Hindu outfits such as the Mahabir Dal. These were also the groups at the

[40] The value of the land was estimated at around Rs. 2000 in 1900. By the time of the suit of 1934, the estimated value was Rs. 400,000.

[41] 'Trouble in Delhi: Alleged Sale of Temple', *HT*, 26 August 1926. The article also notes that the processionists intended to challenge the right of the temple-owner to sell the temple.

[42] *AIR* 1936, Lahore 361.

[43] 'Protecting Hindu Temples: Delhi Citizens' Efforts', *HT*, 25 May 1927.

heart of the Shiv Mandir agitation, and we shall turn to a broader discussion of these groups in the next section.

In July 1927, however, the temple was back at the heart of religious tensions. This time, however, it was between parties not usually considered antagonists in communal mobilizations. It happened that one of the tenants to whom the *mahant* had let a portion of the temple was a Sikh who had installed their holy book in his quarters. When this tenant returned to his room he found that the book had been moved to another place. Suspecting that this was part of an effort to evict him, he immediately called other Sikhs from the neighbourhood, after which, the situation became extremely tense. Only the arrival of armed police pacified the crowd.[44] However, even a few days later Sikhs were considering a course of action to respond to what they considered an act of sacrilege.[45] Ultimately, the issue was resolved after a week, with the major Sikh and Hindu leaders of the city arriving at a compromise and organizing a *langar* (communal dining) and *Akhand Path* (an uninterrupted reading of the entire Sikh holy book).

The fall and subsequent rise of property values between 1920 and 1940. as well as the construction of New Delhi and development of the suburban areas, generated anxieties about urban spaces. These were coupled with a qualitative reconfiguration of the relationship between the public and private. We have seen previously that, with its campaigns against *kuchabandi* and claims on public property, the DMC began to call into question long-established traditions of how *mohallas* controlled space. This was, in other words, a period in which the spatial correlates of collectivity were thrown into question at multiple levels. Temples, mosques, graveyards, and other such sacral spaces came to have a certain appeal as a kind of urban commons. They could be seen as embodying rhythms of time, ethics of mutuality, and a sense of collectivity that other kinds of urban space, because of impermanence, were less able to express.

The outcome, emerging with increasing clarity from the late 1920s through the 1930s, was that sacral spaces could be defended, often violently, as spaces outside this generalized process of commodification. The metaphor through which this defence found expression was that of the public/private divide. Public claims upon these structures were asserted against those of individual *mutawallis* and *mahants* who managed them. British legal and administrative practice undoubtedly contributed to this view of

[44] 'Much Ado about Nothing', *HT*, 6 July 1927.
[45] 'Pahari Imli Temple Incident', *HT*, 9 July 1927.

religious spaces being public and not private.[46] However, the impulse to deploy this framework of separation of the public from the private by ordinary people was activated by a host of insecurities and anxieties emerging from the commodification of urban space. Quite apart from the ways in which the legal structuring of the issue caused matters to lie, custodians often found themselves falling foul of local residents for efforts to alienate sacral space that might have been perfectly acceptable in an earlier period.[47]

I have argued that in the early twentieth century, people in neighbourhoods across Delhi found themselves drawn into contestations with *mahants* and *mutawallis* over what they saw as the illegitimate commodification of temples and mosques. In contrast to this, Malavika Kasturi suggests that most worshippers could not effectively intervene on questions of management because of the long and expensive court procedures involved.[48] She argues that this was the breach into which the Sanatan Dharma Sabha entered, with their efforts to regulate the practices of temples. This claim about the inability of worshippers to intervene in local religious institutions as a result of the expense of court proceedings must be qualified by the fact that (as she notes for the Sanatan Dharma organizations) there were extrajudicial ways of acting on the question through agitation and collective intimidation.[49] Nevertheless, it raises the important point that circles of mobilization beyond the neighbourhood increasingly took up the cause of shrines in the city, and it is to a discussion of these wider circles that I now turn.

From Neighbourhood to Community

From the mid-1920s, sacral sites became critical elements in the imageries of large-scale, imagined collectives. Historian P. K. Datta has argued that the vacuity at the core of communal ideology meant that it operated as 'a

[46] Ritu Birla (2009), *Stages of Capital: Law, Culture, and Market Governance in Late Colonial India* (Durham, NC: Duke University Press), pp. 124–25; Malavika Kasturi (2010), '"All Gifting Is Sacred": The Sanatana Dharma Sabha Movement, the Reform of Dana and Civil Society in Late Colonial India', *Indian Economic and Social History Review*, 47 (1), 107–39; Kozlowski, *Muslim Endowments and Society in British India*.

[47] Kozlowski, *Muslim Endowments and Society in British India*, p. 95.

[48] Kasturi, "All Gifting Is Sacred".

[49] Equally, while individual worshippers might have found it very difficult to see through legal suits, the typical instances examined previously were those of groups of people in the neighbourhood doing so—a possibility that Kasturi does not investigate.

composite point for the mobilization of a large range of tensions'.[50] Tensions around the commodification of sacral sites in urban spaces ought to be seen as yet another element that entered into the construction of notions of religious community.

A few discursive shifts are perceptible in the move from neighbourhood to larger collectivity. As mentioned previously, the priority of public use (as compared to private profit) was the central metaphor through which the neighbourhood battled against commodification. Typical of larger collectivities, however, was an additional emphasis on the details of management. Thus, the Mandir Raksha Committee could suggest that the temples of Delhi were languishing as a consequence of mismanagement by *mahants*.[51] Its memorandum of association registered in 1927 stated that the Raksha Committee was set up 'To protect all Hindu temples, dharmshalas, maths, Satimandirs (Monastries), trusts, and trust properties hereafter called "Hindu public properties."' These had to be 'rescue [d] . . . from the hands of the Pujarees.' It went on to pledge that they would 'realize the surplus funds of Hindu properties [and employ them] towards the upkeep and maintenance of other neglected or unprovided for [sic] Hindu properties.'[52]

The notion of 'Hindu properties' was the correlate of the idea that surplus funds from one endowment ought to be used for other temples as well. Kasturi's important discussion of the reformist Hindu effort to control temple incomes highlights the use of ideas about the publicness of sacred endowments and the corruption of the *mahants*, and that this corruption was an outcome of British colonial rule.[53] The cases that she cites relate to mobilizations spanning much of northern and eastern India.

At play here was the insertion of these sacred sites into a spatial imagination of community which was much wider than had been characteristic of the neighbourhood.[54] This is amply demonstrated by even a cursory mapping of the actions of the Mandir Raksha Committee in Delhi.

[50] Pradip Kumar Datta (1999), *Carving Blocs: Communal Ideology in Early Twentieth Century Bengal* (New Delhi: Oxford University Press), p. 15.

[51] The dealings of the *mahants* with respect to the property of the temple were not the only grounds on which opposition to them was registered. Another prominent accusation was one of immoral behaviour—keeping women on the premises and consuming alcohol.

[52] 'Mandir Raksha Committee', *HT*, 30 August 1927.

[53] Kasturi, "All Gifting Is Sacred", 124–5.

[54] Ritu Birla also suggests that from the mid-1920s, partly as a response to the Mussulman *Wakf* Act, Hari Singh Gour drafted the Hindu Religious and Chritable Trusts Bill in order to demand 'submission of accounts from all Hindu trusts.' Birla, *Stages of Capital*, pp. 135–6.

These ranged from the intramural Pahari Imli to a temple in the south-western suburb of Paharganj and yet again to the western suburb of Teliwara. Indeed, the Delhi chapter of the Mandir Raksha Committee was merely one among a number of such organizations across north India. Their actions also spanned a variety of forms of intervention, from pressing for legislation to instituting civil suits, public protests, and even forcible entry and occupation of temples.[55]

A certain modularity could be suggested for this kind of intervention in the 1920s and 1930s. Something like this is the import of the *Hindustan Times* editorial which claimed:

> gitation in India for the reform and better supervision of endowed religious institutions may be said to have first started among the Sikhs in the Punjab. For many years it had been common knowledge that public religious trusts were being most hopelessly mismanaged in nearly all the provinces . . . and it is to be hoped that other local governments will without avoidable delay consider what steps should be taken for the better control and supervision of public religious institutions belonging to any community or sect in each individual province.[56]

The relationship of the trope of management to commodification in the discourse of these groups is also significant. The emphasis on illegitimate alienation of temple property was shared between neighbourhood-level agitations and those on a countrywide scale. It was only at this level of community-wide mobilization, however, that we see the emergence of a coherent idea of legitimate commodification in counter-position to its illegitimate forms.

This possibility of a legitimate commodification inhered in the form taken by abstract space. Its amenability to representation by account books and leases made temple and mosque property, much like any other, liable to

[55] 'Hindu Temple Reform: Mahants and Chelas', *HT*, 2 July 1927; 'Police Guard Temple', *HT*, 29 March 1927; 'Phus ki Sarai Temple', *HT*, 30 July 1927; 'Paharganj Temple', *HT*, 10 March 1932. DDA, CC Confidential, F no. 47, 1938: Note of Government Pleader, n.d. (*c.*August 1938). Oddly enough, Kasturi suggests that after an agitation in 1924, 'the notion of a pan-Indian movement to forcibly rid temples and maths of trustees soon lost its appeal amongst Sanatani reformers.' She argues for a turn to legal solutions after this point. The existence of an active Mandir Raksha Committee and Mahabir Dal in Delhi and UP must qualify this contention. Kasturi, "All Gifting Is Sacred", 127–8.

[56] 'Hindu Religious endowments', *HT*, 28 May 1931. Kasturi also suggests that the influence of the Akali movement was crucial for the Sanatani reformers. Kasturi, "All Gifting Is Sacred", 126.

comparison across various times and spaces. The idea of 'Hindu public property' (and the concomitant scalar jump from neighbourhood to community) depended upon images of contained commodification. Rather than keeping commodification at bay (a possibility effectively foreclosed for any kind of urban space), it would be better to create an internal circuit of profits coincident with the community. Thus, richer shrines would contribute their 'surplus' to smaller ones. In this way, commodification could be managed and presented as allied with the interests of the community as a whole.

Despite reference to it on occasion, the centralization of 'Hindu properties' was never quite achieved on a large scale.[57] The dynamic described previously can, however, be traced in the emergence of a *wakf* committee in Delhi. The unique importance of urban property for the mosques of Delhi was underwritten not just by the positive fact of owning large amounts of it, but by the negative injunction against holding interest-bearing forms of wealth. According to one account, this was why the Jama Masjid came to acquire such large amounts of urban property in the city after 1857.[58]

Committees with influence beyond individual mosques existed in Delhi well before the twentieth century. The Anjuman Moaiyyid-ul-Islam (established in 1892) and the committees of the Jama Masjid (established in 1862) and Fatehpuri Masjid (established in 1877) each, to different degrees, had extensive spheres of activity. Nevertheless, during the 1920s these were also transformed. Both the Jama Masjid and Fatehpuri Masjid, whose rural estates were confiscated after the Mutiny, saw dramatic increases in their monthly incomes as a consequence of the shifting of the capital to Delhi.[59] The Anjuman, despite its wide remit, was a spasmodically active body usually shaken into action by popular mobilizations rather than the other way around. All three of these were dominated by the old Muslim elite of the city, and their committees and all their members were appointed for life. While these longstanding organizations held sway, *mutawallis* of mosques

[57] Kasturi points towards countervailing forces within the Sanathan Dharma Sabha that were reluctant to pursue the centralization of Hindu property through the path of legislation; "All Gifting Is Sacred", 130–1. She also points towards the denigration of of ostentatious forms of public charity by the Arya Samaj (114).

[58] KB Sheikh Khurshaid Mohammad, *Report on the Delhi Masajid and Delhi Muslim Wakfs Bills*, p. 9.

[59] Jama Masjid, from an income of Rs. 213–13 per month in October 1905 to just over Rs. 4,000 per month in the 1940s. In addition, they had accumulated property worth more than 2 lakhs over this period. For the Fatehpuri Masjid, the income in 1877 was Rs. 400 per month, and this had also risen to around 4,000 per month in the 1940s. From Sheikh Ghulam Mohammad (1941), *Report on the Delhi Mosques* (Calcutta: Government of India Press), and KB Sheikh Mohammad, *Report on the Delhi Masajid.*

around the city in the early twentieth century were quite easily able to exercise significant autonomy with respect to the structures under their care.

Legislation on *wakf* (an Islamic charitable trust) did not transform this situation either. The Mussalman *Wakf* Validating Act of 1913 restored the ability to create *wakfs* in favour of the family—a power which had been nullified by a Privy Council judgement of 1894. As such, it was 'designed to protect [the property of] a fairly small body of landholders or merchant princes.'[60] Kozlowski points out, however, that the debates generated by this Act sparked the first demands for a general accounting of all *wakfs* in country,[61] but it was not until the 1920s that such an accounting could be achieved. The Mussalman *Wakf* Act of 1923, which for the first time introduced the requirement that *wakfs* be registered, was not extended to Delhi even though the opinion canvassed from the major Muslim organizations in the city was in favour.[62] Opinion from these organizations was ignored once again in 1930 when the amendment to the 1913 Act making it retrospectively valid was passed.[63]

Pressure toward more centralized management of mosques and graveyards coalesced, instead, in the form of public mobilizations. One of the few instances in which the Anjuman Moaiyyid-ul- Islam functioned was when the local press threw a spotlight on the acquisition of sacral sites in the construction of the new capital.[64] Even then its operations were considered inadequate by some, and in 1915 a new organization, the Anjuman-i-Muhafiz Auqaf, was established by Sayyid Mohammed Meer, a lawyer from Meerut practicing in Delhi. The new Anjuman claimed by 1924 to have 'filed many suits against dishonest *mutwallies*' in aid of which their members had spent more than Rs. 18,000.[65] By 1940 they managed over 115 mosques and several graveyards.[66]

[60] Kozlowski, *Muslim Endowments and Society in British India*, p. 190. Eric Beverly's work suggests that the discursive impact of this agitation should not be seen as restricted to the interests of this sociological stratum and that it was part of a broader idiom through which some of the legal practitioners involved 'ultimately questioned the legal foundations of the colonial project itself.' Eric Lewis Beverley (2011), 'Property, Authority and Personal Law: Waqf in Colonial South Asia', *South Asia Research*, 31 (2), 155–82.

[61] Kozlowski, *Muslim Endowments and Society in British India*, pp. 174–7.

[62] Various consultations in DDA, CC Records, Home, F no. 66, 1924.

[63] Various consultations in DDA, DC Records, F no. 1, 1921.

[64] See, for instance, Mohammed Ali in *Comrade*, cited previously.

[65] DDA, CC Records, Home, F no. 66, 1924: Representation from the Muslim Endowments Protection Association (Anjuman Mohafiz-i Auqaf) to CC, July 1924.

[66] Mohammad, *Report on the Delhi Masajid*, p. 6.

In 1928, some of the members of the Anjuman Auqaf were involved in an agitation over the demolition of the palace of Zinat-ul Nisa built by Bahadur Shah Zafar. The plot, which was auctioned by the British authorities after the Mutiny, had been sub-divided, let out, and sold on numerous occasions. It was not until the Maharaja of Patiala had consolidated the much-fragmented ownership and begun to demolish the structure to build his own residence in 1928 that there was a call to 'rescue' the palace. The situation in the city was sufficiently tense that the Chief Commissioner felt the need to inspect the place and mollify protesters.[67] Mirza Buland Akhtar, in his speech to a public meeting, claimed that 'The demolition of the building was a sacrilegious act in the eyes of the Muhammadans. It was the last link with the hoary past...'[68]

Through the 1920s and 1930s, then, organizations repeatedly took up the issue of managing sacral sites. They were able to convert what had become everyday occurrences in the city—the demolition and reconstruction of buildings—into moments at which other kinds of solidarities could be innovated. In doing so, however, the mobilizations were shaped by the dynamic of urban space. They were forced to articulate their proposals through the language of management and an orientation towards time and space driven by commodification. Something like this is observable in the dispute that in large measure contributed to the legislation requiring registration and accounting of *wakfs* in Delhi.

In February 1936, Seth Lakshmi Narain Gadodia, a prominent trader of the city, began to rebuild his property located in the busy market neighbourhood of Khari Baoli. His property (called Sarai Bangash) bordered on the western wall of the Fatehpuri mosque. The construction caused much agitation among worshippers, who alleged that there had been an encroachment on the property of the mosque in the course of rebuilding: the stormwater drains were opening onto the wall and were likely to damage it, and a *pushta* (embankment) had been broken and built over. In pursuance of this claim, the managing committee instituted a civil suit which ended with a

[67] 'Zinnat Mahal of Delhi' *HT*, 19 October 1928.

[68] 'Zinnat Mahal of Delhi', *HT*, 7 October 1928. In a letter defending the Maharaja of Patiala, Rao Sardar Khan Punwar of Rohtak bluntly stated: 'Properties change hands... Zeenut-Ul Nissa is long dead and buried and so is Bahadur Shah and I do not understand why people arrogate to this building the status of a mosque in which they allege the King and Queen lived for some time and therefore sacred and the demolition sacrilegious.' 'Zinnat Mahal of Delhi', *HT*, 20 October 1928.

compromise between the committee and the Seth.[69] Far from putting an end to the matter, this was to be the first of eight court cases (civil and criminal) concerning the Fatehpuri Mosque, the last of which was adjudicated only in 1949.[70] On at least two occasions during this period (late 1936 and early 1938), the authorities were worried about the possibility of riots breaking out over the matter.[71]

The very fact that something as prosaic as a disputed embankment could ramify into this particular set of developments is fascinating in itself and has as much to do with the micropolitics of petty jealousies as the macropolitics of the Muslim League, Congress, and other groups in Delhi. However, the facet of the dispute which I highlight here relates to the turn that the case took in 1939 when Mohammed Shafi Bari and Mohammed Idris Bari lodged civil suits against the managing committee of the mosque. In the course of the investigation that followed, the failure to prevent the encroachment was cited as part of a pattern of incompetence—inability to maintain accounts, inadequate supervision of tenants, and allowing the cleanliness and physical structure of the mosque to deteriorate.[72] The judge pronouncing on the suit in the lower court stated that 'the chief cause of the unsatisfactory condition of this *wakf*...is the defective system under which members are taken on the managing committee and once taken are allowed to continue for life.'[73] Even though this judgement of the lower court was eventually overturned, the statement is a significant one. In identifying the problem as the appointment of committee members for life, the judge highlighted a structure of time and stability. The certainty of position entailed in a life-term, in this view, was not suited to respond to the changes and shifts that adroit management required. The instability of the urban fabric, in other words, required echo in the organizational structures that were to manage it.

Sheikh Khurshaid Mohammad, an administrative official tasked with investigating the need for and refinements necessary to legislation about *wakf*, would cite much of this reasoning. His recommendation was that a central *wakf* board with changing personnel ought to administer charitable

[69] DDA, CC Confidential, F no. 65-C, 1938: Report of the Additional District Magistrate on the agitation relating to constructions on the western side of the Fatehpuri Masjid, 29 June 1938.

[70] *AIR* 1949 P&H 141 has a brief account of all the cases instituted.

[71] This is the view of KB Sheikh Khurshaid Mohammad, who in 1941 was asked to investigate the viability of the *wakf* bill in Delhi. See Mohammad, *Report on the Delhi Masajid*, p. 2.

[72] These are all cited in the judgement of Ijaz Ahmad, Judge 1st class at Delhi, 28 October 1940. DDA, CC Confidential, F no. 41, 1942.

[73] Ibid.

endowments.[74] The *wakf* bill which emerged from these deliberations did, in fact, envisage a two-tier system, with a Majlis-e-*Wakf* to sit above the individual *mutawallis*. The members of the Majlis were to be regularly elected and nominated by various bodies, and it was charged with supervisory responsibilities and funded out of a levy upon the *wakfs*. In conjunction with this, *mutawallis* had to register their individual structures and maintain accounts in a prescribed format. This legislation reduced the power of the *mutawallis* in favour of centralization at a higher level. On the Majlis, as many as half of the members could potentially not hail from Delhi at all![75]

From the 1920s onward, sacral structures came to be sites from which visions of community could be articulated. Compared to the neighbourhood, however, when viewed at the scale of community, the treatment of these structures was significantly different. At this level, the ideal of management—the optimal use of property—was inflected with novel content: a wide-spanning scale of operation, the existence of legitimate forms of commodification, and a demand that personnel on managing committees be regularly changed. Thus, even as groups like the Mandir Raksha Committee, Anjuman-e-Muhafiz Auqaf, and the Akali movement attempted to create visions of community based on the perceived non-commodification of sacral space, they were forced to do so through engaging with the questions thrown up by commodification.

A Structure of Abstraction

The role of abstraction in these disputations over sacral space is wonderfully summed up in a single image from the administrative correspondence about the Shiv Mandir agitation (Figure 7.4). This map, scrawled by the Chief Commissioner in his confidential report about the ongoing events in Delhi, is supposed to represent the Town Hall, the centre of municipal administration in Delhi, flanked on the west by a mosque and the attempted encroachment by Sadhu Shyampuri to the east.[76] The image of the state balanced between two religious groups is its irresistible import. The claim that I am making, however, is stronger than one suggesting that the struggle

[74] Mohammad, *Report on the Delhi Masajid*.
[75] This was, in fact, a scaling back from an initial draft of the Bill in which a clear majority was likely to be from outside Delhi. Mohammad, *Report on the Delhi Masajid*, p. 20.
[76] Ibid.

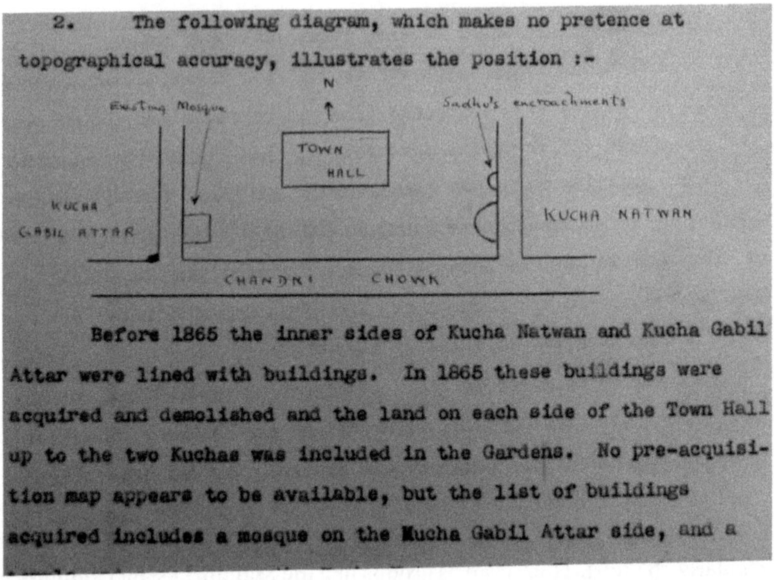
2. The following diagram, which makes no pretence at topographical accuracy, illustrates the position :-

Before 1865 the inner sides of Kucha Natwan and Kucha Gabil Attar were lined with buildings. In 1865 these buildings were acquired and demolished and the land on each side of the Town Hall up to the two Kuchas was included in the Gardens. No pre-acquisition map appears to be available, but the list of buildings acquired includes a mosque on the Kucha Gabil Attar side, and a

Figure 7.4. Diagram of the Shiv Mandir agitation, by the Chief Commissioner. (DDA, CC Confidential, F no. 47, 1938: note by Chief Commissioner, n.d., p. 76.)

is well *symbolized* by the map. Something similar to this map, I would argue, structured the political imagination of the Hindu protagonists of the mobilizations of August 1938.

In order to pursue this claim we must take a short detour to understand the circumstances of the mosque on the western edge. While digging to build a storeroom in the Town Hall in August 1931, workers hit a cement floor.[77] Upon further excavation it began to appear that they had uncovered the remains of a mosque. Excavation was stopped as people from the neighbourhood gathered to physically protect the remains. During subsequent investigations, witnesses (assembled by a Muslim municipal commissioner) from the neighbourhood of Kucha Qabil Attar testified that there had been a mosque on the site before the Mutiny.[78] While these depositions were found contradictory and the records were inconclusive, the Chief Commissioner,

[77] DDA, DC Records, F no. 21, 1931: Secy. Delhi Municipal Committee to DC, 10 August 1931.

[78] At one point the Secretary of the Hindu Sudhar Sabha claimed that the structure was, in fact, a temple. Ibid., Report 11 October 1931.

emphasizing repeatedly that this was an exceptional act of largesse rather than a rightful claim, allowed the mosque to remain.

The Shiv Mandir Agitation of 1938 suggests a structure of politics that, rather than putting forward an authentic claim, sought to repeat the act of largesse in a spatially symmetrical fashion. This is quite independent of what Sadhu Shyampuri might have thought about the matter, as his personal opinions were superceded by the involvement of various Hindu groups in the city.[79] The issue was framed in terms of the restoration of a spatial balance; since a mosque had been permitted, a temple ought also to be permitted. This specific claim that 'there [had] been several successful Muslim encroachments including that west of the Town Hall' was repeatedly made through the negotiations between the administration and Hindu leadership.[80] Even more tellingly, however, in September 1938, L. Lachhman Das, a municipal commissioner negotiating on behalf of a deputation of Hindus, suggested that if the site could not be handed over to the Hindus it should be sold to them at market price.[81] The proposition was reiterated six months later in a meeting of the Deputy Commissioner with Pandit Raj Nath Kunzru, a leader from the United Provinces.[82] The public grant of an alternative site for construction of the temple was another option put forth on these occasions. It mattered little how the symbolic space was acquired or where it was located. The peculiar lack of specific content points to the ways in which abstraction could undergird many such conflicts over sacral space. The Shiv Mandir agitation, even though an instance of a particularly cynical claim, is nevertheless illustrative of the role of abstraction in urban politics.

What it does not illustrate, however, is why youths from across Punjab were prepared to be arrested for this cause. I turn now to the Nabi Karim incident to explore just what the idea of abstraction as developed previously can and cannot help explain about the politics of these movements.

With what we have seen of the impact of commodified urban space on sacral structures, it is not surprising that the Nabi Karim graveyard clashes

[79] Incidentally, the Charandasi sadhu Gulab Das, current *mahant* of the temple at Mohalla Dassan discussed previously, was one of the chief negotiators on behalf of the Varnashram Swarajya Sangh, Delhi Province. DDA, DC Records, F no. 34, 1938: Secy. All-India Brahmana Mahasabha to Chief Commissioner Delhi, 24 September 1938.

[80] DDA, CC Confidential, F no. 47, 1938: Confidential note by CC, n.d., p. 59. That the mosque was the key to the issue was also acknowledged by Asaf Ali, a pro-Congress municipal commissioner. Confidential note by CC, 26 September 1938.

[81] DDA, DC records, F no. 34, 1938: Confidential note of Deputy Commissioner to Chief Commissioner, 21 September 1938.

[82] Ibid., confidential note of Deputy Commissioner to Chief Commissioner, 17 March 1939.

culminated in the setting up of an organization called Anjuman-e-Mahafuz-e Qabur (Graves Protection Association).[83] The name is a significant one and gestures towards the inability to maintain elements of an urban fabric in pristine form. Preservation necessitated political mobilization. This is very much part of the pattern of political mobilizations over localized disputes which threw up organizations with much wider interests.

CID reports about the meetings of the Anjuman-e-Mahfuz-e Qabur suggest that these were often stormy and conflictual affairs. However, they consistently claimed that the structure destroyed in the graveyard was not a temple. But also characteristic was the note struck at one meeting in Paharganj by the Imam of the Paharganj Mosque: ' If the Mohammadans would have gone every week to say their prayers at the graves, the land would not have been sold and no house would have been built at that place.'[84]

The actors brought into play at various points in the Nabi Karim mobilization (and the audience for this declaration of religious orthodoxy and doctrinal purity)—the *chaudharis* and cart-pullers of Paharganj, the residents of Ajmere Gate, the Imam of Paharganj, and the elite Muslim leadership from Gali Qasim Jan to Daryaganj—were an extremely diverse set. Experientially, few elements of everyday life unified these groups. This is, in effect, the reworking of an historiographical puzzle about why riots took the form of conflicts between the poor, while much of the political rhetoric came from the elite.[85] The shared structure of anxieties about urban space that I have been elaborating has not been systematically explored as a possible source of community cohesion.

[83] The organization seems to have emerged within two weeks of the Nabi Karim incident. 'Letter from S Abdul Hamid to Chief Commissioner, 4 June 1937.' Department of Delhi Archives, Chief Commissioner Records, Home, Part B, File no. 124, 1937. It was one of the organizations dealing with *wakf* property that was mentioned in the report that led up to the Delhi Muslim *Wakfs* Act 1943. Mohammad, *Report on the Delhi Masajid*, p. 6.

[84] 'CID Daily Report, 11 June 1937'. Nehru Memorial Museum and Library, Institutional Collections, Delhi CID Records, Installment 2, File no. 55.

[85] Nandini Gooptu argues that the prominence of the theme of deprivation in the mobilizations around the Macchlibazar mosque in Kanpur in 1913 could resonate with the longer-term occupational malaise of the poor. Sandria Freitag suggests that a pre-existing vocabulary of participation in public arenas was the key in bringing different classes into communal mobilizations. Both Gooptu and Chitra Joshi talk about the fragmentary nature of mobilizations around religious themes. Participation in these did not preclude other kinds of solidarities on other occasions. Nandini Gooptu (2001), *The Politics of the Urban Poor in Early Twentieth-Century India* (Cambridge: Cambridge University Press); Sandria B. Freitag (1989), *Collective Action and Community: Public Arenas and the Emergence of Communalism in North India* (Berkeley, CA: University of California Press); Chitra Joshi (2005), *Lost Worlds: Indian Labour and Its Forgotten Histories* (London: Anthem).

The centrality of urban space is often highlighted in accounts of communal mobilization. These claims are, however, accompanied by perfunctory accounts of the urban process, typically suggesting the displacement of class or caste conflicts into communal conflict. When space is discussed, it is in terms of territorial claims laid to it—through processions, for instance—or by analyses of its symbolisms. Studying the material space of the city in conjunction with sacral spaces brings into focus a number of elements relatively neglected by these accounts. Analyses of communal conflict centring on religious structures in urban centres have often isolated these incidents from the other kinds of dispute that centred on sacral spaces. Bringing the whole gamut of conflict into the picture suggests that tussles over shrines were both more frequent and less patterned. Thus they broke out within religious groups, between religious groups expected to be conflictual (Hindus and Muslism or Sikhs and Muslims), between religious groups not expected to be conflictual (Hindus and Sikhs), and between religious groups and the state.

The experience of urban space as mutable was shared by most groups in the city. Correlatively, sacral structures could be seen as points of stability to be defended against commodification. In this way, relationships to everyday space were an important component of the formation of religious communities. Paradoxically, however, this was only possible through incorporating commodification within the framework of communal mobilizations. Thus the metaphors through which mobilization around urban sacral space proceeded—those of management and the relationship between public and private—were based on the generalization of abstract space in the city. The commodity form assumed by urban land must, in short, remain a significant point of analysis even for struggles that ostensibly had little to do with property.

Conclusion

> We have no desire to raise the controversy of public versus private enterprise. We feel that the housing problem in Delhi is so vast and so diverse that there is scope for state enterprise as well as for private enterprise.
>
> ...
>
> A house itself is a commodity...
>
> Report of the Delhi Improvement Trust Enquiry Committee, vol. 1, 1951

By the time the Delhi Improvement Trust Enquiry Committee (also known as the Birla Committee) was set up in 1951, the landscape of Delhi had been transformed once again. In the intervening period, the wartime shortage of building materials, rent control, and the events of Partition had led to a flurry of transformations at the level of individual ownership as well as in the discursive and structural aspects of property in the city. We have already seen how rent control, once it was introduced in the 1940s, had the effect of stimulating sales and sharpening antagonism between landlords and tenants. In the aftermath of Partition, refugees physically captured houses left empty by the largely forced exodus of Muslims from Delhi. Refugees also lobbied for government provision of land—a claim which the post-colonial state found impossible to ignore. Taken together, these developments created a palpable crisis of housing in Delhi.

The Birla Committee's response was to set itself the task of reviving the property market. Private enterprise was presented as the most important means of raising capital for construction. Apart from specifying that a Master Plan for urban development must be drawn up, the major role envisioned for the state was to step in when private sources of capital were not forthcoming. The state's intervention was to take certain forms: easy credit for builders as well as purchasers of houses, the organization of credit associations and cooperative societies, and more standardized building plans so that 'it would be easier for the banker to know how much risk he was

Possessing the City: Property and Politics in Delhi, 1911–1947. Anish Vanaik, Oxford University Press (2020).

DOI: 10.1093/oso/9780198848752.001.0001

taking in advancing money against a certain type of house'.[1] This book has explored how a number of these elements—forms of representation, finance for property development, and real-estate companies—emerged in Delhi over the previous half century.

The Market

Three central issues have been addressed throughout these chapters. First, the largely empirical questions of what happened in the property market after the announcement of Delhi as the capital, and who were the builders active in Delhi. Based on a combination of existing reports and an original dataset, I have argued that Delhi saw a modest boom in construction after the announcement of the shift of the capital. This was followed by a pronounced trough in the 1920s and a boom in the 1930s (particularly in the middle of that decade) which was sustained until a few years into World War II. This series of perturbations, rather than mere increase in population, explains the pattern of Delhi's urban development over this period.

With the levels of building and construction outlined, it is difficult to see Old Delhi as a static landscape which preserved trends from the nineteenth century or earlier.[2] Shahjahanabad and its principal extramural suburbs were transformed over this period. These were transformations that were not, for the most part, planned by the state. Cycles of boom and trough in construction in the suburbs of Delhi, for instance, did not correspond to planned urban expansion by the state. In fact, much construction took place in advance of major layouts, and where layouts were established (by the Municipal Committee or the DIT) they were not developed in a uniform fashion. In some localities the pace of building was steady over long periods (Karol Bagh), and at other places concentrated into relatively short bursts of intensive construction (as in Rehgarpura during the peak of the 1930s boom). In short, it is the rhythms in which capital streamed onto urban land, more than demography, that explain the pattern of property development in Delhi.

[1] *Report of the Delhi Improvement Trust Enquiry Committee* (1951) (New Delhi: Ministry of Health, Government of India), p. 17.

[2] Hosagrahar has, of course, made the same point with reference to the individual house.

But who were the people actually carrying out the property development? Particularly on the outskirts of the city, the initial stages of property development could often take the form of proliferating *bastis* into which working-class immigrants to the city arrived. For some owners of the land on which these *bastis* were located—relative outsiders in the city's power structure—property development helped carve out routes into the centre of urban politics. For others, property played a more supplementary role. This was true, for instance, of small traders in the city for whom house property might have been a useful place to park a windfall or a source of steady income in the form of rent. The 1920s changed much of this.

Crisis in the spheres of finance and commerce prompted a reorientation of the property market. As pressure from the formal banking sector began to restrict the sphere of the indigenous money market, some of the largest firms in bazaar banking wound up their banking operations and shifted capital to property rentals and sales. For many in the middle classes it became difficult to access credit against their property, and they were forced to sell. Alongside these upheavals, new organizations also emerged. In particular, from the mid-1930s a nascent sector concentrating primarily on property development came into existence. Often these were joint stock limited liability companies such as Housing and General Finance Ltd, but a large number of them were short-lived, appearing in the record for a few years before dropping out of sight. The trend in the 1920s was towards a squeeze on the middle and the emergence of larger actors in the property market.

From within the state, the response to the crisis of the 1920s was a novel focus on the middle classes. The instrument of choice was the cooperative housing society. A peculiarly schizoid approach to housing cooperatives emerged: a discursive championing of the collective consolidation of middle-class incomes, but a practical refusal to support such efforts by granting land at subsidized rates. Many cooperative societies established by members of the middle classes failed. Nor was the DIT particularly successful at creating cooperatives. The idea of cooperatives as a solution to the provision of housing, however, took firm root in Delhi, not least because it was championed by a section of people—government employees—who were among the most consistently politically active.

There were, in short, many twists in the trajectory of real-estate development over this period. The unfolding logic of commodification, particularly during the increased construction of the 1930s, tended towards a consolidation of larger forms of private capital in real estate.

The State

The second issue that I have explored is the relationship between the state and the property market. This was, I argue, both a central relationship with respect to how the urban fabric was created as well as one in which, on balance, the property market was the more significant end. One of the elements that anchored the state in the property market was its role as the guarantor of the representations of property. Refining and clarifying title and lease documents, for instance, was an oft-articulated concern of the state. A careful examination of individual representations of space, however, points to the significance of time in these documents. Inasmuch as commodified space was inserted into cycles of accumulation, forms of temporality were necessarily embedded in each of the kinds of representation of space studied. Whether this took the form of a pattern of revision (maps) or, as with auctions, through shifts in the underlying form of uncertainty being represented, time was a crucial dimension.

The element of temporality embedded within representations of commodified space allowed for their compilation into narrative forms. From microscale reports about individual structures to accounts about city-wide policy, narratives about property were ubiquitous. In turn, these narratives were used to refine individual representations of space. Control of this narrative circuit differentiated the state from other actors in the market, potentially allowing it to act with a surer footing. Even though the colonial state (through its various agencies) was the largest landowner in the city, this narrative circuit was the basis for the most significant role which the state was prepared to play. In fact, the colonial state was often reluctant to leverage its extensive holdings to intervene in ways that ran counter to market trends. In contrast, 'narrating' property, and leveraging its role as archiver and guarantor of the key forms of representation of commodified space, were seen within the state as more acceptable ways of relating to the property market.

The reluctance to actively shape and regulate the property market was not for want of the capacity to do so. In effect, what the construction of Imperial Delhi and subsequent power of the New Delhi Municipal Committee demonstrated was precisely such a capacity: to enunciate a central vision and control the operations of the market. The exceptional symbolic value of New Delhi prompted a strategy for that part of the city very different from that adopted for other parts of the city. In the areas of operation of the DMC and the DIT the determination to head off excessive popular autonomy and strictures dictating government 'on the cheap' meant that the market had much freer rein.

The results were paradoxical. On the one hand, in a manner analogous to the formulations of govermentality theory, the market was made an intimate element of statecraft. Thus, even where exchanges between the formidably multiple agencies of the state in Delhi were concerned, the actual valuations through which decisions were taken about allocation of resources were determined through the market. This held true across all parts of the city, old and new. On the other hand, the state could also view the property market as a stumbling block against its own aims. In the face of private speculation, the state was portrayed as requiring protection from the property market. Ultimately, the state saw itself as both the protector of the principle of private property as well as in need of protection from the market to carry out its more welfarist ambitions. Irresolvable disputes about establishing the correct 'market value' of land, or concerns about confiscating 'unearned increment' away from house-owners, all point to the deep dilemmas thrown up by this double bind.

Struggles

This underlying bind in which the state so often found itself was only resolved in the context of different kinds of struggle and action by classes and groups within the city. This question of how various political struggles in the city were shaped by, and responded to, the commodification of land is the third running theme of this book. The impact of the market on housing in Delhi was an issue that regularly took political forms. Some of these were from within the state itself. Thus, sanitary discourse could evolve a deeply material feel for the city, and advocate measures in the collective interest that ran counter to the logic of the market. The hypervisibility endowed upon Delhi as a consequence of its becoming the capital of British India was another factor which could introduce non-market considerations where the urban fabric was concerned.

Both these impulses within the state that ran counter to the market, however, were articulated within the context of an authoritarian disdain for the rise of democracy and mass politics. The DIT, in fact, was built upon these foundations. In contrast to the denigration of mass politics, the concerns of urban elites found a ready resonance within state agencies. In the early years of the twentieth century, DMC was very much a place in which the interests of landlords and builders were served—to the point where violations of even municipal bye-laws were supported by municipal commissioners. The committee of DIT, which was explicitly designed to reduce the voice of municipal commissioners elected on an expanded franchise, allowed disproportionate representation to business interests and local elites such as Lala Shri Ram. Additionally, urban elites also had access to municipal and governmental personnel through more direct and less legal channels, with forms of corruption and illegality forming yet another interface between the state and the elite.

The rise of mass politics in the city, however, was the horizon against which these machinations had to define themselves. Were there forms of mass agitation that expressed opposition to the commodification of urban land? The answer here must be 'yes'. In fact, opposition to the commodification of urban land was expressed, perhaps, in too many diffuse ways for it to be a sharp and unified political demand. For Congress nationalists, engaging with politics in the city necessarily brought them up against questions of rent and the conflict between tenants and landlords. Neither in the *kiraya* committees of the 1930s nor in the upheavals over rent control in the 1940s was the Congress a major voice in favour of tenants against landlords. Indeed, the leadership seems to have been eager to walk a tightrope between reassuring landlords of their legitimate claims and supporting masses of tenants. Unsurprisingly, the organization often chose to officially opt out of battles in which they were pitted against each other.

The demand for state-subsidized housing was also raised consistently by organizations active on the issue of caste. Where Arya Samajist organizations seem to have been most concerned to occupy a position as brokers, Congress workers, operating within a particular vein of Gandhian politics, were prepared to go further and demand that the Municipal Committee provide decent housing to sweepers in the city. The peculiarities of the Gandhian approach to caste, however, meant that the basis of this demand would be the continuation of the sanitation work by dalits. Conversely, the demand for decent housing did not, in this version, take on a universalist aspect as a right of every citizen.

The most radical, sustained, and successful agitations for housing protected from the operations of the market came, in fact, from government clerks. Apart from successfully demanding the allocation of subsidized housing, clerks pushed on to force authorities to grant better infrastructure in their neighbourhoods. Again, cooperative credit arrangements evolving from the 1930s were seized by lower-middle-class clerks in Delhi, as they had been elsewhere in the country.[3] Even during the rent-control agitations, clerks who lived in rented accommodation were the voices who most steadily pushed for the enactment of rent control legislation. While workers in other state agencies readily followed the template established by government clerks—municipal clerks, for instance, petitioned successfully for housing—there is little evidence of wider solidarities around housing being built around these efforts. Struggles over housing, then, remained a fragmented and insufficient counterweight to the state's commitment to the maintenance of private property in the city.

Struggles over the commodification of urban land were not, however, played out solely on the terrain of housing. Other seemingly unrelated conflicts, such as those over sacral space discussed in Chapter 7, were shaped by the commodification of urban land. In a landscape where space was increasingly assumed to generate profit, religious property posed unique problems and resolutions. Religious spaces could, on the one hand, appear as pockets of non-commodified space within the city, but at the same time they were subject to pressures and demands for 'managing' property that were similar to any other plot in the city. These contradictory pressures yielded paradoxical outcomes. Keeping sacral spaces free from the flexibility of a landscape of accumulation was presented as requiring ever wider and more abstract notions of community: the Hindu, Muslim, or Sikh community as a whole, rather than more tangible units like the neighbourhood. These abstract communities were created in close conjunction with the idea of a legitimate commodification that could sustain communal property. On the other hand, this call to abstract community was twinned with an appeal to the tangible and shared experience of the slipping away of collective space. This tangibility helped to stitch together mobilizations that sharpened the forms of religious antagonism that had developed over the late nineteenth and twentieth centuries.

Politics over a variety of issues in the city, then, was shaped by the commodification of urban land. In an ironic reversal, demands for containing or controlling commodification were much more effectively articulated in struggles that were not directly about the market, such as those over sacral space. Here there emerged ideas of commons, a public to which property managers had to be accountable, and a vigorous opposition to the idea of accumulation for private profit. The articulation of these demands with

[3] Nikhil Rao (2013), *House, but No Garden: Apartment Living in Bombay's Suburbs, 1898–1964* (Minneapolis, MN: University of Minnesota Press).

respect to religious property, however, had pathological consequences in the form of sharpening communal antagonism. Collective action undertaken explicitly on the issue of housing was far more fragmented, and the demand for action independent of market considerations was correspondingly weaker.

Conclusion

By the end of the colonial period the process of understanding urban space through the lens of ownership and private development was well established. To return to the Birla Committee, in light of the manner in which the housing question emerged in Delhi, it is neither surprising to find that a non-local figure (and industrialist) G. D. Birla should be chosen to head a committee about housing in Delhi, nor that the committee would steer away from the idea that most housing should be provided by the state. Alongside the numerous other factors that were unique to this moment—the discourse about refugees, and the relationship between the Congress establishment and the state—there remained significant lines of continuity between the pre- and post-1947 social formation. Prominent among the continuities was the acceptance of the connections between the representation of commodified space, the availability of credit, and cycles of property development. In declaring the house to be a commodity, the Birla Committee was acknowledging not just the centrality acquired by urban property to any question regarding land disposal, but also the densely packed sedimentation of this principle into the everyday experience of urban life in Delhi.

APPENDIX

The Database of Construction

The data tables on which the graphs are based are compiled from the proceedings of the Delhi Municipal Committee (DMC). The Building Sub-Committee (BSC) of the DMC was convened on a weekly basis. The proceedings of the latter were confirmed, with appropriate alterations, every week by the Ordinary Meeting (OM) of the DMC. Within the municipal area of Delhi, all construction required the permission of the DMC which was provided by the OM in this way. The proceeding volumes of the DMC were usually organized into quarters (January–March, April–June, and so on). The database contains information from proceedings in forty-nine quarters (out of the total of 149 quarters) between 1911 and 1947. These amount to more than 15,000 individual applications to build.

Collecting the Data

The applications consist of brief accounts of the construction envisaged and other information about the locality, ward, owner, and so on. Each of these would be sanctioned or rejected by the BSC; two such proceedings are shown in Figure A.1. The subsequent OM would consider the proceedings of the BSC and could reverse any of its decisions.

To create the database, I recorded the following information from each application: the ward in which construction was proposed, the name, sex, and religion (based on the name) of the applicant, the locality in which construction was proposed, information about the nature of construction, whether it was approved by BSC and whether it was approved by OM, and the quarter in which the application was considered by the DMC.

The nature of construction was recorded through a broad classification into large structures and small structures. A large structure would be described with one of the following words in the application: house, shop, godown, *katra* (multi-apartment structure around a large courtyard), building, and a miscellaneous collection of other descriptions (temple, mosque, substation, and so on). If the information was available, the number of storeys being built and the highest storey of the building were recorded.

Small constructions consisted of a large variety of structures ranging from a storey to a trough. They also included verandahs, *chajjas* (overhanging eaves), *chajja* verandahs, portion, *barsati* (free-standing rooms on the roof), *saiban* (sheds), latrines, colonnade, room, and so on.[1] In the case of every small construction and

[1] The following is a near-comprehensive list of the descriptive terms from the DMC registers which were entered under the 'small constructions' category: *baithak*, *balakhana*, *baradari*,

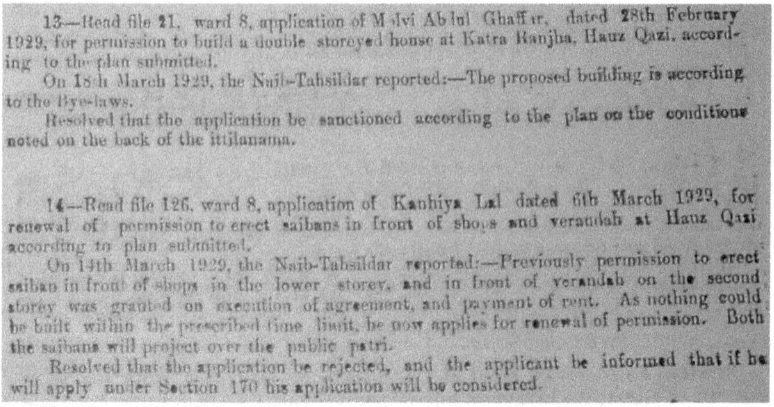

13—Read file 21, ward 8, application of Mulvi Abdul Ghaffar, dated 28th February 1929, for permission to build a double storeyed house at Katra Ranjha, Hauz Qazi, according to the plan submitted.

On 18th March 1929, the Naib-Tahsildar reported:—The proposed building is according to the Bye-laws.

Resolved that the application be sanctioned according to the plan on the conditions noted on the back of the ittilanama.

14—Read file 126, ward 8, application of Kanhiya Lal dated 6th March 1929, for renewal of permission to erect saibans in front of shops and verandah at Hauz Qazi according to plan submitted.

On 14th March 1929, the Naib-Tahsildar reported:—Previously permission to erect saiban in front of shops in the lower storey, and in front of verandah on the second storey was granted on execution of agreement, and payment of rent. As nothing could be built within the prescribed time limit, he now applies for renewal of permission. Both the saibans will project over the public patri.

Resolved that the application be rejected, and the applicant be informed that if he will apply under Section 170 his application will be considered.

Figure A.1. Applications to the Building Sub-Committee of the DMC. (TH, DMC Progs, BSC, 22 March 1929, confirmed at OM, 3 April 1929.)

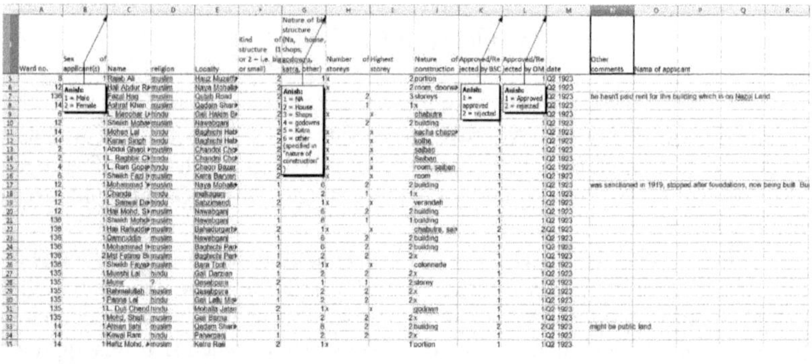

Figure A.2. A spreadsheet recording entry of construction data.

the miscellaneous large ones, the nature of the particular structure for which permission was required was also recorded. The entry format is shown in Figure A.2.

In instances where more than one kind of construction was sanctioned, the principle followed was to make only one entry against the largest structure discernible. Thus, an application for a shop and a room would not be entered under the

chabutra, *chajja*, *chajja* verandahs, *chajjlis*, *chhatri*, *chaubara*, *chaukhat*, *chhal*, *chhappar*, *chowkidar*'s hut, colonnade, covered drain, culvert, *dalan*, *dasa*, *dehliz*, *deorhi*, *dohashma* room, door, drain, flooring of shops, frontage of shops, gateway, hinged wooden flap, *hujra*, iron flap, *jastposh kotha*, *jhanp*, *kacha kotha*, *katehra*, *kham kotha*, *khancha* wall, *khaprail*, kiln, kitchen, *kotha*, *kothi*, *kothri*, latrine, *mamti*, overway, *piao*, pillars, privy, *panjdarah*, *purdah* wall, *pushta*, *raoti*, roof, *rukar*, *saiban*, *sehdara*, shed, sitting room, skylight, staircase, steps, *tatti*, temple in the house, tin shed, *toredar chabutra*, *toredar* step, verandah, wall, well.

'room' category but only under the 'shop' category. Where the term 'repairs' was used, no entry was made at all.

Analysing the Data

After entry of all the information, the most significant issue prior to further analysis concerned the changes in the boundaries of various wards. This was only a problem for the wards outside the walled city. Initially these consisted of numbers 12, 13, and 14. By the end of the period, Wards 13 and 14 had been subdivided, and a new area—Karol Bagh—added, leading to wards 12–16 being the extramural wards. To circumvent this problem, rather than using the ward numbers the names of the localities were employed to organize the data of the extramural wards. Thus, Sabzimandi, Sadar North, Sadar South, Paharganj, and Karol Bagh were used as the spatial units. Data entered under different ward numbers were reassigned based on the locality information recorded.

Further analysis and all the graphs were prepared in Microsoft Excel.

Bibliography

Manuscript and Archival Sources

British Library, London, UK

India Office Collection, MSS Eur D724: Hume Papers

Centre of South Asian Studies, Cambridge, UK

Hume Papers

Department of Delhi Archives, New Delhi, India

Chief Commissioner's Records (various departments), 1913–47
Chief Commissioner's Confidential Records, 1914–46
Commissioner's Office Records, 1878–1912
Deputy Commissioner's Office Records, 1900–47
Private archives (various collections)

National Archives of India, New Delhi, India

Home (Municipalities)

Manuscript Section, Nehru Memorial Museum and Library, New Delhi, India

Individual Collections, B. K. Chandiwala
Institutional Collections, Delhi CID Records

Town Hall, Delhi, India

Proceedings of the Delhi Municipal Committee 1911–47

Printed Primary Sources

Administration Report of the Delhi Improvement Trust for Years 1937–39 (1940) (New Delhi: Delhi Improvement Trust).

Banking Enquiry Committee for the Centrally Administered Areas, 1929–30 (1930) (Calcutta: Government of India, Central Publication Branch).

Census of India, 1901–41.

Comrade, 1911–13.

Hindustan Times, 1924–46.

Mohammad, KB Sheikh Khurshaid (1942). *Report on the Delhi Masajid and Delhi Muslim Wakfs Bills* (New Delhi: Government of India Press).

Report of the Delhi Improvement Trust Enquiry Committee, 1951 Vol. 1 (1951) (New Delhi: Ministry of Health, Government of India).
Report of the Indian Taxation Enquiry Committee, 1924–25, Vol. 1 (1926) (Madras: Government of India, Central Publication Branch).
Report on the Administration of the Delhi Crown Lands (1910) (Lahore: Civil and Military Gazette Press).
Report on the Administration of the Delhi Municipality, various volumes, 1911–44.
Report on the Administration of the Delhi Province, various volumes, 1921–39.
Report on the Relief of Congestion in Delhi (1937) (Simla: Government of India Press).
The Times of India, 1911–47.

Printed Secondary Sources

Ahuja, Ravi (2009), *Pathways of Empire: Circulation, 'Public Works' and Social Space in Colonial Orissa, c.1780–1914* (Hyderabad: Orient BlackSwan).
Anderson, M. R. (1992), 'Public Nuisance and Private Purpose', *SOAS Law Department Working Paper 1* (Law School of Oriental and African Studies).
Barrow, Ian J. (2003), *Making History, Drawing Territory: British Mapping in India, c.1756–1905* (New Delhi: Oxford University Press).
Bayly, C. A. (1975), *The Local Roots of Indian Politics: Allahabad, 1880–1920* (Oxford: Clarendon Press).
Bayly, C. A. (2012), *Rulers, Townsmen, and Bazaars: North Indian Society in the Age of British Expansion, 1770–1870*, 3rd edn. (New Delhi: Oxford University Press).
Beverley, Eric Lewis (2011), 'Property, Authority and Personal Law: Waqf In Colonial South Asia', *South Asia Research*, 31 (2), 155–82.
Bhadra, Gautam (1988), 'Four Rebels of Eighteen-Fifty-Seven', in Ranajit Guha and Gayatri Chakravorty Spivak (eds.), *Selected Subaltern Studies* (Delhi: Oxford University Press), pp. 129–70.
Bharat Sevak Samaj (1958), *Slums of old Delhi: Report of the Socio-Economic Survey of the Slum Dwellers of Old Delhi City* (Delhi: Atma Ram and Sons).
Bhattacharya, Neeladri (1986), 'Colonial State and Agrarian Policy', in Sabyasachi Bhattacharya and Romila Thapar (eds.), *Situating Indian History: For Sarvepalli Gopal* (Delhi: Oxford University Press).
Birla, Ritu (2009), *Stages of Capital: Law, Culture, and Market Governance in Late Colonial India* (Durham, NC: Duke University Press).
Brenner, Robert (1985), 'Agrarian Class Structure and Economic Development in Pre-Industrial Europe' in T. H. Aston and C. H. E. Philpin (eds.), *The Brenner Debate: Agrarian Class Structure and Economic Development in Pre-Industrial Europe* (Cambridge: Cambridge University Press), pp. 10–63.
Chakrabarty, Dipesh (2002), *Habitations of Modernity: Essays in the Wake of Subaltern Studies* (Chicago, IL: University of Chicago Press).
Chakravarty-Kaul, Minoti (1996), *Common Lands and Customary Law: Institutional Change in North India over the Past Two Centuries* (Delhi: Oxford University Press).

Chandavarkar, Rajnarayan (1994), *The Origins of Industrial Capitalism in India: Business Strategies and the Working Classes in Bombay, 1900–1940* (Cambridge: Cambridge University Press).

Chandavarkar, Rajnarayan (1998), *Imperial Power and Popular Politics: Class, Resistance and the State in India, c.1850–1950* (Cambridge: Cambridge University Press).

Chatterjee, Partha (1993), *The Nation and its Fragments: Colonial and Postcolonial Histories* (Princeton, NJ: Princeton University Press).

Chatterjee, Partha (2004), *The Politics of the Governed: Reflections on Popular Politics in Most of the World* (New York: Columbia University Press).

Chattopadhyay, Swati (2000), 'Blurring Boundaries: The Limits of "White Town" in Colonial Calcutta', *Journal of the Society of Architectural Historians*, 59 (2), 154–79.

Chattopadhyay, Swati (2005), *Representing Calcutta: Modernity, Nationalism and the Colonial Uncanny* (London: Routledge).

Chibber, Vivek (2013), *Postcolonial Theory and the Specter of Capital* (London: Verso).

Codell, Julie (2018) 'On the Delhi Coronation Durbars, 1877, 1903, 1911.', *BRANCH: Britain, Representation and Nineteenth-Century History*, 11 July 2018.

Cohn, Bernard S. (1964), 'The Role of the Gosains in the Economy of Eighteenth and Nineteenth Century Upper India', *Indian Economic and Social History Review*, 1 (4), 175–82.

Cohn, Bernard S. (1992), 'Representing Authority in Victorian India', in E. J. Hobsbawm and T. O. Ranger (eds.), *The Invention of Tradition* (Cambridge: Cambridge University Press), pp. 165–209.

Dalrymple, William (1994), *City of Djinns: A Year in Delhi* (London: Flamingo).

Datta, Partho (2012), *Planning the City: Urbanization and Reform in Calcutta, c.1800–c.1940* (New Delhi: Tulika Books).

Datta, Pradip Kumar (1999), *Carving Blocs: Communal Ideology in Early Twentieth Century Bengal* (New Delhi: Oxford University Press).

Dobbin, Christine E. (1972), *Urban Leadership in Western India: Politics and Communities in Bombay City, 1840–1885* (Oxford: Oxford University Press).

Dossal, Mariam (2010), *Theatre of Conflict, City of Hope: Mumbai, 1660 to Present Times* (New Delhi: Oxford University Press).

Dube, S. (1998), *Untouchable Pasts: Religion, Identity, and Power among a Central Indian Community, 1780–1950* (Albany, NY: SUNY Press).

Dyos, H. J. (1968), 'The Speculative Builders and Developers of Victorian London', *Victorian Studies*, 11 (Supplement: Symposium on the Victorian City), 641–90.

Edney, Matthew H. (1997), *Mapping an Empire: The Geographical Construction of British India, 1765–1843* (Chicago, IL: University of Chicago Press).

Engels, Friedrich (1972), *The Condition of the Working Class in England: From Personal Observation and Authentic Sources* (London: Panther).

Engels, Friedrich (1988), 'The Housing Question', in Karl Marx and Friedrich Engels (eds.), *Collected Works* (New York, NY: International Publishers).

Freitag, Sandria B. (1989), *Collective Action and Community: Public Arenas and the Emergence of Communalism in North India* (Berkeley, CA: University of California Press).

Frykenberg, R. E. (1993), 'The Coronation Durbar of 1911', in R. E. Frykenberg (ed.), *Delhi through the Ages: Selected Essays in Urban History, Culture and Society* (Delhi: Oxford University Press), pp. 225–46.

Ghosh, Anindita (2016), *Claiming the City: Protest, Crime and Scandals in Colonial Calcutta, c.1860–1920* (New Delhi: Oxford University Press).

Glassman, Jim (2006), 'Primitive Accumulation, Accumulation by Dispossession, Accumulation by "Extra-Economic" Means', *Progress in Human Geography*, 30 (5), 608–25.

Glover, William J. (2008), *Making Lahore Modern: Constructing and Imagining a Colonial City* (Minneapolis, MN: University of Minnesota Press).

Gooptu, Nandini (2001), *The Politics of the Urban Poor in Early Twentieth-Century India* (Cambridge: Cambridge University Press).

Gordon, A. D. D. (1978), *Businessmen and Politics: Rising Nationalism and a Modernising Economy in Bombay, 1918–1933* (New Delhi: Manohar).

Goswami, Manu (2004), *Producing India: From Colonial Economy to National Space* (Delhi: Permanent Black).

Grewal, J. S. (1975), *In the By-Lanes of History: Some Persian Documents from a Punjab Town*, 1st edn. (Simla: Indian Institute of Advanced Study).

Guha, Ranajit (1963), *A Rule of Property for Bengal: An Essay on the Idea of Permanent Settlement* (Paris: Mouton).

Gupta, Narayani (1981), *Delhi between Two Empires, 1803–1931: Society, Government and Urban Growth* (Delhi: Oxford University Press).

Haila, A. (1990), 'The Theory of Land Rent at the Crossroads', *Environment and Planning D: Society and Space*, 8, 275–96.

Hall, Peter (2002), *Cities of Tomorrow: An Intellectual History of Urban Planning and Design in the Twentieth Century*, 3rd edn. (Oxford: Blackwell).

Harvey, David (1989a), *The Condition of Postmodernity: An Enquiry into the Origins of Cultural Change* (Oxford, England; Cambridge, MA: Blackwell).

Harvey, David (1989b), *The Urban Experience* (Oxford: Blackwell).

Harvey, David (1999), *The Limits to Capital*, new edn. (London: Verso).

Harvey, David (2003), *Paris, Capital of Modernity* (New York: Routledge).

Harvey, David (2003), *The New Imperialism* (Oxford: Oxford University Press).

Heitler, Richard (1972), 'The Varanasi House Tax Hartal of 1810–11', *Indian Economic and Social History Review*, 9 (3), 239–57.

Hosagrahar, Jyoti (1992), 'City as Durbar: Theater and Power in Imperial Delhi', in Nezar AlSayyad (ed.), *Forms of Dominance: On the Architecture and Urbanism of the Colonial Enterprise* (Aldershot: Avebury).

Hosagrahar, Jyoti (2005), *Indigenous Modernities: Negotiating Architecture and Urbanism* (London: Routledge).

Irving, Robert Grant (1981), *Indian Summer: Lutyens, Baker, and Imperial Delhi* (New Haven, CT: Yale University Press).

Jager, Johannes (2003), 'Urban Land Rent Theory: A Regulationist Perspective', *International Journal of Urban and Regional Research*, 27 (2), 233–49.

Joshi, Arun (1975), *Lala Shri Ram: A Study in Entrepreneurship and Industrial Management* (New Delhi: Orient Longman).

Joshi, Chitra (2005), *Lost Worlds: Indian Labour and its Forgotten Histories* (London: Anthem).

Kasturi, Malavika (2010), '"All gifting is sacred": The Sanatana Dharma Sabha Movement, the Reform of *Dana* and Civil Society in Late Colonial India', *Indian Economic and Social History Review*, 47 (1), 107–39.

Kidambi, P. (2001), 'Housing the Poor in a Colonial City: The Bombay Improvement Trust, 1898–1918', *Studies in History*, 17 (1), 57–79.

Kishore, Raghav (2015), 'Urban "Failures": Municipal Governance, Planning and Power in Colonial Delhi, 1863–1910', *Indian Economic and Social History Review*, 52 (4), 439–61.

Kozlowski, Gregory C. (1985), *Muslim Endowments and Society in British India* (Cambridge: Cambridge University Press).

Kumar, Sunil (2002), *The Present in Delhi's Pasts* (New Delhi: Three Essays Press).

Lackman, Conway L. (1977), 'The Modern Development of Classical Rent Theory', *American Journal of Economics and Sociology*, 36 (1), 51–63.

Lefebvre, Henri (1998), *The Production of Space*, trans. Donald Nicholson-Smith (Oxford: Blackwell).

Legg, Stephen (2007), *Spaces of Colonialism: Delhi's Urban Governmentalities* (Malden, MA; Oxford: Blackwell).

McGowan, Abigail (2013), 'Ahmedabad's Home Remedies: Housing in the Re-Making of an Industrial City, 1920–1960', *South Asia: Journal of South Asian Studies*, 36 (3), 397–414.

Mehra, Diya (2013), 'Planning Delhi *ca.*1936–1959', *South Asia: Journal of South Asian Studies*, 36 (3), 354–74.

Nair, Janaki (2005), *The Promise of the Metropolis: Bangalore's Twentieth Century* (Delhi: Oxford University Press).

Oldenburg, Veena Talwar (1984), *The Making of Colonial Lucknow, 1856–1877* (Princeton, NJ: Princeton University Press).

Pernau, Margrit (2013), *Ashraf into Middle Classes: Muslims in Nineteenth-Century Delhi* (Delhi: Oxford University Press).

Pershad, Rai Sahib Madho (1921), *The History of the Delhi Municipality, 1863–1921* (Allahabad: The Pioneer Press).

Pinch, William R. (1996), *Peasants and Monks in British India* (Berkeley, CA: University of California Press).

Prakash, Gyan (1999), *Another Reason: Science and the Imagination of Modern India* (Princeton, NJ: Princeton University Press).

Prasannan, Parthasarathi (2015), 'The History of Indian Economic History', in Daniele Boldizzoni and Pat Hudson (eds.), *Routledge Handbook of Global Economic History* (London: Routledge).

Prashad, Vijay (2000), *Untouchable Freedom: A Social History of a Dalit Community* (Oxford: Oxford University Press).

Ramaswamy, Sumathi (2001), 'Maps and Mother Goddesses in Modern India', *Imago Mundi*, 53, 97–114.

Rao, A. (2009), *The Caste Question: Dalits and the Politics of Modern India* (Berkeley, CA: University of California Press).

Rao, Nikhil (2013), *House, But No Garden: Apartment Living in Bombay's Suburbs, 1898–1964* (Minneapolis, MN: University of Minnesota Press).

Ray, Rajat Kanta (1979), *Urban Roots of Indian Nationalism: Pressure Groups and Conflict of Interests in Calcutta City Politics, 1875–1939* (New Delhi: Vikas).

Ray, Rajat Kanta (1988), 'The Bazaar: Changing Structural Characteristics of the Indigenous Section of the Indian Economy before and after the Great Depression', *Indian Economic and Social History Review*, 25 (3), 263–318.

Ray, Rajat Kanta (1995), 'Asian Capital in the Age of European Domination: The Rise of the Bazaar, 1800–1914', *Modern Asian Studies*, 29 (3), 449–54.

Roy, Tirthankar (2004), 'Flourishing Branches, Wilting Core: Research in Modern Indian Economic History', *Australian Economic History Review*, 44 (3), 221–40.

Sarkar, Sumit (2004), *Beyond Nationalist Frames: Relocating Postmodernism, Hindutva, History* (Delhi: Permanent Black).

Sehrawat, Samiksha (2013), *Colonial Medical Care in North India: Gender, State, and Society, c. 1840–1920* (New Delhi: Oxford University Press).

Sharan, Awadhendra B. (2014), *In the City, Out of Place: Nuisance, Pollution, and Dwelling in Delhi, c.1850–2000* (New Delhi: Oxford University Press).

Singh, Malvika (2013), *Perpetual City: A Short Biography of Delhi* (Delhi: Aleph).

Smith, Charles W. (1989), *Auctions: The Social Construction of Value* (London: Harvester Wheatsheaf).

Smith, Neil (2008), *Uneven Development: Nature, Capital and the Production of Space*, 3rd edn. (Athens, GA: University of Georgia Press).

Spodek, Howard (2012), *Ahmedabad: Shock City of Twentieth-Century India* (Hyderabad: Orient BlackSwan).

Srivastava, Sanjay (2015), *Entangled Urbanism: Slum, Gated Community, and Shopping Mall in Delhi and Gurgaon* (New Delhi: Oxford University Press).

Stokes, Eric (1959), *The English Utilitarians and India* (Oxford: Clarendon Press).

Tinker, Hugh (1954), *The Foundations of Local Self-Government in India, Pakistan, and Burma* (London: Athlone Press).

Trevithick, Alan (1990), 'Some Structural and Sequential Aspects of the British Imperial Assemblages at Delhi: 1877–1911', *Modern Asian Studies*, 24 (3), 561–78.

Vanaik, Anish (2008), 'Changing the Plot: Property Relations in Delhi 1857–1920' (Jawaharlal Nehru University).

Index

Notes: Figures and tables are indicated by an italic "*f*" and "*t*" following the page number.

For the benefit of digital users, indexed terms that span two pages (e.g., 52–53) may, on occasion, appear on only one of those pages.